Adaptive Pattern Recognition and Neural Networks

Yoh-Han Pao

Case Western Reserve University

▲▼▲ **Addison-Wesley Publishing Company, Inc.**

Reading, Massachusetts • Menlo Park, California • New York
Don Mills, Ontario • Wokingham, England • Amsterdam
Bonn • Sydney • Singapore • Tokyo • Madrid • San Juan

Many of the designations used by manufacturers and sellers to distinguish their products are claimed as trademarks. Where those designations appear in this book, and Addison-Wesley was aware of a trademark claim, the designations have been printed in caps or initial caps.

The programs and applications presented in this book have been included for their instructional value. They have been tested with care, but are not guaranteed for any particular purpose. The publisher does not offer any warranties or representations, nor does it accept any liabilities with respect to the programs or applications.

Library of Congress Cataloging-in-Publication Data

Pao, Yoh-Han
      Adaptive pattern recognition and neural networks/Yoh-Han Pao.
         p.   cm.
      Includes bibliographies and index.
      ISBN 0-201-12584-6
      1. Pattern recognition systems. 2. Neural computers. I. Title.
  TK7882.P3P36 1989   88-7760
  006.4–dc19   CIP

This book was prepared under the supervision of the author, using the TEX typesetting language.

To Helen

Foreword

Pattern recognition, artificial intelligence, and neural modeling have a common history that started in the 1950s. Contemporary neurocomputing technology is an area of information sciences that takes its models from the biological nervous systems. In contrast to the digital computers that make use of the high precision of numerical algorithms, thereby often defining various functions recursively, neural networks tend to embed the computational functions in the physical network itself—there exists a neural cell (neuron) or connection (synapse) for every elementary computing operation. In this sense, the neural networks are more akin to analog computers. In an analog computer, the problem structure (often of a dynamical or optimizational nature) is transferred, one-to-one, into the computer hardware, using analog computing elements such as integrators, summers, and multipliers.

One particular problem in the construction of system-theoretic models for the nervous system and perceptual operations is that the elementary system component, the neuron, is not known accurately enough to fully define the basic system equations. There are several reasons for this; first of all, a biological neural cell can only be studied in vivo, since it needs many kinds of psychological and chemical controls in order to operate correctly. On the other hand, there exist thousands of inputs, many of which are different kinds of chemicals, to every neural cell, and all of these cannot be controlled or forced to wanted values in a natural way. Consequently, direct measurement of the "transfer function" of a neuron can only be made in a very coarse manner, which may not yield sufficiently reliable results on which to base a complex system theory. It is characteristic to the research of artificial neural networks that the theorists must guess or imagine the forms of the basic "transfer functions" and the adaptive system equations, thereby using common sense for their formulation, and experimenting with different analytical functions, in order to implement natural-like phenomena. This kind of approach has sometimes raised anger among the experimental physiologists and psychologists; but what can be done? It is necessary to concretize the functions in some way, or otherwise there would exist nothing to study theoretically. The nicest formulation of the understanding of neural modeling that I have heard was made by the famous psychologist Donald MacKay; in 1986 he said to me: "When you talk to the biologists, you might say that if one makes certain modeling assumptions, one cannot avoid seeing these [natural-like] phenomena."

Over the years, a number of books on pattern recognition have been published. Contrary to that, although plenty of edited books on neuro-computing have been published, there has been a lack of textbooks that deal with the subject in a systematic way, covering everything from the background and fundamental modeling assumptions to demonstration of the various results and applications.

Professor Pao, who has worked in this field and especially with models of distributed associative memory since the early 1970s, has undertaken an ambitious project of describing both pattern recognition and neural networks within the same framework. The central theme in this book is adaptation of the networks and algorithms to given signals and data. The author first refers to various decision theories, the Bayesian philosophy as well as the fuzzy-set formalism. This then naturally leads to neural net implementation of discriminant functions, associative memory, and self-organization. Finally, various processing steps are linked in an attempt to proceed towards hierarchical systems, and to introduce linguistic patterns into the theory.

This book will certainly serve as a valuable text for advanced undergraduate and graduate courses in pattern recognition and neural networks, and strengthen the fundamentals for academic as well as practical research.

Teuvo Kohonen

Professor, Helsinki University of Technology
Research Professor the Academy of Finland

Preface

This book rests on three premises. The first premise is that pattern-recognition science and technology is important, useful, and interesting. Knowledge of pattern recognition is *important* because the occurrences of human existence seem to take form in the format of patterns. The formation of language, the utterance of speech, the drawing of pictures, and the understanding of images all involve patterns. No one aspect, or any sequence of aspects, of a pattern determine the significance of that pattern. Instead, there is a great deal of compensation among all aspects of the pattern, so the significance of a pattern can be grasped only if all aspects are available simultaneously for consideration.

Pattern recognition is important not only in human perception, but also in cognition. Humans assess situations in terms of the pattern of circumstances that constitutes the situation, and they act in accordance with what that pattern might represent or what it might portend. Therefore, ultimately, pattern recognition is important because much of human experience involves its practice. It is *useful* not only because it is intrinsically an essential part of human behavior, but also because computer-implemented pattern-recognition capabilities can enable machines to carry out perception tasks. Pattern-recognition research is also *interesting*, but that is a subjective matter.

The second premise is that knowledge of pattern recognition is often highly specialized. Contributions to the field have come from many different research areas, from various disciplines. This in itself is a healthy indication of the breadth and depth of interest in the topic and the vigor of the associated research. An ancillary effect, however, is that investigators often have knowledge that pertains to only their own tightly knit research group.

The third premise is that the interests of research and education might be better served if more coherent and coordinated presentations of knowledge of pattern recognition were available. Comparative and relational discussions of the research in and results of the various focus areas would be particularly helpful for pattern-recognition research as a whole. This is a particularly opportune time for such discussions, because contributions to the understanding of pattern recognition are now being made by a variety of disciplines including artificial intelligence, cognitive science, computer engineering, neurobiology, (traditional) pattern recognition, philosophy, and psychology. These advances are coordinated to some extent under the aegis of neural-net research, but a wider coordination would be helpful.

This book is made up of two parts. Part 1 is concerned with basic concepts; Part 2 is concerned with adaptive pattern recognition as implemented with networks of elemental processors, interconnected in manners reminiscent of biological neural nets. The rationale for this book lies in the interaction between the two parts. Neural-net implementations of pattern-recognition algorithms are interesting not only because they allow iterative procedures to be implemented rapidly, but also—and perhaps primarily—because a neural-net perspective on pattern information processing stimulates us to be creative in visualizing new approaches. The considerations presented in Part 1 provide guidance for and constraints in our new creativity.

Chapter 1 is concerned with the nature of the activity itself—namely, how is a pattern to be described? In pattern recognition, when are we concerned with estimating beliefs or with estimating similarities? We also describe the differences between classification and the more general task of estimating attribute values.

Chapter 2 considers the basic issue of dealing with uncertainty in pattern recognition, principally from the perspective of Bayesian statistics. We also describe how seemingly deterministic discriminants can in fact be based on statistical considerations. Criticisms of the Bayesian approach are also addressed.

Fuzzy set theory can provide an interface between the qualitative symbolic (linguistic) features that humans seem to prefer and quantitative measurements. A synopsis of the salient aspects of fuzzy set theory germane to pattern recognition is contained in Chapter 3, as are several examples illustrating the roles that fuzzy set theory plays in pattern recognition.

Moving into the domain of linguistically valued features, we describe in Chapter 4 how inductive learning of rules for the recognition of such patterns might be carried out. Three approaches are described: the ID3, the Pao-Hu, and the Procedure M methods. Each is appropriate in different circumstances. The ID3 method is efficient; the Pao-Hu method is suitable for parallel processing; and the Procedure M method builds a semantic-net description of the object, which it uses as the basis for recognition.

In Part 2, Chapter 5 describes one form of a generalized Perceptron, principally the Rumelhart–Hinton–Williams multilayer semilinear feedforward net based on the generalized delta rule, and back propagation of error. The action of that type of net is examined in detail, and also is viewed from the perspective of synthesizing a new spatially dependent tensor metric in input pattern space.

Chapter 6 reviews the development of associative memories over the years. It covers matrix and holographic associative memories, and the Hopfield net.

Chapter 7 contains a brief discussion of how unsupervised learning or clustering might be carried out with neural-net computing.

Chapter 8 shows how a modification of the generalized delta rule net can result in dramatically enhanced rates of learning and decreased system errors. The modification consists of enhancing the input pattern representation through use of a nonlinear functional link. We also show that the functional link net unifies the architectures of nets for associative recall, supervised learning, and unsupervised learning.

Chapter 9 provides an echo to Chapters 3 and 4. In Chapter 3, we made an argument for the use of fuzzy logic in pattern recognition, emphasizing the role of the membership function in providing an interface between qualitative, vaguely defined, concepts and quantitative measurements. In Chapter 4, we described several methods for inductive learning of rules in terms of qualitative entities. Now, in Chapter 9, we make a connection between fuzzy logic and neural-net computing.

Chapter 10 addresses applications of adaptive pattern recognition as implemented with neural nets. Although many interesting specific instances are well worth attention, our approach is to focus attention on basic and generic issues, rather than to examine the specific applications. Eight issues are addressed, including how to deal with structures within patterns, with degrees of belief, with the concept of time, and with the possibility of using adaptive pattern recognition for discovering simple solutions to some truly difficult problems. We also discuss three application areas, primarily by articulating the issues involved and the insights gained to date. Extensive references are provided.

This book should be useful to scientists and engineers who have experience in the "hard-science" aspects of information processing and who wish to obtain an introduction to the fields of adaptive pattern recognition, fuzzy-set theory, and neural-net computing, especially in applications. This book also should be of interest to researchers in behavioral and biological sciences because it shows how existing knowledge in several interrelated computer-science areas intermesh to provide a base for practice and further progress in matters germane to their research. This book can serve as a text for a senior undergraduate or first-year graduate course on pattern recognition. It approaches the matter of pattern information processing with a broad perspective, so the student should learn to understand and follow important developments in several research areas that affect pattern information processing.

Finally, this book can also be used in an introductory course on neural computing. It explains basic concepts by emphasizing information-processing issues and applications.

Cleveland, Ohio

Yoh-Han Pao

Acknowledgments

I take this opportunity to express my thanks to the many people who have, in various ways, helped me to attain my objective of preparing this manuscript.

Going back into the mists of history, I thank Professor J.A.M. Howe of Edinburgh University for the hospitality shown me in the summers of 1971 and 1972 when, as a NATO Senior Science Fellow, I started work on associative memories. Along the way, I have received important understanding and encouragement from several people. These supporters include the late Professor K.S. Fu, Professor Donald Michie, Professor Gerald Sussman, Professor C.H. Hu, Professor L.F. Pau, and Professor J.L. Sklansky, to name a few. I am grateful for those enjoyable and strengthening interactions.

I also want to express my affection and high regard for a small group of people who worked closely with me in preparing the manuscript. My heartfelt thanks go to Victor Chen, M.S. Klassen, Kam Komeyli, Dennis Lee, Dejan Sobajic, Georges Zwingelstein, and—in particular—Christene Griffen and Donna Buggs, who mastered the idiosyncrasies of an impressively complex package and were able to design and prepare the manuscript to our satisfaction. In this connection, I appreciated the help I received from Cheryl Wurzbacher of Addison-Wesley. I also thank Georges Zwingelstein for designing and implementing most of the illustrations, Robin Pao and Jeff Leane for help in researching references, and Helen Pao for help in important ancillary tasks, including that of preparing the index.

I also thank Randy Beer, Hillel Chiel, David Helman, Leon Sterling, Farrokh Khatibi, and other colleagues for their interest in this endeavor and in the subject matter covered in this manuscript. I also would like to acknowledge the following people who reviewed the early drafts of the book: Mr. Jack Sexton (Ford Aerospace Corporation), Professor Jack Sklansky (University of California at Irvine), Professor Azriel Rosenfeld (University of Maryland), Professor Dana Anderson (University of Colorado).

Finally, as a general matter, I want to thank George S. Dively for offering his friendship and for establishing the endowed Chair that I have the honor and good fortune to occupy and that, over the years, has helped me to enrich our research environment, greatly to the benefit of many.

Contents

Appendices

PART 1

Scope and Description

CHAPTER 1

Nature of the Activity

1.1 Introduction

The addition of parallel distributed processing to traditional pattern recognition has given rise to a new, different, and more powerful methodology, *adaptive pattern recognition*. This methodology has ties to several other research activities. For example, it is very much part of neural-net computing, but not all of neural-net computing is adaptive pattern recognition. It also has some special, important ties to artificial intelligence.

In this introductory chapter, we describe motivations for the study of pattern recognition in general, and of adaptive pattern recognition in particular. We then present certain basic aspects of pattern recognition; these matters are central to a good understanding of the fundamental concepts of pattern information processing; they increase in importance as pattern recognition increases in capability.

1.2 Motivation for the Study of Adaptive Pattern Recognition

In this section, we shall examine pattern recognition in general, and adaptive pattern recognition in particular. In so doing, we shall see that these disciplines' methods are distinctive and complement those of other information-processing disciplines.

Situations in this world generally cannot be assessed in terms of isolated facts or even in terms of a body of isolated facts. Rather, we find that we need to describe situations in terms of *patterns* of interrelated facts. Sometimes, the interrelation is implicit, in the sense that we know

3

that all those facts pertain to the same object or situation. In other cases, a pattern may be meaningful only because of explicit relationships among the various features of the pattern.

It is interesting to observe that our perceptive powers seem to be well adapted to such pattern-processing tasks. For example, we are able to recognize speech utterances and images such as handwriting in a robust manner, despite major variations, distortions, or omissions. A related trait is the ability of humans to retrieve information on the basis of associated cues, consisting of only a part of a pattern. A few whistled notes can evoke a memory of an entire tune; a glimpse of the back of a head in a crowd can remind us in detail of an old friend.

This same capability to cope easily with patterns of associated items is found not only in perception, but also in tasks that clearly involve both perception and cognition. Thus, it seems that nature decreed that information be in pattern format, and humans seemingly adapted well to that circumstance. (Incidentally, we know from observation that many other forms of life also adapted well in this regard.)

Part of the motivation for the study of pattern recognition stems from our desire to understand the basis for these powers in humans. There is also a strong engineering-based pragmatic motivation. As we learn how to build computers to help us in the performance of tasks, we strive to make them "intelligent" so that they might be more compatible with the manner in which we normally behave. We would like to have computer-based machines with perception and cognition capabilities that would enable them to understand what we say, to read what we write, and, in general, to respond in intuitively understandable ways. *In other words, we would like to build into our machines the same pattern-information-processing capabilities that we ourselves possess.* This would enable us to use the machines more easily and would undoubtedly make the machines more efficient in handling real world tasks.

This second combination of circumstances provides great motivation for understanding how pattern-formatted information might be handled. Traditional pattern recognition worked on supplying that understanding; other disciplines, including artificial intelligence, psychology, and neuro-biology, also undertook activities directed toward that objective.

To understand more clearly the role of adaptive pattern recognition, we shall look at both traditional artificial intelligence and traditional pattern recognition. These two research disciplines have several common objectives, the most important of which are to "understand" perceptual and cognitive processes in humans and to implement similar capabilities in machines. The two disciplines had common starting points, but then developed increasingly different interests, different styles, and different areas of emphasis.

The work of traditional artificial intelligence, for example, is based on the *representation hypothesis*—the idea that the world can be represented symbolically. From this viewpoint, perception and cognitive processes consist of acquiring, manipulating, associating, and modifying symbolic representations. The approach seems to be natural for representing certain high-level mental functions, but may be inappropriate and perhaps even unnatural for dealing with tasks involving combined perception and cognition. In addition, such high-level symbolic representations seem to be far removed from anything we know about processes in biological neural systems.

In contrast to all this, traditional pattern recognition experienced some early disappointments with the Percepton approach, then proceeded to concentrate on the mathematical or computer-science aspects of pattern-formatted information processing. There is, for example, emphasis on statistical pattern recognition, and there is also considerable interest in the use of mathematical linguistics in the classification of patterns with syntactic structures. Use of fuzzy logic provides one link between pattern recognition research and humanlike behaviour.

Thus, although the two disciplines shared interesting objectives, both left major categories of problems untouched. We hasten to add that this does not mean that advances were not made or that they were not useful. It is a matter of record that valuable progress has occurred, rather ironically, more has been attained in the area of useful practical engineering than in that of "understanding" human perception and cognition.

More recently, groups of researchers have been experimenting with parallel distributed models of computation (see, for example, the two volumes on PDP by Rumelhart and McClelland [1986]). These models are based on use of large numbers of elemental processors interconnected in manners reminiscent of human neural nets, and they can exhibit powerful learning, memorization, and associative-recall capabilities for pattern-formatted information. Such subsymbolic-level processing seem to be appropriate for dealing with perception tasks and perhaps even with tasks that call for combined perception and cognition. Moreover, because the structure and the processing modes of these models seem to be conceptually compatible with what we know of biological neural-nets, it is often possible to derive inspiration from neurobiological or psychological studies, even though the objective might be engineering. By the same token, when engineering performance mirrors human performance, it might be that, in fact, similar systems considerations apply in the biological neural net as in the computer neural net, and mutually useful hints can be obtained in this manner.

Artificial neural-net computing is presently the confluence of the interest and energies of several disciplines, including neurobiology, psychology, philosophy, and computer researchers. It is an extremely active research area.

One important aspect of this discipline is its central concern with the manipulation of *pattern-formatted information*. The introduction of parallel distributed processing allows for *adaptive* learning and classification in ways not hitherto feasible.

Neural-net research gives rise to two important related research goals. One of these is to build bridges of understanding between neural net computing and symbolic processing. The other is to coordinate, interpret, organize, and make coherent the various parts and pieces of pattern-recognition expertise that reside in statistical pattern recognition, syntactic pattern recognition, fuzzy logic, and (now) neural-net computing. It is important to organize these pieces into a related, coherent body of knowledge, so that education in this matter can be achieved efficiently and so that research will not be wasteful. We need to organize and develop a coherent approach to *adaptive pattern recognition*, an approach that will recognize the contributions of the past and yet will be compatible with the rapid pace of future progress in neural-net research. *All these matters constitute our motivation for the study of adaptive pattern recognition.*

This book is a contribution to this study. It comprises two parts. Part 1 is concerned with those basic insights developed by traditional pattern recognition that we deem to be of lasting value and that need to be incorporated in adaptive pattern recognition. Part 2 is concerned with neural-net implementations of some of these basic approaches and techniques. As we proceed from pattern recognition to adaptive pattern recognition, we shall see that much is the same and yet much is changed—so radically changed that the visage of pattern recognition is irrevocably altered.

The remaining sections of this chapter deal with basic introductory matters. In Section 1.2, we discuss the circumstances and manners in which a pattern might be said to *represent* an object. Also, we describe pattern recognition in terms of mappings. Section 1.3 is concerned with the *focus* of the task. It is important to differentiate between classification on the basis of similarity and that on the basis of belief, although in general both similarity and belief need to be estimated. The matter of *objectives* is quite different from that of focus. Different objectives of pattern recognition are discussed in Section 1.4. Finally, we examine different pattern-representation formats and the corresponding different pattern-recognition techniques in Section 1.5. That discussion provides an overview of and an introduction to the remaining material in this book.

1.3   Description of Computer-Based Pattern Recognition in Terms of Opaque and Transparent Mappings

Zadeh [1977] once proposed that we think of pattern recognition in terms of mapping a pattern correctly from pattern space into class-membership space.

He said that pattern recognition as carried out by nature can be thought of in terms of an *opaque* mapping. A new situation, or pattern, is correctly recognized and classified by an observer. However, the procedure by which a pattern is mapped into the correct class membership is an opaque one; not only are the details of the process inaccessible to other observers, but also the process is generally not even understood by the recognizer himself. *The task of implementing computer-based pattern recognition is to replace the opaque mapping with a transparent mapping that we can describe precisely to a computer.*

This abstract depiction of computer-implemented pattern recognition is illustrated in Figures 1.1(a) and 1.1(b).

In Figure 1.1(a), we see that an object, X, may have many instantiations, $\underline{x}$. That is, object X may appear in many different guises, all of which nevertheless represent it. In nature, there is some opaque mapping $R_{op}(\underline{x})$ that maps all these patterns into c_X, the class designation X. That is, any and all of these patterns are recognized and are classified into the category of object X. Humans achieve all this processing in an opaque manner through their perceptual and cognitive apparatus.

In computer-implemented pattern recognition, on the other hand, the opaque mapping has to be replaced by an explicitly described procedure— a transparent mapping; the overall procedure may be described by the mapping $R_{tr}(f(\underline{x})) \rightarrow \underline{c}(\underline{x}) = X$, as illustrated in Figure 1.1(b).

We see that the entire procedure comprises two distinct steps. In the first step, we describe a specific manifestation of object X in terms of appropriate features; that is, we go from $\underline{x}$ to $f(\underline{x})$. Then, in the second step, the machine carries out an unambiguous procedure to achieve a transparent mapping, $R_{tr}(f(\underline{x}))$, to go from $f(\underline{x})$ to $\underline{c}(\underline{x}) = X$.

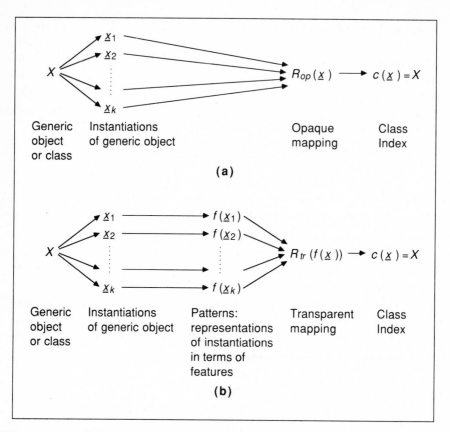

Figure 1.1   Schematic representation of component steps in pattern recognition. (a) As carried out in nature. (b) In computer-implemented pattern recognition.

Of the two operations, the first is much more difficult to devise. In other words, once $f(\underline{x})$ is known, theoretical guidance is available for synthesizing mathematical transformations for achieving the desired $R_{tr}(f(\underline{x})) \rightarrow c(\underline{x})$ result, albeit to varying degrees of satisfaction. In contrast, there is no a priori basis for the choice of the transformation $f(\underline{x})$. This is but another way of saying that, in general, we do not know what aspects of a representation are germane to the pattern-recognition act.

Consider, for example, the act of a human recognizing an object to be an apple. This capability is learned over a period of time through seeing, smelling, touching, peeling, eating, picking, sorting, and buying apples. Finally, the person is able to recognize apples, but in ways that she cannot quite describe adequately. The mapping is essentially opaque.

In contrast, for computer-implemented pattern recognition, we need to be concerned not only about $R_{tr}()$, but also about the appropriate choice of $f()$. Even if we have excellent sensors for quantifying measures of color, fragrance, texture, and so on, it is nevertheless difficult to know which of those features are essential, which are helpful, and which might be redundant or irrelevant. The choice of features for the description of objects–which may be concepts or physical objects or situations or events—is a difficult but essential preprocessing task in the implementation of computer-based pattern recognition.

To some extent, there is no right or wrong choice, as long as sufficient information has been included in the set of feature values. However, inappropriate choices lead to the need for complex decision rules or mappings, $R_{tr}()$, whereas incisive choices result in simple and comprehensive rules.

The task of determining $f()$ is a crucial part of implementing computer-based pattern recognition, and the problem remains with us in adaptive pattern recognition. Often, however, we have the opportunity to discover adaptively which of the $f()$ features are important and which are irrelevant.

It is ironic that, for many years, we strived for transparent mappings, yet some of the algorithms of neural net adaptive pattern recognition are not quite transparent. The algorithm may be indeed clearly stated, but the details of the computing carried on by the network are not easily accessible, and the effects are not easily traced.

1.4 Focus of the Task

The focus of the pattern-recognition act varies with circumstances. In some cases, *similarity* is of primary concern; in others, the task is one of estimating *beliefs*. The distinction is important, although in general both similarity and belief need to be estimated.

When we are certain that we have never seen a particular pattern before, it is reasonable to classify that pattern on the basis of similarity. That is, we classify the new pattern as belonging to the class of object A if it is most similar to patterns that belong to class A. This focus is especially appropriate if there is negligible or no overlap in pattern space—that is, if every pattern description maps unambiguously into one and only one class membership index.

This situation is illustrated schematically in Figure 1.2(a). The objects A and B may each be represented by many different patterns,but their pattern descriptions do not overlap in feature space. The patterns are mapped unambiguously in a many-to-one manner to class-membership designations. For such circumstances, a computer-based deterministic procedure for estimating similarities is of prime importance. Such a procedure allows us to distinguish between classes and to generalize within each class. *The usual classification rule is that, if pattern x is most similar to patterns of class A, then pattern x belongs to class A.*

In contrast to the deterministic situation illustrated in Figure 1.2(a), another extreme exists where we know that every pattern that we encounter could belong to any one of several previously identified classes.

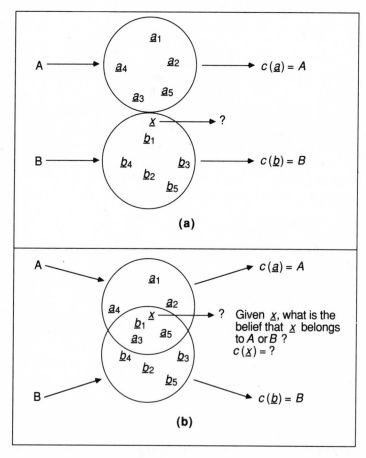

Figure 1.2   Estimating similarities and beliefs. (a) Generalization through estimating similarities: Is x more similar to a patterns or to b patterns? (b) Estimation of belief that pattern belongs to a certain class, given that it is valid for that pattern to be representing either of two classes.

That is, it is just as valid that a pattern $\underline{x}$ represents object A as it is that $\underline{x}$ represents object B, and so on, as illustrated in Figure 1.2(b). But given that we encounter $\underline{x}$, what are the weights of the relative beliefs that $\underline{x}$ represents object A, or object B, or any of the other objects? In this case, the focus is on *estimating beliefs* rather than on estimating similarities.

In reality, actual pattern-recognition tasks lie between the two extremes. Even if the patterns were separable in some feature space, there would still be the troublesome problem of what happens in detail at regional boundaries, where some overlap might occur. Conversely, it is extremely unlikely that complete overlap will occur in all of the feature space for two or more classes of patterns; thus measures of similarity might generally be as useful as are belief estimates.

We shall return to these issues in Section 1.5, where we discuss pattern-representation formats. In Chapter 2, we shall see that deterministic procedures may be viewed as approximations to the statistical case, and we shall derive theoretical support from that view. Similarly, the material in Chapter 5, on the learning of a neural-net discriminant, may also be justified on that basis. In the latter case, however, additional probabilistic measures may be provided by the neural net if that is desired.

1.5 Objectives of Pattern Recognition

In principle, as well as in practice, pattern recognition is concerned not only with classification, but more generally, also with estimates of attributes. In fact, class membership might be viewed as being only one of many attributes of possible interest.

This has not always been the accepted view. The more familiar view of pattern recognition is based on the narrowly defined classification model. In the classification model, we would be concerned with

- Performing feature extraction; that is, deciding how the manifestation $\underline{x}$ of the object X should be described symbolically in the form of $f(\underline{x})$

- Learning the transparent mapping $R_{tr}()$; that is, using a set of labeled training-set patterns to infer decision rules

- Exercising the mapping $R_{tr}(f(\underline{x}))$ to carry out the actual classification act

This view, depicted in Figures 1.3(a) and 1.3(b), is too limited and too restrictive. It neither encompasses the diverse uses of pattern-recognition

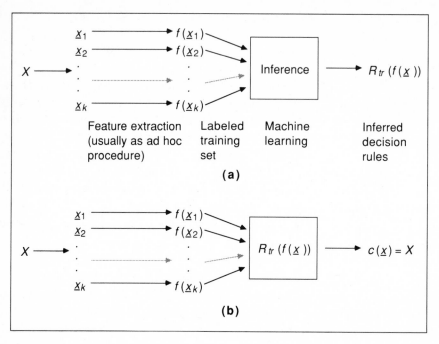

Figure 1.3   The classification model of computer-implemented pattern recognition. (a) Learning the classification rule using a labeled training set. (b) Using the learned mapping to carry out classification.

methods in solving real-world problems, nor does justice to the many new and valuable results from research in fields related to traditional pattern recognition.

Figures 1.4(a) and 1.4(b) illustrate an alternate and more adequate view. In this view, the emphasis is on pattern attributes. The manifestations x of object X are described in terms of $f(x)$. The mapping $R_{tr}(f(x))$ takes each pattern $f(x)$ into an appropriate $A(x)$. This mapping describes an estimation model of pattern recognition, rather than the traditional classification model. The mapping is learned, as usual, through a finite number of pattern samples, each labeled with a corresponding attribute value or with corresponding attribute values if there is more than one attribute. The learned mapping not only is able to reproduce all the training-set pattern–attribute associations, but also must be able to accommodate any new pattern, so that correct attribute values are estimated through the mapping $R_t r()$. If class label is considered to be the principal and only attribute of interest, then this estimation model reduces to the usual classification model.

Figure 1.5 depicts an even more general situation. It illustrates what is at stake in estimating attributes when more than one class is involved, and when classes overlap in feature space. In Figure 1.5, $x_1, x_2, \ldots, x_k$, are different manifestations of the object X, and $f(x_1), f(x_2), \ldots, f(x_k)$ are the corresponding symbolic pattern representations of these manifestations. A transparent mapping $R_{trx}()$ maps these descriptions onto an attribute space, taking $f(x_1)$ onto $A(x_1), f(x_2)$ onto $A(x_2)$, and so on. Similarly $y_1, y_2, \ldots, y_m$ are manifestations of object Y, and $f(y_1), f(y_2), \ldots, f(y_m)$ are pattern representations of these manifestations. Another transparent mapping, R_{try}, maps $f(y_1)$ onto $A(y_1)$, $f(y_2)$ onto $A(y_2)$ and so on. The attribute of interest is the same in each case; that is, the *name* of the attribute is the same, and the estimated values are $A(x_1), \ldots, A(x_k)$, and $A(y_1), \ldots, A(y_m)$. For a given new pattern, the task is to determine which

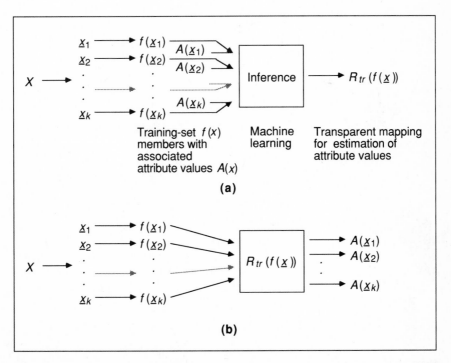

Figure 1.4   Schematic illustration of a more general estimation model of pattern recognition. (a) Using a labeled training set to learn a transparent mapping for estimating attribute values. (b) Using the learned transparent mapping for estimation of attribute values.

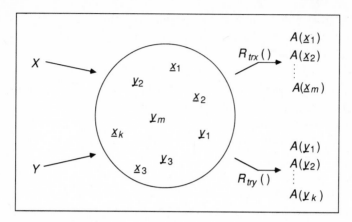

Figure 1.5   Schematic illustration of attribute-value estimation in the presence of uncertainties.

of the mappings, R_{trx} or R_{try}, should be used to provide estimates of the value of attribute A. In classification, the output is usually a set of discrete class indices, whereas in estimation the output is usually a continuous-valued variable.

1.6   Pattern-Representation Formats

The essence of pattern recognition is the concurrent processing of a body of information, all items of which are available at the same time. In general, a *pattern* is a data structure of features, including information on feature name and feature value or values, and explicit or implicit information on relationships among features, if these exist.

In the language of the previous sections, the matter of immediate interest is the nature of the procedure $f()$ used to describe a "physical" object in terms understandable to a machine.

Generally, a pattern can be expressed as a conjunction of statements of the form

$$(\langle\text{feature-name}\rangle\langle\text{feature value, belief in value}\rangle$$
$$\langle\text{relationships with other features}\rangle)$$

The pattern itself would be of the form

$$statement_1 \wedge statement_2 \wedge \ldots \wedge statement_n$$

where $\wedge$ denotes the Boolean logic operator AND.

This format is cumbersome, however, and not all its facets are necessary for all circumstances.

In the past, two traditional areas of pattern recognition—the decision-theoretic and the syntactic—influenced the choice of pattern representation modes, and, in most cases, patterns were either arrays of numbers or linear sequences of nonnumeric symbols.

These formats are not terribly restrictive because they can be arrived at by a number of different routes. Therefore, the formats alone do not dictate how classification or estimation procedures should be inferred and executed. But it is useful to understand how researchers arrived at these formats, and what the various quantities mean in any particular instance.

To clarify some of these issues, we present, in Figure 1.6, a categorization of pattern formats based on the nature of features values and corresponding processing procedures. Other schemes of categorization also are possible; this particular one should be useful for illustrating the relationships among the various topics treated in this book.

The first important differentiation is the question of whether feature values are numeric or nonnumeric. For example, in encoding weather information in the form of a pattern, we might have feature-name and feature-value associations in the form of

$$weather \equiv ((temperature\ in\ °C: 18.2)$$
$$(rainfall\ in\ past\ 24\ hours\ in\ mm:\ 0.2)$$
$$(barometric\ height\ in\ mm\ Hg:\ 759.8)$$
$$(relative\ humidity\ in\ percent:\ 70))$$

If we agree to fix the order of the features and let the names of features be implicit, such patterns can be presented as lists of real numbers, for example,

$$weather \equiv (18.2,\ 0.2,\ 759.8,\ 70)$$

This type of simplified pattern representation has found considerable favor with researchers, for good reason. Under such circumstances, the patterns, each described in terms of N real-number components, can also be viewed as vectors in N-dimensional space; each pattern then corresponds to a point in that space. With the adoption of this view, a great deal of familiar mathematics becomes available for use in pattern recognition. For example, such spaces are metric spaces; that is, it is meaningful

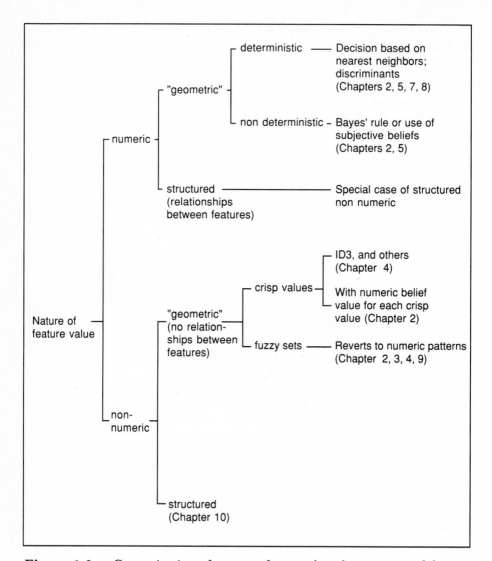

Figure 1.6   Categorization of pattern formats based on nature of feature value.

to think of *distances* between two points in such spaces, the Euclidean distance being one example of such a measure. Two patterns that represent objects very nearly alike might be expected to be very close to each other in pattern space. As another example, much is known about coordinate transformations in such space, and sometimes we can make use of this knowledge by carrying out transformations to see whether we can obtain a more convenient representation. Thus, we see that numeric features values can lead to a *geometric* view of patterns in pattern space.

It is also important to differentiate between deterministic and nondeterministic numeric representations. Although the formats may be similar in the sense that the patterns are lists of real number in both cases, the emphasis in the latter case is on the probability of occurrence of the pattern.

Despite the convenience of working with real-numbered feature values, there are circumstances where it is just not possible to have them. For example, certain aspects of an apple might be described in terms of a pattern:

apple-1: ((category fruit)(color red)(taste sweet))

Or, a person might be described as

person-1: ((height medium)(build heavy)(age middle aged))

Both these representations are "flat" in the sense that the values are simple elemental nonnumeric symbols and there are no embedded data structures.

Again, if we agree to fix the order of the features and let the names of the features be implicit, then we can represent such patterns as lists of nonnumeric symbols, so we have

$$\text{apple-1} = (\text{fruit, red, sweet})$$
$$\text{person-1} = (\text{medium, heavy, middle aged})$$

There is a drastic difference between patterns with numeric and nonnumeric (linguistic) feature values, because there is no straightforward way of ascribing a metric for measuring distances between patterns in the latter case. Of the many ways that have been explored for use in special cases, one of these consists of associating arbitrary numbers to correspond to—that is, to represent—feature values for linguistic features. Distances can then be determined, but these values are artificial and are not meaningful.

For example, the *values* of the feature named "color" might be red, green, or yellow. It is not meaningful to code these nonnumeric symbolic values into, say, 2, 3, and 4 respectively. The results might be misleading. In another approach, pattern recognition is based on exact match, and "distance" might be measured on the basis of the number of nonmatching ($\langle feature - name\rangle\langle feature - value\rangle$) associations. This corresponds to using the Hamming distance metric. In yet another approach, each $(\langle feature-name\rangle\langle feature-value\rangle)$ pair is retained as a feature and the value of that feature is a number representing belief or certainty factor. This third approach is probably the most meaningful.

There is a significant difference between the *apple* and the *person* patterns. In the case of the *apple* pattern, each of the features can take on any one of a number of discrete nonnumeric values. Color, for example, might be red, green, or yellow, and taste might be sweet or tart—and, for all practical purposes, these values are irreducibly nonnumeric. In contrast, for the *person* pattern, although the values for *height* might be tall, medium, or short, and the values of age might be old, middle-aged, or young, nevertheless in some cases it might be possible to relate such nonnumeric values to more quantitative measurements. In such cases, we can define *tall* as a fuzzy set of values defined in the domain of quantitative measurements of height and we can then revert to a numeric representation. These matters are discussed in Chapter 3.

Proceeding to the final major category in Figure 1.6, there are circumstances where the principal objective of the pattern-recognition act is to determine whether certain regularities occur in the pattern being considered or, equivalently, whether the observed pattern of symbols could have been generated with use of certain *production rules* or *generation rules*. Under such circumstances, it would be irrelevant whether all such patterns were of uniform size or whether features were always ordered in the identical sequence. Indeed, under such conditions, it would be more natural to regard patterns as streams of nonnumeric symbols.

Conventional pattern recognition has had considerable success in dealing with streams of simple symbols. In that area of pattern recognition, called *syntactic pattern recognition*, techniques of mathematical linguistics are used for recognition and classification. Patterns are considered to be sentences, and the classification act is described in terms of parsing a sentence to see whether it satisfies a certain grammer—that is, belongs to a certain class. Although researchers have been most successful in classifying syntactic structures that obey context-free grammars, we might argue that such exercises are almost not within the core of pattern recognition, because the nature of information processing in such cases is quintessentially sequential rather than parallel. These special context-free circumstances are in contrast to the more general and more difficult cases where structure cannot be determined without considerations of context and semantics. In the latter circumstances, processing is again more parallel in nature and pattern-based techniques are needed.

1.7 Comments and Bibliographical Remarks

Researchers generally recognize that, in the abstract, the science of pattern recognition is concerned with three major issues, these being

1. The appropriate description of objects, physical or conceptual, in terms of a representation space

2. The specification of an interpretation space

3. The mapping from representation space to interpretation space

This abstraction sets the scope and the structure for the development of the science of pattern recognition. Our motivation for advancing that body of knowledge is our belief that general principles developed for the abstract will be widely applicable over many diverse domains of application.

The matter of representation was and still is an important issue. If we restrict ourselved to *geometric* representations, then statistical methods such as that based on the Karhunen–Loêve transformation can indeed determine what combination of feature values provides measures for discriminating between classes and what other combinations are largely irrelevant and might be ignored. Such statistical analyses are largely irrelevant, however, if we depart from *geometric* representations and other matters that need to be considered.

Texts such as those of Duda and Hart [1973], Chen [1973], Ullman [1973], Tou and Gonzalez [1974] and Devijver and Kittler [1982] deal primarily with geometrically represented patterns and emphasize the statistical aspects of decision making to varying degrees.

Sometimes, however, even though some aspects of the objects are clearly important *features*, it develops that those features are not important in themselves. Rather it is the structural relationships among the features that contain critically important information. That realization gave rise to a large body of literature on *syntatic* and *structural* pattern recognition.

Whereas statistical pattern recognition made use of the results of statistical communication and estimation theory, syntactic pattern recognition built on earlier work in mathematical linguistics and on the results of research in computer languages. These matters are discussed in several texts and edited volumes, including those by Watanabe [1972], Fu [1974; 1977] and Gonzalez and Thomason [1978].

Syntactic pattern recognition as developed by its principal proponents, however, became limited to "before–after" relationships and could
not cope with more general structures.

The augmented-transition-network (ATN) approach for analysis of
languages provides one evolutionary way out of the confines of context-
free grammars [Woods 1970] and might be considered to be relevant to
pattern recognition, as long as one feels bound to the methods of syntactic
pattern recognition.

Texts by Pavilidis [1977], Miclet [1986] and Simon [1984, 1986] address
the matter of representation more liberally, with emphasis on examining
what structural information should be and might be represented.

Simon's text describes well a variety of signal-preprocessing and data-
representation methods available to us for representing patterns. Some
of these methods deal with structures explicitly, but others are helpful
in that they are concerned with representations that can accommodate
structural information. Typical of the latter class of material is the discussion of ordinal representation space, Peano–Hilbert scan in an n-ordinal
space, and the properties of neighborhood graphs in an ordinal space.

The purpose of pattern recognition is to carry out a mapping from
representation space to *interpretation space* [Simon, 1984], and an important aspect of pattern recognition is to determine the *operator* that will
carry out this mapping.

Against this background of gains in research, there still remains the
question of how the requisite operators are to be learnt. Certainly, they
can be handcrafted and installed in specific pattern recognition systems,
but what are the general principles for autonomous inference of such operators or discriminators, even if, for example, we are content to limit
ourselves to geometric representations?

Rosenblatt [1959; 1962] did suggest a general approach to the automatic learning discriminants for pattern classification, the Perceptron
approach. Earlier related work had also been reported by Farley and
Clark [1954]. Subsequent work [Ridgeway 1962] generalized the Perceptron structure to that of the the committee machine, made of layers of
interconnected threshold-logic units (TLU). A good account of the underlying principles for the committee machine and related devices was given
by Nilsson [1965] in his monograph on *Learning Machines: Foundations
of Trainable Pattern-Classifying Systems*. That account showed that the
structure and function of such devices were well understood and there
was no question that such devices could perform very well when trained
properly.

At the time, Nilsson's discussion of the layered machine (that is, of Perceptrons with "hidden" layers), indicated clearly his understanding of the power of the generalized Perceptron approach. The only remaining questions were whether training could be carried out successfully and what the training procedures might be. Unfortunately, however, at the time, no one knew of a practicable method for training layered machines made up layers of TLUs. Part of the problem was that the only threshold function considered seriously for those machines was the binary on/off function; if a unit was not "on," there was no easy way for the other units to know how far it was from being "on," and there was no mechanism for adjusting parameters in a systematic manner.

In 1969, Minsky and Papert published a discussion of the Perceptron. Although the monograph is, even to this day, a correct and enlightening discussion of certain aspects of pattern information processing, the overall effect was disastrous to further progress in Perceptron-related research. Even in 1984, Simon, in his otherwise excellent book *Patterns and Operators* dismissed the Perceptron under the heading "Birth and Death of a Myth."

In the interim, the Perceptronlike approach survived in mostly linear form, and was even taught and practised as such, as a variant of the Widrow–Hoff algorithm [Widrow 1960, 1962; Duda and Hart 1973]. Sklansky and Wassel [1981] also provided valuable mathematics background for the training of piecewise linear networks.

In 1986, Rumelhart, Hinton, and Williams published their account of how multilayered Perceptrons might be trained with use of the generalized delta rule, and new ground is now being broken in the exploration of means for autonomous learning of mappings from representation space to interpretation space.

The actions of the "internal layers" might be viewed as successive transformations of the original representation until we attain a final representation in which the desired separations can be achieved with use of a hyperplane. In this book, we show that we can enhance the initial representation without explicit use of hidden layers, and can effect the desired classification with a hyperplane directly. In a sense, Rosenblatt could have been correct if the initial representation had been chosen with care.

Although it is rarely acknowledged explicitly, estimating the values of attributes is often the principal objective of pattern recognition. That is, often the question is not whether or not x belongs to class A. Rather, the question is *what is the value of attribute* A *of* x. It is in this role that network processing of patterns will excel.

1.8 References and Bibliography

1. Chen, C.H., 1973. *Statistical Pattern Recognition*, Hayden, Washington, D.C.

2. Devijver, P. and J. Kittler, 1982. *Pattern Recognition: A Statistical Approach*, Prentice-Hall, Englewood Cliffs, NJ.

3. Duda, R.O. and P.E. Hart, 1973. *Pattern Classification and Scene Analysis*, Wiley, New York.

4. Farley, B.G. and W.A. Clark, 1954. Simulation of self-organizing systems by digital computer, *IRE Transactions on Information Theory*, 4, pp. 76–84.

5. Fu, K.S., 1974. *Syntactic Methods in Pattern Recognition*, Academic Press, New York.

6. Fu, K.S., 1977. *Syntactic Methods in Pattern Recognition: Applications*, Springer-Verlag, New York.

7. Gonzalez, R.C. and M.G. Thomason, 1978. *Syntactic Methods in Pattern Recognition*, Addison-Wesley, Reading, MA.

8. Harel, David, 1987. *Algorithms: The Spirit of Computing*, Addison-Wesley, Reading, MA.

9. Miclet, L., 1986. *Structural Methods in Pattern Recognition*, Springer-Verlag, New York.

10. Minsky, M. and S. Papert, 1969. *Perceptron: An Introduction to Computational Geometry*, MIT Press, Cambridge, MA.

11. Nilsson, N.J., 1965. *Learning Machines*, McGraw-Hill, New York.

12. Pavilidis, T., 1977. *Structural Pattern Recognition*, Springer-Verlag, New York.

13. Ridgeway, W.C., 1962. An adaptive logic system with generalizing properties, *Stanford Electronics Laboratories Technical Report 1556-1*, Stanford University, Stanford, CA.

14. Rosenblatt, F., 1961. The theorems of statistical separability in the perceptron, In *Mechanisation of Thought Processes*, Proceedings of Symposium No. 10 held at the National Physical Laboratory, Nov. 1958, Vol. 1, pp. 421–456, H.M. Stationery Office, London.

15. Rosenblatt, F., 1962. *Principles of Neurodynamics: Perceptrons and The Theory of Brain Mechanisms*, Spartan, New York.

16. Rumelhart, D.E. and J.L. McClelland, 1986. *Parallel Distributed Processing: Explorations in the Microstructure of Cognition*, Vols. 1 and 2, MIT Press, Cambridge, MA.

17. Rumelhart, D.E., G.E. Hinton, and R.J. Williams, 1986. Learning internal representations by error propagation in parallel distributed processing. In D.E. Rumelhart and J.L. McClelland (Eds.), *Explorations in The Microstructures of Cognition*, Vol 1. *Foundations*, pp. 318–362, MIT Press, Cambridge, MA.

18. Simon, J.C., 1986. *Patterns and Operators: The Foundation of Data Representation*, McGraw-Hill, New York. Original French-language edition, 1984, Masson, Editeur, Paris.

19. Slansky, J. and G.N. Wassel, 1981. *Pattern Classifiers and Trainable Machines*, Springer-Verlag, New York.

20. Tou, J.T. and R.C. Gonzalez, 1974. *Pattern Recognition Principles*, Addison-Wesley, Reading, MA.

21. Ullman, J.R., 1973. *Pattern Recognition Techniques*, Butterworths, London.

22. Watanabe, S. (Ed.), 1972. *Frontiers of Pattern Recognition*, Academic Press, New York.

23. Widrow, B. and M.E. Hoff, 1960. *IRE Wescon Convention Record*, Part 4, pp. 96–104, Institute of Radio Engineers, New York.

24. Widrow, B., 1962. Generalization and information storage in networks of Adaline 'Neurons,' in M.C. Yovits, G.T. Jacobi, and G.D. Goldstein (Eds.), *Self-Organizing Systems*, pp. 435–461, Spartan Books, Washington, D.C.

25. Woods, W.A., 1970. Transition network grammars for natural language analysis, *Communications of the ACM*, 13, pp. 591–606.

26. Zadeh, L.A., 1977. Fuzzy sets and their application to classification and clustering. In J. Van Ryzin (Ed.), *Classification and Clustering*, pp. 251–299, Academic Press, New York.

CHAPTER 2

Estimating Class Membership: The Bayesian Approach

2.1 Introduction

The classical Bayesian approach to pattern recognition is adequately covered in existing treatises. It might seem that that body of material could serve as a basis for "statistical pattern recognition" for all times. However, more recently, as pattern recognition *in various guises* has surfaced as a critical issue in different areas of information processing research, researchers have reexamined the scope and validity of this approach. In addition, as traditional pattern recognition becomes severely perturbed and stimulated by the onset of parallel distributed processing, it is well to reexamine the basic theoretical percepts of statistical pattern recognition so as to understand how uncertainty might be dealt with in the parallel distributed processing forms of pattern recognition.

In this chapter, we begin with a brief review of the concepts on which the classical Bayesian approach is based. Then, we show how classification on the basis of decision functions can be related to classification on the basis of the identity of nearest neighbors, or on the basis of discriminants. These relationships are important both conceptually and pragmatically, because sometimes it is much easier to learn discriminants than decision functions. As we shall see in Chapters 5, 7, and 8, discriminants can be inferred in parallel-processing manner. There are circumstances, however, where similar parallel distributed processing may also be viewed in terms of synthesis of decision functions; the metric synthesis viewpoint described in Chapter 5 is an example.

Criticisms of Bayesian pattern recognition are not really directed at *pattern recognition* per se, but are aimed at the very nature of Bayesian statistics. One type of criticism challenges the validity and the relevance of the Bayes' relationship for expressing the a posteriori probability in terms of the a priori probability and class conditional probabilities. The argument is either that the expression is of limited utility because the a priori probabilities are rarely known, or that the expression is insufficient because it does not provide means for including subjective measures of belief.

We shall comment on these criticisms. In one instance, we describe ways of avoiding need for knowledge of the a priori probabilities. For example, we can design the data-gathering operation appropriately, or we can evaluate "odds" in favor of one class membership versus another without explicitly estimating absolute values of probabilities.

Such discussions are also related to the subject matters of Chapters 3 and 4. In Chapter 3, for example, we show how the fuzzy-set-theory approach does provide one means of interjecting subjective views into pattern description and classification. In Chapter 4, we deal with patterns that have linguistic symbolic features, and we show how, in some cases, they can be converted into numeric-valued patterns through use of subjective belief functions.

There are other critics of Bayesian statistics. According to those critics, the Bayesian methodology is incapable of merging supporting or contradictory evidence from several different sources, and is incapable of dealing with missing information. On close examination, the question is not whether Bayesian methodology is capable of handling such matters, because it is, in fact, quite capable of doing so. The real question is whether humans would combine evidence or chain probabilities in the same manner. That is quite a different issue, and we shall see in Chapters 5, 8, and 10 that neural nets are eminently suited to capturing and representing human judgement.

The material covered in this chapter is crucial to an in-depth understanding of the methods of adaptive pattern recognition. All phenomena are ultimately statistical in some sense, and optimal adaptation can be obtained only if the statistical implications of the training-set data are understood and are used correctly.

2.2 General Considerations

The Bayesian approach is appropriate when there is no ambiguity about the pattern itself. We see the pattern clearly and know that it resembles *exactly* a pattern that we have seen before, perhaps quite frequently.

However, we also know that any one of several causes (or hypotheses) might have been responsible for the manifestation of this pattern. Therefore, our task is one of *classification*; namely, we have to decide which one of the possible causes is in fact responsible for this particular pattern. Over time, some of our decisions will be wrong. The issue in statistical pattern recognition is not whether we will make errors. Rather, the issue is how we can minimize the overall incidence or the overall cost of the errors.

In the following discussion, let $\underline{x}$ be the pattern in question and let $c_i, i = 1, 2, \ldots, I$, be the various possible classes of which $\underline{x}$ might be a member. The physical situation considered is that in which the observer awaits the occurrence of a pattern. That event is random in the sense that the next sample—namely, the next pattern—could be any $\underline{x}$, which, in addition, could be from any one of the I classes. Despite the stochastic nature of an individual event, the statistics of the overall phenomenon can be well described in terms of the following probabilities or relative frequencies. In particular, let

$$P(c_i) \equiv \text{the a priori probability that a pattern belongs to} \atop \text{class } c_i, \text{ regardless of the identity of the pattern} \tag{2.1}$$

$$P(\underline{x}_k) \equiv \text{the probability that a pattern is } \underline{x}_k, \text{ regardless} \atop \text{of its class membership} \tag{2.2}$$

$$P(\underline{x}_k|c_i) \equiv \text{the class conditional probability that the pattern} \atop \text{is } \underline{x}_k, \text{ given that it belongs to class } c_i \tag{2.3}$$

$$P(c_i|\underline{x}_k) \equiv \text{the a posteriori conditional probability that the} \atop \text{pattern's class membership is } c_i, \text{ given that the} \atop \text{pattern is } \underline{x}_k \tag{2.4}$$

$$P(c_i, \underline{x}_k) \equiv \text{the joint probability that the pattern is } \underline{x}_k \text{ and that} \atop \text{its class membership is } c_i \tag{2.5}$$

In these definitions, we have taken $\underline{x}_k$ and c_i to be *discrete* quantities, and the normalization conditions are

$$\sum_i P(c_i) = 1$$

$$\sum_k P(\underline{x}_k) = 1$$

Because of the very definition of these quantities, the joint probability can be expressed in two different but equivalent ways; namely,

$$P(c_i, \underline{x}_k) = P(\underline{x}_k|c_i)P(c_i) \tag{2.6}$$

and

$$P(c_i, \underline{x}_k) = P(c_i|\underline{x}_k)P(\underline{x}_k) \tag{2.7}$$

From these expressions, we obtain

$$P(c_i|\underline{x}_k) = P(\underline{x}_k|c_i)P(c_i)/P(\underline{x}_k) \tag{2.8}$$

The Bayes' relation (2.8) can be used for estimating values of the a posteriori probability $P(c_i|\underline{x}_k)$ if those statistics are not known directly and if the class conditional probabilities and a priori probabilities are known.

In the Bayes' approach to pattern classification, the a posteriori probability is treated in the same manner as are all the other probability measures. The a posteriori probability is an *objective probability*—a statistical quantity—and it indicates *chance or relative frequency of occurrence in a random experiment.*

In a simple case, given $\underline{x}_k$, we would evaluate $P(c_i|\underline{x}_k)$ for all the classes $i = 1, 2, \ldots, I$, and decide in favor of that class i for which $P(c|\underline{x}_k)$ is the largest. More generally, our approach would be to construct *decision functions* $g_i(\underline{x}_k)$, one for each class, and the decision rule would be as follows.

Definition 2.1 The Bayes' Decision Rule. *Decide x_k belongs to class $c = c_j$, if and only if*

$$g_j(\underline{x}_k) > g_i(\underline{x}_k) \tag{2.9}$$

for all $i = 1, 2, \ldots, I, i \neq j$, where $g_i(\underline{x}_k)$ is the decision function for class i.

In principle and in practice, $g_i(\underline{x}_k)$ could be $P(c_i|\underline{x}_k)$ itself or some function of $P(c_i|\underline{x}_k)$. We can synthesize risk functions from such conditional-probability functions, and *we can then make decisions on the basis of minimum risk or maximum gain.* We note that the Bayes' decision rule is distinct from the Bayes' relation (2.8). It is the use of the latter that is sometimes controversial.

Let us suppose that not all decision errors can be made with equal impunity. Let us define ℓ_{ij} to be the loss sustained if we decide class membership is c_i when in reality it is c_j. Then the risk undertaken in deciding that $\underline{x}_k$ belongs to c_i is

$$R_i(\underline{x}_k) = \ell_{ii}P(c_i|\underline{x}_k) + \sum_{j \neq i} \ell_{ij}P(c_j|\underline{x}_k) \qquad (2.10)$$

For a two-class problem,

$$\begin{aligned} R_1(\underline{x}_k) &= \ell_{11}P(c_1|\underline{x}_k) + \ell_{12}P(c_2|\underline{x}_k) \\ R_2(\underline{x}_k) &= \ell_{21}P(c_1|\underline{x}_k) + \ell_{22}P(c_2|\underline{x}_k) \end{aligned} \qquad (2.11)$$

and the decision rule would be to decide the $\underline{x}_k$ belongs to class c_1 if and only if

$$R_1(\underline{x}_k) < R_2(\underline{x}_k) \qquad (2.12)$$

or

$$(\ell_{12} - \ell_{22})P(c_2|\underline{x}_k) < (\ell_{21} - \ell_{11})P(c_1|\underline{x}_k) \qquad (2.13)$$

or

$$\frac{P(c_1|\underline{x}_k)}{P(c_2|\underline{x}_k)} > \frac{\ell_{12} - \ell_{22}}{\ell_{21} - \ell_{11}} \qquad (2.14)$$

If we assume that there is no loss if we guess correctly, and that it is equally costly to guess incorrectly in either way, then

$$\ell_{11} = \ell_{22} = 0 \quad \text{and} \quad \ell_{12} = \ell_{21}$$

For that case, we recover the maximum a posteriori probability decision rule, which is to decide in favor of c_1 if and only if $P(c_1|\underline{x}_k) > P(c_2|\underline{x}_k)$.

Example 2.1 The English-Speaking Traveler. As an illustration, consider the case of an English-speaking traveler visiting an European country where the native language is not English. In fact, to our traveler's surprise and distress, few of the native population speak English. At first, he feels disoriented; after a while, however, he is told that, statistically speaking,

- One out of 10 natives speak English

- One out of five persons encountered is likely to be a tourist

● One out of two tourists speak English

Using Bayesian statistics, he is then able to infer other statistical estimates and is able to cope with the situation in detail, optimizing the overall chances of attaining his objectives.

The statistics of the situation can also be illustrated schematically in terms of relative areas covered by regions within a square of unit area, as shown in Figure 2.1. In that illustration, let the square of unit area represent the total population in the locale visited by the traveler. This is the universe of discourse; the probability of any one person, encountered by the traveler, being in this universe is unity.

The lightly shaded area, rectangle A, represents the relative size of the native population; in a random encounter, it would also represent the probability that the person so encountered is a native.

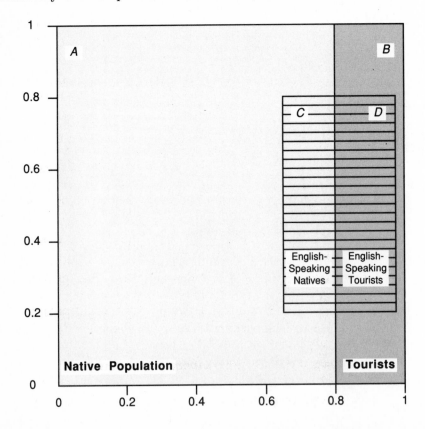

Figure 2.1   Graphical representation of probabilities in the English-speaking traveler example.

Similarly, the darker shaded area, rectangle B, represents the relative size of the tourist population and the a priori probability of a person met on the street in a random encounter being a tourist. Of both populations, some members speak English and others do not. Thus, for the native population, the English-speaking components are represented by the lighter horizontally hatched area, rectangle C, and the English-speaking tourists by the darker hatched area, D.

The statistical estimates given to the traveler may be stated as follows in terms of probabilities, and can also be visualized in terms of the geometrical representation of Figure 2.1.

$$P(t) \equiv \text{the probability that a randomly encountered} \atop \text{person is a tourist} = 0.2 \text{ (represented by area } B) \tag{2.15}$$

$$P(e|n) \equiv \text{the conditional probability that the person can} \atop \text{speak English, given that she is a native} = 0.1 \atop \text{(represented by area } C \text{ divided by area } A) \tag{2.16}$$

$$P(e|t) \equiv \text{the conditional probability that the person can} \atop \text{speak English, given that she is a tourist} = 0.5 \atop \text{(represented by area } D \text{ divided by area } B) \tag{2.17}$$

Other quantities of interest, which can be inferred, include

$$P(n) \equiv \text{the probability that the person is a native} \atop \equiv 1 - P(t) = 0.8 \text{ (represented by area } A) \tag{2.18}$$

$$P(e) \equiv \text{the probability that the person speaks English,} \atop \text{regardless of whether she is a native or a tourist} \atop \equiv P(e|n)P(n) + P(e|t)P(t) = (0.1)(0.8) + (0.5)(0.2) \atop = 0.18 \text{ (represented by areas } C \text{ and } D) \tag{2.19}$$

$$P(\bar{e}|n) \equiv \text{the conditional probability that the person } cannot \atop \text{speak English, given the fact that she is a native} \atop \equiv 1 - P(e|n) = 0.9 \text{ (represented by (area } A \text{ minus} \atop \text{area } C) \text{ divided by area } A) \tag{2.20}$$

$$P(\bar{e}|t) \equiv \text{the conditional probability that the person } cannot \atop \text{speak English given that she is a tourist} \atop \equiv 1 - P(e|t) = 0.5 \text{ (represented by (area } B \text{ minus} \atop \text{area } D) \text{ divided by area } B) \tag{2.21}$$

The joint probability $P(n \wedge e)$ is equal to $P(e|n)P(n)$, as represented by (area C)/(area A) multiplied by (area A)—that is, area C. It is also equal to $P(n|e)P(e)$, as represented by (area C)/(sum of areas C and D) multiplied by the (sum of areas C and D)—that is, again area C. Therefore,

$P(n \wedge e) \equiv$ the joint probability that the person is a native

   and speaks English

   $\equiv P(e|n)P(n) = (0.1)(0.8) = 0.08$ (represented by   (2.22)

   area C)

$P(t \wedge e) \equiv$ the joint probability that the person is a tourist

   and speaks English   (2.23)

   $\equiv P(e|t)P(t) = (0.5)(0.2) = 0.1$

This example illustrates a typical situation, in which the traveler knows a lot about the statistics of the situation and is yet not able to give an estimate for $P(n|e)$ or $P(t|e)$. That is, when he encounters an English speaking person, he cannot say whether it more likely that the person is a native or that she is a tourist.

These quantities can be inferred, however, through use of the Bayes' relationship (2.8).

$P(n|e) \equiv$ the conditional probability that the person is a

   native, given that she speaks English

   $\equiv P(e|n)P(n)/P(e) = (0.1)(0.8)/0.18 = 0.44$, and   (2.24)

   (area C divided by the sum of areas C and D)

$P(t|e) \equiv$ the conditional probability that the person is a

   tourist, given that she speaks English   (2.25)

   $\equiv P(e|t)P(t)/P(e) = (0.5)(0.2)/0.18 = 0.56$

The traveler now can use these estimates as the basis for deciding whether the English-speaking person he has just encountered is more likely to be a native or a tourist. Depending on the consequencies of a wrong guess, he might want to bias his decision somewhat, in which case he might want to base his decision on functionals of these probabilities.

This simple example has illustrated the concepts of joint and conditional probabilities, as well as the use of the Bayes' relationship. *It is also an example of pattern recognition, involving a pattern of one feature with*

feature name of "linguistic capability" and with discrete feature values of
e (English speaker) and $\bar{e}$ (non–English speaker).   ■

Example 2.2 The Social Activities Director.   Let us consider a case where
a decision needs to be based on a function of probability measures rather
than on a posteriori probabilities alone. A social events director who
has an important outdoor event scheduled for Saturday is confronted on
Thursday afternoon with a weather forecast of 60 percent probability of
rain on Saturday.

The director's options are limited: she can postpone the event to some
future Saturday, or she can take a chance and go ahead with the event on
this Saturday.

If the director guesses that the weather will be fair and it is indeed
fair, then there is considerable gain in terms of participation fees, good
publicity, and enhanced reputation of the director. The loss in this case
is a negative quantity, because there is in fact considerable gain.

If the director guesses that the weather will be fair and instead rain
inundates the participants, the loss is in terms of discomfort to these
people, damage to equipment, possibly additional expense due to having
to cancel the event at or near the start of the event and having to conduct
it again at some future weekend, and some decrease in confidence in the
director's good sense.

If the director decides that it will rain and it does not, then the loss
is real and large, including loss of revenue, loss of positive publicity, and
decrease in regard for the director's judgement.

Finally, if the director decides that it will rain and it indeed does rain,
there is no net loss or gain.

As described in Section 2.2, let ℓ_{ij} be the loss sustained when we
decide in favor of condition i but nature decides in favor of condition j.

Let subscript 1 represent fair weather and subscript 2 denote rain.
And let

$$\ell_{11} = -1$$

$$\ell_{12} = 2$$

$$\ell_{21} = 3$$

$$\ell_{22} = 0$$

These assigned values represent an attempt to quantify the losses in the four cases. We note that $\ell_{11} = -1$ represents a gain. The value of ℓ_{21} is taken to be larger than that of ℓ_{12}, meaning that of the two unfortunate eventualities, it is worse to decide that it will rain and then have the weather be fair.

Let $P(c_1|\underline{x})$ represent the forecast probability of the weather being fair on Saturday and let $P(c_2|\underline{x})$ represent the forecast probability for rain falling. We write the forecast values in terms of a posteriori conditional probabilities, not only because we can make our point more easily in the manner, but also because in fact they are indeed conditional probabilities, in the sense that "given a set of meterological data, the probability for rain is …."

If the director decides on the basis of minimum risk, then, according to (2.14), her decision would be to decide in favor of "fair"; that is, she will go ahead with the event as long as $R_1 < R_2$, or equivalently, if

$$\frac{P(c_1|\underline{x})}{P(c_2|\underline{x})} > \frac{\ell_{12} - \ell_{22}}{\ell_{21} - \ell_{11}} = \frac{2 - 0}{3 - (-1)} = \frac{2}{4} = 0.50$$

In the present case, we have

$$\frac{P(c_1|\underline{x})}{P(c_2|\underline{x})} = \frac{0.4}{0.6} = 0.66 > 0.5$$

so the director decides in favor of going ahead with the scheduled event.

Note that, if the minimum risk decision is made for each case, then minimum risk is obtained for the overall system average. In this case, the actual pattern $\underline{x}$ is a set of metereological readings, and the pattern processing has proceeded far enough that we know the a posteriori probabilities for $\underline{x}$ to be in class "rain" or "fair." For this example, the decision was based on the objective of minimum risk rather than of maximum a posteriori probability.   ∎

2.3 Knowledge Required for Training

In this section, we are concerned with the process of acquisition of knowledge required for support of the classification act. We also consider the nature, extent, and representation of that knowledge.

This knowledge is acquired during the training or learning phase of pattern recognition. It is worth noting that, in statistical geometric pattern recognition, although the patterns themselves are simply lists of real numbers, a great deal of knowledge is required in support of the classification act. In fact, in principle, an infinite amount of knowledge is required; in practice, however, we deal with matters in a more pragmatic manner, and resort to approximate procedures.

The principal aspects of these matters can be illustrated readily for uni-dimensional patterns that belong to one of two possible classes. Let x be the name of the feature, and let the set of patterns observed during the learning process be $\{x_1, x_2, x_3, \ldots x_M\}$. Each of these patterns is a labeled pattern in the sense that the training knowledge is in the form of (pattern, class membership) associative pairs.

After a training session, the knowledge base of the classifer might be that depicted schematically in Figure 2.2(a). Knowledge in this form, however, would be essentially useless because, in statistical pattern recognition—at least in this rudimentary pure form—it is necessary that we have previous information on *any* pattern we are asked to classify. Since it is extremely unlikely that any new pattern will have precisely one of the values of the set $\{x_1, x_2, x_3, \ldots x_M\}$, the knowledge acquired in the so-called learning session would be quite irrelevant. Furthermore, we would have to have an infinitely long training session to be sure of learning all the possible pattern values that might be encountered in practice.

Of course, we know that, in practice, statisticians proceed differently. In the training phase, we can quantize pattern space into cells of finite size, and can group all patterns within each cell to yield a value positioned at the center of the cell. In the classification phase, we would proceed in a similar way to consider any pattern falling within a cell as being positioned at the center of that cell. Alternatively, we might find a continuous-function representation of the discretized data in the form of class-dependent probability density distribution functions. The representation would be "optimum" in the sense that the curve fitting would be carried out on the basis of least mean square error.

The distributions obtained in those two manners are displayed in Figures 2.2(b) and 2.2(c), respectively. *It is clear that, in both cases, we have solved the problem of being able to recognize the input pattern, and the only remaining task is that of classification.* In Figure 2.2(b), every new pattern has to fall within one of the quantization cells, and it is then considered to be identical to the pattern at the center of the cell. In Figure 2.2(c), the inferred continuous probability density function provides a probability $p(x)dx$ for the occurrence of a pattern being within the interval x and $x + dx$.

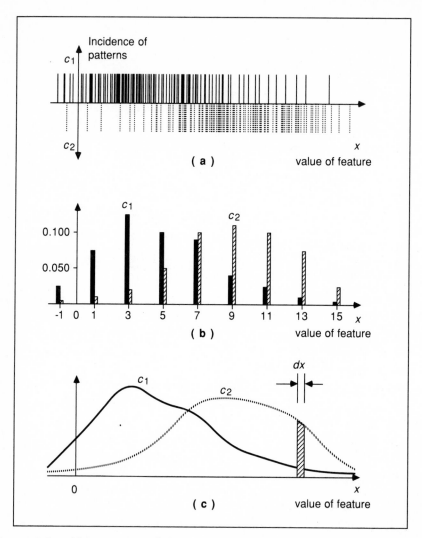

Figure 2.2   Using quantized discrete distributions or continuous-distribution functions to provide approximate representations of discrete data.

Note that the discrete and continuous distributions displayed in Figures 2.2(b) and 2.2(c) are not independently normalized class conditional distributions, but rather are the more useful joint probability distributions. In other words, the discrete probability values displayed in Figure 2.2(b) and listed in Table 2.1 are normalized with respect to the entire net of observations. The value of 0.039 in the cell with $x = 9.0$ is the probability that the next new pattern will be in that cell and (jointly)

Table 2.1 Discrete Joint Probabilities

x	$P(x, c_1)$	$P(x, c_2)$
-1	0.025	0.005
1	0.076	0.012
3	0.125	0.022
5	0.102	0.048
7	0.091	0.099
9	0.039	0.111
11	0.025	0.102
13	0.012	0.076
15	0.005	0.025

belong to class c_1. Similarly, the value of 0.111 in the same cell is the probability that the next new pattern will be in that cell and belong to class c_2. That is, for the discrete case,

$$P(x = 9.0, c_1) = P(x = 9.0|c_1)P(c_1) = 0.039$$

and

$$P(x = 9.0, c_2) = P(x = 9.0|c_2)P(c_2) = 0.111$$

also

$$\sum_{x_k} \sum_{i=1,2} P(x_k|c_i)P(c_i) = \sum_{i,k} P(x_k, c_i) = 1 \tag{2.26}$$

This type of information is useful because, from expression (2.8), we see that for continuous-valued patterns the a posteriori probability may be written as

$$P(c_j|\underline{x}_k) = p(\underline{x}_k|c_j)P(c_j)/p(\underline{x}_k) \tag{2.27}$$

However, $p(\underline{x})$ does not depend on class, and classification on the basis of maximum a posteriori probability can be made readily on the basis of joint probabilities alone.

Generalizing, this means that we decide $\underline{x}_k$ belongs to c_i if and only if

$$\frac{P(c_i|\underline{x}_k)}{P(c_j|\underline{x}_k)} = \frac{p(\underline{x}_k|c_i)P(c_i)}{p(\underline{x}_k|c_j)P(c_j)} = \frac{p(\underline{x}_k, c_i)}{p(\underline{x}_k, c_j)} > 1 \tag{2.28}$$

If learning is achieved through recording of a set of labeled random samples, then classification can be carried out even if we have no knowledge of the class conditional probabilities $p(\underline{x}_k|c_i)$ and of the a priori probabilities $P(c_i)$ separately.

This discussion shows clearly that the format of the training session is important. If we were informed that, for example, the next N pattern are all of class c_i, and we then proceeded to assign the patterns to the different cells in accordance with their feature values, we would merely obtain $p(\underline{x}|c_i)$ separately. We would then need to obtain the various $P(c_i)$ values separately, and that might not be easy or even feasible. Similar remarks apply to the continuous case.

In the training session, it is preferable that the patterns be generated normally (that is, seemingly randomly) in accordance with the environment of the problem. Of course, each of the patterns would need to be labeled, so that the classifier could be trained properly.

For continuous representations, the density distributions are $p(\underline{x}|c_j)$ $P(c_j)$ and the normalization condition is that

$$\sum_i \int_v d\underline{x} p(\underline{x}|c_i) P(c_i) = 1 \qquad (2.29)$$

2.4 System Error in the Case of Continuous Distributions

We have seen that representation of pattern information with use of continuous class conditional or joint distributions is actually a way of interpolating and extrapolating pattern data. Note that classification on the basis of maximum a posteriori probability constitutes an optimum classification procedure. In addition if an optimum procedure is followed for each value of $\underline{x}$, then the entire systemwide practice is also optimum. However, optimum decision does not imply that there is no error. One is merely assured that the overall system error is at a minimum.

In statistical pattern recognition, the question is not whether we make any errors; the only concern is that we make as few errors as possible.

The continuous joint probability distributions are particularly convenient for illustrating the origin and nature of the system error. For example, in a binary classification task, if we make decisions on the basis of the maximum a posteriori probability rule, then, for an $\underline{x}$, we decide

$\underline{x} \in c_1$ *if and only if* $P(c_1|\underline{x}) > P(c_2|\underline{x})$ *and* $\underline{x} \in c_2$ *otherwise*   (2.30)

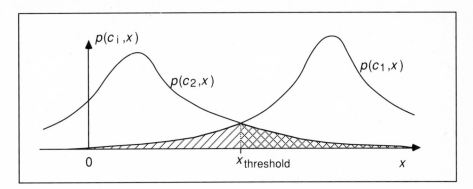

Figure 2.3   Illustration of a threshold discriminant based on statistics.

For any $\underline{x}$, then, the probability density of making an error is given by

$$\text{Probability density of error} = P_e(\underline{x}) = \min\{P(c_1|\underline{x}), P(c_2|\underline{x})\} \quad (2.31)$$

In particular, for a one-dimensional case that is well behaved in the sense that the statistics can be described in terms of two smooth unimodal distributions representing (approximately) the two joint probability distributions $p(c_i, x)$, we might have a situation such as that shown schematically in Figure 2.3.

Let $x_{\text{threshold}}$ be the value of x where the two joint probability distributions intersect. Then, according to expression (2.8), we decide $x \in c_1$ if and only if $x > x_{\text{threshold}}$, else $x \in c_2$. The special case of $x = x_{\text{threshold}}$ might be decided either way.

The probability of error averaged over all values of x is

$$\begin{aligned}
\text{system error} &= \langle \text{probability of error} \rangle_{\text{averaged over system}} \\
&= \int_{-\infty}^{x_{threshold}} P(c_1|x)p(x)dx + \int_{x_{threshold}}^{\infty} P(c_2|x)p(x)dx \\
&= \int_{-\infty}^{x_{threshold}} \frac{p(x|c_1)P(c_1)}{p(x)} p(x)dx \\
&\quad + \int_{x_{threshold}}^{\infty} \frac{p(x|c_2)P(c_2)}{p(x)} p(x)dx \qquad (2.32) \\
&= \int_{-\infty}^{x_{threshold}} p(x, c_1)dx + \int_{x_{threshold}}^{\infty} p(x, c_2)dx
\end{aligned}$$

$\equiv$ shaded areas in Figure 2.3(b)

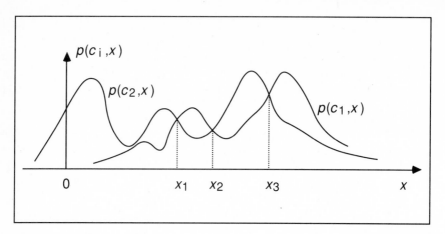

Figure 2.4   Thresholds used as discriminants in the case of multimodal distributions.

It is interesting that, in this case, the act of classification ultimately does not require detailed knowledge of the probability distributions. All that is required is knowledge of one number, $x_{threshold}$, which serves as a *discriminant*. More complex situations are correspondingly more difficult, and in such cases the knowledge of several discriminant values might be required, as shown in Figure 2.4, where $x \in c_1$, if $x_1 < x < x_2$ or $x > x_3$. For higher dimensions, the thresholds are lines, surfaces, or hypersurfaces. *Although the classification act is based on statistics, it appears to be completely deterministic.* We are reminded of the statistical origins only when we remember that there is a system error.

2.5 The Nature and Role of Discriminants

In general, a discriminant is a function or operator that, when applied to a pattern, yields an output that is either an estimate of the class membership of that pattern or an estimate of the values of one or more of the attributes of the pattern. In other words, the action of a discriminant is to produce a mapping from pattern space to attribute space.

In a sense, the existence of discriminants constitutes the essence of pattern recognition. The action of a discriminant is all-encompassing; the entire pattern is processed at the same time, in a *gestalt* manner, rather than sequentially, one feature at a time.

In this section, we develop two themes in our study of discriminants.

1. We show that it is possible to start with statistical pattern recognition and Bayes' decision rule and to end up in practice using discriminants, seemingly processing in a deterministic manner, with no mention of statistics.

2. We also show that, for numeric-valued patterns, the discriminants are based on one of two concepts. In one case, the discriminant consists of a measure of distance, and patterns are classified in accordance with the class membership of nearest neighbors, or with the nearest prototype or cluster center. In the other case, the discriminants are hypersurfaces, and patterns are classified in accordance whether they are on one side or another of a hypersurfaces or of a set of hyperplanes. Use of such discriminants is also tantamount to the use of hyperplanes to divide pattern space into volumes of unique class membership.

In conjunction with our exposition of the first type of discriminant, we mention briefly the existence and use of a well-known algorithm, the ISODATA algorithm [Ball and Hall 1966], for exploring the structure of clusters of patterns in pattern space and discovering the most representative positions of prototypes. In conjunction with discussion of the second type of discriminants, the hypersurfaces, we mention briefly the related approaches of Widrow–Hoff and the linear Perceptron. This theme leads to the material of Chapter 5 on semilinear neural nets and the autonomous learning of discriminants that function as hypersurfaces to partition pattern space into nonoverlapping volumes, each of a single class membership.

Once we have transformed Bayes' decision rule into the action of discriminants, the learning task during the training session is correspondingly transformed into learning the metric of pattern space, or learning the position of prototypes, or learning the position of hyperplanes or of more generalized hypersurfaces.

Seemingly, all notion of statistics is forgotten and everything is deterministic. Of course, in reality, this is not so. As pointed out in the previous section, in statistical pattern recognition, our aim is not to eliminate mistakes, but rather to ensure that the overall system error is minimal. This is the definition of optimal performance. *Correspondingly, we must take care to ensure that such optimal behavior is preserved in the learning of these discriminants.* This is why we need to keep statistics in mind as we move from traditional pattern recognition to adaptive pattern recognition, as implemented in neural nets.

Classification on Basis of Distance to Neighbors or to Prototypes

Let the distribution of patterns among all the possible classes be described by the joint probability density functions $p(\underline{x}, c_i)$. That is, the joint probability density that a pattern be $\underline{x}$ *and* be in class c_i is

$$p(\underline{x}, c_i) = p(\underline{x}|c_i)P(c_i) \tag{2.33}$$

and the normalization condition is

$$\sum_i P(c_i) = 1 \tag{2.34}$$

In the absence of loss factor considerations, Bayes' decision rule would take the form of a maximum a posteriori probability rule and we decide $\underline{x}$ belongs to c_i if and only if

$$p(\underline{x}, c_i) > p(\underline{x}, c_j) \qquad \text{for all} \quad j \neq i \tag{2.35}$$

For the one-dimensional case, let the distribution be Gaussian; that is,

$$p(x, c_i) = (\sigma_i \sqrt{2\pi})^{-1} \exp\left[-\frac{1}{2}(x - \mu_i)^2/\sigma_i^2\right] P(c_i) \tag{2.36}$$

where μ_i is the mean, and σ_i is the standard deviation, of the distribution.

To make our point, let us assume that, for two contiguous overlapping distributions, the *a priori* probabilities $P(c_i)$ and $P(c_j)$ are equal in magnitude, and that the widths of the distributions are also equal; that is, $\sigma_i = \sigma_j = \sigma$.

Then, the decision rule would be that we decide x belongs to c_i if and only if

$$\frac{\exp\left[-\frac{1}{2}(x - \mu_i)^2/\sigma^2\right]}{\exp\left[-\frac{1}{2}(x - \mu_j)^2/\sigma^2\right]} > 1 \tag{2.37}$$

or if and only if

$$(x - \mu_i)^2 < (x - \mu_j)^2 \tag{2.38}$$

The quantities $(x - \mu_i)^2$ and $(x - \mu_j)^2$ may be interpreted to be the (one-dimensional) Euclidean distances of x from the "centers" of the i and j distributions. This analysis is the conceptual foundation for the use of "distances," and for classification on the basis of which distribution center or cluster center is the nearest.

As we can see, this approach may not be sound practice, there being the possibility of considerable error unless all the $P(c_i)$ are equal to one another and unless all the σ_i are equal to one another. *In other words, classification on the basis of nearest prototype or cluster center may be near optimum only if appropriate additional weightings are introduced.* The idea of classification on the basis of nearest neighbor is even further compromised. However, this analysis provides some idea of how statistical distributions and likelihood relate to the concepts of similarity and "distances."

More generally, for the N-dimensional case, the general multidimensional Gaussian density can be written as

$$p(\underline{x}|c_i) = \left((2\pi)^{N/2} \left| \sum_i \right|^{1/2} \right)^{-1} \exp\left[-\frac{1}{2}(\underline{x} - \underline{\mu}_i)^t \sum_i{}^{-1} (\underline{x} - \underline{\mu}_i) \right] \quad (2.39)$$

where $\underline{x}$ is an N-component column vector, $\underline{\mu}_i$ is the N-component *mean vector*, Σ is the N-by-N *covariance matrix*, $(\underline{x} - \underline{\mu}_i)^t$ is the transpose of $(\underline{x} - \underline{\mu})$, Σ^{-1} is the inverse of Σ, and $|\Sigma|$ is the determinant of Σ.

For such cases, if all the classes have the same covariance matrix— that is, if $\Sigma_i = \Sigma$ for all i, and if $P(c_i) = P(c)$ for all i—then we decide that $\underline{x}$ belongs to c_i if and only if

$$(\underline{x} - \underline{\mu}_i)^t \sum{}^{-1} (\underline{x} - \underline{\mu}_i) < (\underline{x} - \underline{\mu}_j)^t \sum{}^{-1} (\underline{x} - \underline{\mu}_j) \quad (2.40)$$

This result corresponds to using the measure of the *Mahalanobis distance* [Chen 1973] rather than the Euclidean distance. Because of the unequal $P(c_i)$ and the different scatters represented by the Σ_i, however, use of Mahalanobis distance alone as a discriminant would not lead to optimal results.

Nevertheless, it is interesting to note how we can proceed from a fully statistical classification problem where there is no question of the identity of the pattern, to go smoothly to the situation where *the primary concern is that of similarity between patterns, and seemingly no thought is given to statistics.*

Classification on the Basis of Discriminant Vectors or Hyperplanes

The multidimensional normal density for the joint probabilities also provides a conceptual justification for the use of discriminants in the form of surfaces that serve to seperate patterns of one class from patterns of other classes. In the linear case, those surfaces are hyperplanes, and discriminants can also take the form of vectors normal to those planes.

Reverting to joint probabilities, we express the decision rule again as deciding $\underline{x}$ belongs to c_i, if and only if

$$p(\underline{x}, c_i) > p(\underline{x}, c_j) \qquad \text{for all} \quad j \neq i$$

This means that the boundary between a specific pair of classes is described analytically by the condition that, for all patterns $\underline{x}$ on the boundary, we have

$$\frac{P(c_i)\left((2\pi)^{N/2}\left|\Sigma_i\right|^{1/2}\right)^{-1} \exp\left[-\frac{1}{2}(\underline{x} - \underline{\mu}_i)^t \Sigma_i^{-1}(\underline{x} - \underline{\mu}_i)\right]}{P(c_j)\left((2\pi)^{N/2}\left|\Sigma_j\right|^{1/2}\right)^{-1} \exp\left[-\frac{1}{2}(\underline{x} - \underline{\mu}_j)^t \Sigma_j^{-1}(\underline{x} - \underline{\mu}_j)\right]} = 1 \quad (2.41)$$

Taking the natural logarithm of both sides and assuming that $\Sigma_i = \Sigma_j$, we obtain, after canceling out the nonlinear terms,

$$\underline{x}^t \sum\nolimits^{-1}(\underline{\mu}_j - \underline{\mu}_i) + (\underline{\mu}_j - \underline{\mu}_i)^t \sum\nolimits^{-1} \underline{x} = 2\ell n P(c_i)/P(c_j) \qquad (2.42)$$

Remembering that Σ^{-1} is a symmetric matrix, this expression further reduces to

$$2\underline{x}^t\left[\sum\nolimits^{-1}(\underline{\mu}_j - \underline{\mu}_i)\right] - 2\ell n P(c_i)/P(c_j) = 0 \qquad (2.43)$$

or

$$\underline{x}^t \underline{a} = \ell n P(c_i)/P(c_j) \qquad (2.44)$$

The analytical expression (2.41) describes a surface in N-dimensional space, separating the c_i class patterns from the c_j class patterns. That hypersurface is our discriminant.

With the use of some simplifying assumptions, we obtain expression (2.43), which can also be understood in terms of some geometrical constructs. Expression (2.43) describes a hyperplane rather than a more general hypersurface. In addition, the plane is described in terms of its normal $\underline{a}$.

That is, expression (2.44) states that in order to classify such patterns, we need to find a discriminant vector $\underline{a}$. If the scalar product of the pattern vector $\underline{x}$ and $\underline{a}$ is greater than $\ell n P(c_i)/P(c_j)$, we decide that the pattern belongs to c_i; otherwise, it belongs to c_j. Of course, in our case, we know that $\underline{a}$ is related to the underlying statistical information through the relationship

$$\underline{a} = \sum^{-1}(\underline{\mu}_j - \underline{\mu}_i) \tag{2.45}$$

More generally, the distributions are not necessarily normal and we know neither the hyperplane nor the discriminant vector and associated threshold, which is $\ell n P(c_i)/P(c_j)$ in this simple case. This derivation, however, provides a conceptual link between the Bayesian approach and the practice of using hyperplanes or vectors as discriminants. This link not only lends legitimacy to such practices, but also can provide guidance on how to modify or improve the use of such practices, should we need to do so.

From a historical point of view, both the Widrow–Hoff algorithm for finding a discriminant vector [Widrow and Hoff, 1960] and the approach of the linear version of the Perceptron algorithm [Duda and Hart, 1973] are easily understood as specialized versions of this general discriminant vector approach. *Since neither $\underline{a}$ nor $\ell n P(c_i)/P(c_j)$ are known, these values are learned through iterative procedures.*

These iterative procedures are well known and will not be treated here. A generalized Perceptron procedure is presented in Chapter 5, and this discussion provides a background for that material and for the material contained in Chapter 8.

Example 2.3 describes the task of obtaining a linear discriminant in terms of a simple network device learning appropriate values of weights. We also use this example to show how enhancement of the original pattern with nonlinear terms can enable the same simple network to learn a discriminant even when the two distributions are not linearly separable in their original form. This enhancement procedure is an essential feature of the Functional Link net approach described in Chapter 8.

Example 2.3 A Network Perspective to the Learning of Discriminants.
In this section, we have shown that for a two category classification problem, we can derive an analytical description for the optimal discriminant surface provided the class conditional probability distribution densities and the a priori probabilities are known.

To fix ideas, we consider a special case of two-dimensional patterns with Gaussian distributions. The normal distributions are taken with their principal axes along the x_1 and x_2 coordinate axes, or equivalently, the covariance matrices are diagonal.

The means of the two distributions are $\underline{\mu}_1 = \{\mu_{11}, \mu_{12}\}$ and $\underline{\mu}_2 = \{\mu_{21}, \mu_{22}\}$ and the diagonal components of the covariance matrices are $\{\sigma_{11}, \sigma_{12}\}$ and $\{\sigma_{21}, \sigma_{22}\}$.

Thus the class conditional probability densities are

$$P(\underline{x}|c_1) = N_1 \exp\left[-\frac{1}{2}(x_1 - \mu_{11})^2/\sigma_{11}^2 - \frac{1}{2}(x_2 - \mu_{12})^2/\sigma_{12}^2\right]$$

and

$$P(\underline{x}|c_2) = N_2 \exp\left[-\frac{1}{2}(x_1 - \mu_{21})^2/\sigma_{21}^2 - \frac{1}{2}(x_2 - \mu_{22})^2/\sigma_{22}^2\right] \quad (2.46)$$

where N_1 and N_2 are normalizing factors.

Expression (2.41) gives an analytical expression for the line that provides an optimal separation of the two classes, namely

$$\begin{aligned} -(x_1 - \mu_{11})^2/\sigma_{11}^2 + (x_1 - \mu_{21})^2/\sigma_{21}^2 - (x_2 - \mu_{12})^2/\sigma_{12}^2 \\ + (x_2 - \mu_{22})^2/\sigma_{22}^2 = 2\ell n[P(c_1)N_1/P(c_2)N_2] \end{aligned} \quad (2.47)$$

If the components of the standard deviations are all equal, that is, $\sigma_{11} = \sigma_{12} = \sigma_{21} = \sigma_{22} = \sigma$, then we attain not only separability, but also *linear separability* in the manner described by expression (2.44). The discriminant can be written as

$$\begin{aligned} 2(\mu_{11} - 2\mu_{21})x_1 + 2(\mu_{12} - \mu_{22})x_2 = (\mu_{11}^2 - \mu_{21}^2) + (\mu_{12}^2 - \mu_{22}^2) \\ + 2\sigma \, \ell n P(c_1)/P(c_2) \end{aligned} \quad (2.48)$$

or

$$\begin{aligned} x_2 = \left(\frac{\mu_{21} - \mu_{11}}{\mu_{12} - \mu_{22}}\right)x_1 + [(\mu_{11}^2 - \mu_{21}^2) + (\mu_{12}^2 - \mu_{22}^2) \\ + 2\ell n P(c_1)/P(c_2)]/2(\mu_{12} - \mu_{22}) \end{aligned} \quad (2.49)$$

This is the equation for a straight line of the form

$$y = mx + b \quad (2.50)$$

where m is the slope of the line and b is the intercept on the y axis.

We see that we can go from statistical probability distributions to a linear discriminant. We can also view equation (2.48), however, in terms of a neural net to be described in Chapters 5 and 8. With input x_1 and x_2, the net learns that the weights need to be $2(\mu_{11} - \mu_{21})$ and $2(\mu_{12} - 2\mu_{22})$, respectively. The sum of the linearly weighted inputs are then compared to

$$(\mu_{11}^2 - \mu_{21}^2) + (\mu_{12}^2 + \mu_{22}^2) + 2\sigma \ell n P(c_1)/P(c_2)$$

and the pattern is class c_1 or class c_2, depending on whether the sum of the weighted inputs is greater or less than this number.

The situation is very different if the standard deviations are not equal, and in this case we have the more general expression

$$
\begin{aligned}
(2\mu_{11}/\sigma_{11}^2 &- 2\mu_{21}/\sigma_{21}^2)x_1 \\
&+ (1/\sigma_{11}^2 - 1/\sigma_{21}^2)x_1^2 + (2\mu_{22}/\sigma_{22}^2 - 2\mu_{12}/\sigma_{12}^2)x_2 \\
&+ (1/\sigma_{12}^2 - 1/\sigma_{22}^2)x_2^2 = (\mu_{11}^2/\sigma_{11}^2 - \mu_{21}^2/\sigma_{21}^2) \\
&+ (\mu_{22}^2/\sigma_{22}^2 - \mu_{12}^2/\sigma_{12}^2) + \ell n[P(c_1)N_1/P(c_2)N_2]
\end{aligned}
\tag{2.51}
$$

The discriminate is a quadratic function of the variables x_1 and x_2 and is no longer a straight line.

In other words, the two populations can be separated with one line, but the line is a general curved line rather than a straight line. The populations are not linearly separable, but nonlinearly separable. If we insist on using a linear discriminant, we would make many errors and the decision process would not be optimal.

However, if we make the substitution

$$z_1 = 2(\mu_{11}/\sigma_{11}^2 - \mu_{21}/\sigma_{21}^2)x_1 + (1/\sigma_{11}^2 - 1/\sigma_{21}^2)x_1^2$$

and

$$z_2 = 2(\mu_{22}/\sigma_{22}^2 - \mu_{12}/\sigma_{12}^2)x_2 + (1/\sigma_{22}^2 - 1/\sigma_{12}^2)x_2^2 \tag{2.52}$$

to obtain the expression

$$z_1 + z_2 = C \tag{2.53}$$

where C is the right hand side of expression (2.51), we see that the distributions are linearly separable in $\{z_1, z_2\}$ space.

When confronted with a nonlinearly separable problem, we can achieve linear separability by enhancing the input pattern, in this case by adding the additional components x_1^2 and x_2^2 to the input pattern. No extraneous information is added, but the net is able to use the additional nonlinear terms to achieve linear separability. These matters will be further clarified in Chapter 8.

2.6 Criticisms of the Bayesian Approach

In considering criticisms of the Bayesian approach to pattern recognition, it is helpful to distinguish between those aimed centrally at Bayesian statistics itself and those concerned with only the appropriateness of the use of Bayesian approach in pattern recognition. Some issues are intertwined and cannot be discussed separately.

A subtle issue needs to be addressed at this juncture. The question is whether decisions are to be made solely by humans, or solely by machines, or by both, sometimes by the one and other times by the other but always in ways understandable to both.

According to one view, machines should be able to behave cognitively in ways similar to humans. Therefore, if humans decide on the basis of some subjective belief rather than of objective probabilities, then machines should have that capability also. This shift of emphasis from *probability* to *belief* is the focus of much of the controversy regarding the validity and adequacy of Bayesian statistics as a formalism for reasoning about partial beliefs under conditions of uncertainty.

In the Bayesian formalism, belief statements regarding class membership obey the following three basic assumptions of (objective) probability theory:

$$0 \le P(c_i) \le 1$$
$$P(\text{certainty}) = 1 \tag{2.54}$$
$$P(c_i \text{ or } c_j) = P(c_i) + P(c_j)$$

In the third assumption, the hypothesis regarding class membership is mutually exclusive; that is,

$$c_i \text{ and } c_j \text{ are incompatible}$$

From these assumptions, we have

$$P(\sim c_i) = 1 - P(c_i) \tag{2.55}$$

where $\sim c_i$ means "not c_i".

This relationship is not necessarily true of non-Bayesian beliefs.

One type of attack on the Bayesian method centers on the use of the inversion formula,

$$P(c_i|\underline{x}) = \frac{P(\underline{x}|c_i)P(c_i)}{P(\underline{x})} \tag{2.56}$$

written in this case for discrete values of $\underline{x}$. The same criticism applies to distributions.

A formal mathematician would dismiss this expression as a straightforward identity resulting from the definition of the conditional probabilities, because it is clear that

$$P(c_i|\underline{x}) = \frac{P(c_i,\underline{x})}{P(\underline{x})} \quad \text{and} \quad P(\underline{x}|c_i) = \frac{P(c_i,\underline{x})}{P(c_i)} \tag{2.57}$$

However, over the years controversy has swirled around the separate issues of whether expression (2.57) is valid or adequate.

Regarding validity, the argument is that $P(c_i|\underline{x})$ should represent a *belief* rather than an objective probability, and that it would be remarkable if that subjective belief always came out to be equal to the one given by the right hand side of expression (2.56). It is interesting that even Bayesians rarely defend expression (2.56) on the basis of it being a straightforward mathematical identity; they prefer to consider it a normative rule for updating beliefs in response to evidence, basic to the Bayesian approach.

We can clarify this viewpoint by discussing the updating process in terms of odds and likelihood ratios. Given evidence $\underline{x}$, the task is to estimate the strength of our belief that $\underline{x}$ belongs to class c_i. Dividing expression (2.56) by the complementary form for $P(\sim c_i|\underline{x})$, we obtain

$$\frac{P(c_i|\underline{x})}{P(\sim c_i|\underline{x})} = \frac{P(\underline{x}|c_i)}{P(\underline{x}|\sim c_i)} \frac{P(c_i)}{P(\sim c_i)} \tag{2.58}$$

We define the a priori odds on c_i to be

$$O(c_i) = \frac{P(c_i)}{P(\sim c_i)} = \frac{P(c_i)}{1 - P(c_i)} \tag{2.59}$$

and the likelihood ratio to be

$$L(\underline{x}|c_i) = \frac{P(\underline{x}|c_i)}{P(\underline{x}|\sim c_i)} \tag{2.60}$$

Then, the a posteriori odds

$$O(c_i|\underline{x}) = \frac{P(c_i|\underline{x})}{P(\sim c_i|\underline{x})} = \frac{P(c_i|\underline{x})}{1 - P(c_i|\underline{x})} \qquad (2.61)$$

are given by the product

$$O(c_i|\underline{x}) = O(c_i)L(\underline{x}|c_i) \qquad (2.62)$$

That is, the Bayesian rule states that, in light of new evidence $\underline{x}$, the overall strength of belief that $\underline{x}$ belongs to c_i can be described as the product of two factors: the prior odds $O(c_i)$ and the likelihood ratio $L(\underline{x}|c_i)$. The first factor measures the *causal* or *prospective* support given to the hypothesis $c = c_i$ by background knowledge alone. The second factor represents the additional support or retrospective support given to $c = c_i$ by the newly acquired evidence $\underline{x}$.

Incidentally, from (2.61), we can also write

$$P(c_i|\underline{x}) = \frac{O(c_i|\underline{x})}{1 + O(c_i|\underline{x})} = \frac{L(\underline{x}|c_i)O(c_i)}{1 + L(\underline{x}|c_i)O(c_i)}$$

This relation is often convenient because only likelihood ratios of the conditional probabilities and prior odds are required.

From a subjectivist's point of view, estimating the quantities $P(\underline{x}|c_i)$, and especially the likelihood ratios $P(\underline{x}|c_i)/P(\underline{x}| \sim c_i)$, usually is much easier than is estimating the belief $P(c_i|\underline{x})$. The latter task usually requires much "expertise" and experience, whereas learning the *local* relationships $P(\underline{x}|c_i)$ is principally a matter of isolated observation.

The preceding discussion has dealt with circumstances where there are indeed firm objective statistical measures of likelihoods and odds. The only controversial matter would be the use of the inversion formula. This is in contrast to other situations where *belief* measures are considered to be subjective and attention is concentrated on how such subjective measures can provide a basis for reasoning, or where *belief* is based on possibilities rather than on probabilities. Some of these issues will be discussed in Chapter 3.

Other criticisms of Bayesian statistics claim that this approach is incapable of dealing with, for example,

- Pooling of evidence

- Multivariabled hypotheses

- Uncertain evidence

The truth is that, in most of these more complicated situations, we are confronted with the need for a great number of additional data or for making additional assumptions of independence of evidence. Given either of the data or the assumptions, Bayesian statistics can deal with those circumstances as well as can any other method.

On the more central issue of whether the Bayesian approach is suitable for use in pattern recognition, we see that it constitutes a formalism for reasoning about partial beliefs under conditions of uncertainty. Therefore, in principle, in pattern recognition, the scope of use of the Bayesian approach should be independent of the format of the patterns and of the nature of the pattern-processing procedures. In practice, however, much of Bayesian pattern-recognition research has been in the context of patterns with numeric-valued features; much less progress has been attained with Bayesian methods in dealing with patterns that have explicit structural relationships among features.

2.7 Comments and Bibliographical Remarks

In the presence of uncertainties, the act of classification in pattern recognition rests on our degree of belief that the pattern in question is indeed a member of a certain class rather than not. But this statement merely begs the question of how a *degree of belief* is to be determined and indeed what is the theoretical structure in support of the definition, manipulation, and utilization of such quantities.

In general, the physical scientist has no difficulty with the concept of objective probability defined in terms of relative frequency of occurrence. In addition, there is no difficulty with Bayes' relationship, which is a self-evident mathematical relationship between different ways of describing the probability of the joint occurrence of two propositions E and H.

Difficulties arise when one takes into account that, in practice, at least up to now, decisions are made by humans and are based in general on subjective probabilities rather than on objective probability. Indeed, belief should be considered to depend on three entities: the two propositions E (the evidence), H (the hypothesis), and the state of mind of the decision maker [Good 1950]. Therein lies the source of the large body of literature dealing with the mysteries of subjective probabilistic reasoning.

The fact of the matter is that it is difficult to be rigorous and subjective at the same time. In other words, a rigorous theory of logic and a subjective approach to probability do not lead to a rigorous theory of belief, but rather result in a large and lively body of controversy.

In this latter day, it is difficult to envision the hindering effect that Bayesian statistics might have had on innovative trends in statistics research in the 1920s and 1930s, but there are some strong statements indeed in literature [Fisher 1930; Dempster 1968] on this matter.

A more temperate and informative statement is that made by Dempster in the foreword of Shafer's book *A Mathematical Theory of Evidence*:

> I differ from Shafer in that I am comfortable with the view that subjective, epistemic probability is the essential concept, while chance or physical probability is only a subspecies which scientific tradition has come to regards as "objective". Moreover, I believe that Bayesian inference will always be a basic tool for practical everyday statistics, if only because questions must be answered and decisions must be taken, so that statisticians must always stand ready to upgrade his vaguer forms of belief into precisely additive probabilities. It is nevertheless very important to study theories which permit discrimination of circumstances where knowledge is secure enough to permit fair bets from other circumstances where the concept of fair bet becomes increasingly meaningless. [Shafer 1976, pp. vii–viii]

Attacks on the Bayes' relationship have ranged from the supposition it must be wrong because Bayes did not publish it in his lifetime to the more practical objection that it is not likely to be useful because the a priori or inital probabilities cannot be estimated. It is important to recognize and reject the more spurious attacks. With respect to the latter objection, we quote from Good to provide a useful perspective:

> If it is desired to decide which of two or more alternative hypothesis is likely to be correct in the light of experimental results, then the natural method is to use Bayes' theorem. Objections have frequently been raised against Bayes' theorem on the ground that the initial probabilities of the hypotheses cannot be estimated, or that they do not exist. The view held here is that the initial probabilities may always be assumed to exist within the abstract theory, but in some cases you may be able to judge only that they lie in rather wide intervals. This does not prevent the application of Bayes' theorem: it merely makes it less effective than if the intervals are narrow.

> *It is hardly satisfactory to say that the probabilities do not exist when the intervals are wide, while admitting that they do exist when the intervals are narrow.* This is, however, quite a common practice even when the interpretation is in terms of degrees of belief. There may be some convenience in the practice, but it is out of place in a discussion on fundamentals, and it will not be adopted here. [Good 1950, p. 40]

In our opinion, the truly difficult issues have not been settled yet. There are many ways of introducing subjective issues into the theory of reasoning. Shafer, for example, concerns himself with the possibility of shaping a mathematical approach for handling subjective beliefs in a manner that would accommodate subjective modes of delineating "belief." Fuzzy-set–logic proponents, on the other hand, essentially abandon probabilities concerns and concentrate on subjective measures of *possibility*—that is, on the degree to which an object is *compatible* with a concept or a class. These issues remain to be elucidated.

Turning to another issue, in our opinion the difference between classification and estimation is not delineated as clearly as it might be and should be. In fact, the acts are quite different. In the first case, we observe a pattern that has a random aspect and decide which of two, or more, possible causes produced it. This is the type of problem that Thomas Bayes studied in the middle of the eighteenth century. In the second case, the focus is on the value of some attribute, and we try to estimate the value of this attribute. In the literature, the discussion of estimation has emphasized the determination of the most efficient tests and the extrapolation, interpolation, and smoothing of data sequences [Fisher 1925; Neyman and Pearson 1933; Kolmogoroff 1941; Wiener 1949].

In pattern recognition, however, both the estimation and the classification acts have to be regarded as mappings from representation space to an interpretation space, and the topologies of such spaces need to be considered in the estimation act. This situation is in contrast to the conventional estimation act, where the N-dimensional real-number space is almost automatically assumed to be the only type of space of interest.

Thus, in pattern recognition, the choice of representation space needs to be made with estimation in mind. Not only should the representation bring out interclass differences, but also the topology of that space should be such that points in the neighborhood of a reference point should have attribute values that can be estimated on the basis of knowledge of the reference point and knowledge of the topology of that neighborhood. An ordinal representation [Simon 1984] in terms of (say) fractals [Mandelbrot 1982] would require estimation procedures different from that for Euclidean-space representations.

Considerations of topology are also important in clustering, for purposes of classification.

2.8 References and Bibliography

1. Ball, G.H. and D.J. Hall, 1966. ISODATA, an iterative method of multivariate data analysis and pattern classification, *Proceedings of the IEEE International Communications Conference*, Philadelphia, PA, June.

2. Chen, C.H., 1973. *Statistical Pattern Recognition*, Hayden, Washington, D.C.

3. Dempster, A.P., 1968. A generalization of Bayesian inference, *Journal of the Royal Statistical Society*, Vol. 30B, pp. 205–247.

4. Duda, R.O. and P.E. Hart, 1973. *Pattern Classification and Scene Analysis*, Wiley, New York.

5. Fisher, R.A., 1925. Theory of statistical estimation, *Proceedings of the Cambridge Philosophical Society*, Vol. 22, p. 700.

6. Fisher, R.A., 1930. Inverse probability, *Proceedings of the Cambridge Philosophical Society*, Vol. 26, Part 4, pp. 528–535.

7. Good, I.J.,1950. *Probability and the Weighing of Evidence*, Charles Griffin and Company, London.

8. Kolmogoroff, A., 1941. Interpolation and extrapolation, von Stationärin Zufälligen folgen, *Akademua nauk SSSR, Izvestua. Seriia Matemischeskaia*, Vol. 5, pp. 3–14.

9. Mandelbrot, B.,1982. *The Fractal Geometry of Nature*, Freeman, San Francisco, CA.

10. Neyman, J. and E.S. Pearson, 1933. On the problem of most efficient tests of statistical hypotheses, *Philosophical Transactions of the Royal Society of London*, Vol. A231, p. 289.

11. Shafer, G., 1976. *A Mathematical Theory of Evidence*, Princeton University Press, Princeton, NJ.

12. Simon, J.C., 1986. *Patterns and Operators: The Foundations of Data Representation*, McGraw-Hill, New York. Original French-language edition, 1984, Masson, Editeur, Paris.

13. Widrow, B. and M.E. Hoff, 1960. *Western Electric Show and Convention Record*, Part 4, pp. 96–104, Institute of Radio Engineers.

14. Wiener, N., 1949. *Extrapolation, Interpolation and Smoothing of Stationary Time Series*, MIT Press, Cambridge, MA. (Originally published as a classified report in 1940 to Section D2, National Defense Research Committee.)

CHAPTER 3

Vague Features and Vague Decision Rules: The Fuzzy-Set Approach

3.1 Introduction

The purpose of this chapter is to provide an informal introduction to the use of fuzzy-set theory in the task of pattern recognition.

Fuzzy-set theory is an active research area, highly mathematical in nature. Proponents of that methodology believe that fuzzy-set theory can provide a robust and consistent foundation for information processing, including pattern-formatted information processing. But nonexperts can find the massive body of mathematical publications to be mystifying rather than helpful. In addition, the body of published discussions on pattern-recognition–related applications is relatively small and rather fragmented.

We believe that fuzzy-set theory plays at least two roles in pattern recognition. In one role, it serves as an interface between the linguistic variables seemingly preferred by humans and the quantitative characterizations appropriate for machines. In this role, it might also serve as a bridge between the symbolic processing of artificial intelligence and the parallel distributed processing approaches favored by adaptive pattern recognition.

In another role, it emphasizes the possibility-distribution interpretation of the concept of fuzziness. The value of that role is that it legitimizes and provides a meaningful interpretation for some distributions that we believe are useful, but might find difficult to justify on the basis of objective probabilities. The two roles are not distinct, but the differences are interesting and worth noting.

Section 3.2 is concerned with basic concepts. Section 3.3 is concerned with operations on fuzzy sets, and examines how crisp mathematical concepts might be extended into fuzzy sets. Some instances of the use of fuzzy-set theory in pattern recognition are described in Section 3.4.

3.2 Basic Concepts

In this section we describe the two roles that fuzzy-set theory plays in adaptive pattern recognition and introduce the basic concepts involved.

The Interface Role

In the context of the interface role, a feature (actually the *name* of a feature) is defined in terms of a membership function. The membership function in turn is defined in the domain of some measurement variable, and the value of the membership function indicates the extent to which a particular value of the variable is compatible with the concept of that feature. Skeptics argue that this practice is not very different from assigning a subjective probability to the value of a feature, but practioners of fuzzy-set theory respond by saying that the membership-function values are to be interpreted more in terms of a possibility distribution rather than in terms of a probability distribution.

As an example of an instance of the first role, we consider the situation of an employer thinking of the characteristics he would prefer in candidates for a particular job opening in his company.

In particular, consider the position of a supervisor in a building supplies company. Experience with previous holders of that position indicate that the preferred applicant would be someone who is "reasonably tall," has had about "a year or two of college education," and is inclined to be "physically active." The prescreening process can be automated through use of pattern recognition. A candidate profile can be expressed in terms of features, and an appropriate decision rule can be used to sift out the more promising applicants.

In conventional pattern recognition, the features used for this purpose might be

- Height (in feet)
- Years of education (in years)
- Physical activity (in hours per week)

A decision rule is then learned through a training procedure, so that applicants with appropriate combination of promising traits are classified as candidates, and others are not.

In a sense, there is nothing wrong with this procedure, but some people believe that such a procedure constitutes a serious mismatch between humans and machines and that we should do better if we wish to have machines perform more in accordance with human expectation. *Therein lies a role for fuzzy sets.*

The proposition is that the feature "reasonably tall" is a vague or a fuzzy quantity and should be retained as such. Not only is this the way humans represent knowledge, but also it is with such types of entities that humans reason. It is probably very important that we retain this abstraction explicitly and not have that concept fragmented into a feature named "height" and an opaque decision rule. Otherwise, a rule that might have been perfectly reasonable and well understood at the time it was formulated might become "lost" in the vastness of a computer memory separated from the circumstances that led to its formulation. Neither the fact of the "height" feature nor the nature of the decision rule can ever reconstitute the simple human thought that the candidate for the job should be "reasonably tall."

In the fuzzy-set theory approach, we retain "reasonably tall" as a vague quantity and retain height as a variable in a domain of deterministic crisp measurements. We provide an interface between the two views by defining "reasonably tall" as a fuzzy set in the domain of "height" with use of a membership function.

We now provide a definition for a fuzzy set. Then, we use the fuzzy set "reasonably tall" as an example to clarify this theory.

Definition 3.1 *If X is a collection of objects x, then a fuzzy set $\tilde{A}$ in X is a set of ordered pairs:*

$$\tilde{A} = \{(x, \mu_{\tilde{A}}(x)) | x \in X\}.$$

The entity $\mu_{\tilde{A}}(x)$ is called the membership function, *the value of which is the grade of membership of x in $\tilde{A}$. It is also the degree to which the deterministic measurement x is compatible with (the vague concept of) $\tilde{A}$.*

$\mu_{\tilde{A}}(x)$ maps X to the membership space M. If M contains only two points, 0 and 1, then $\tilde{A}$ is not fuzzy. The range of the values of the membership function is a subset of the nonnegative real numbers with a finite least upper bound. If this bound is unity (that is, $sup\{\mu_{\tilde{A}}(x)\} = 1$), the fuzzy set $\tilde{A}$ is called normal. We can always normalize nonempty fuzzy set $\tilde{A}$ by dividing $\mu_{\tilde{A}}(x)$ by $sup\{\mu_{\tilde{A}}(x)\}$. In many instances, it is convenient to work with $\mu_{\tilde{A}}(x)$ normalized in this manner; under other circumstances, normalization needs to be carried out differently to satisfy problem-prescribed constraints. Elements with zero degree of membership are usually not listed.

This definition in terms of an ordered set of pairs can be extended to include the case of a continuous membership function defined over the interval of X that constitutes the support of $\tilde{A}$. Examples 3.1 and 3.2 show how a membership function can be defined in a discrete or a continuous manner. There are also other notations that are used in more formal discussions, especially for continuous membership functions, but that we need not consider in our brief discussion.

Example 3.1 Defining a Fuzzy Set in Terms of a Set of Associated Pairs. Let

$$\tilde{A} = \text{``reasonably tall''}$$

Then we might define $\tilde{A}$ as a fuzzy set,

$$\tilde{A} = \{(5.7, 0.36)(5.8, 0.56), (5.9, 0.83), (6.0, 1.00), (6.1, 0.83), (6.2, 0.56),$$
$$(6.3, 0.36)\}$$

In this case, "reasonably tall" is a vague feature of a pattern that we intend to retain in that form. However, we define it as a set of associations of the nature of (value of height, membership in concept of "reasonably tall") where the membership is expressed in terms of the value of a membership function. ∎

The fuzzy set, however, need not be restricted to the format of a discrete set of associated pairs—that is, for a discrete set of height values. The representation could also be continuous, as indicated in the following example.

Example 3.2 Defining a Fuzzy Set in Terms of Functional Relationships. As depicted in Figure 3.1,

$$\tilde{A} = \text{``reasonably tall''}$$

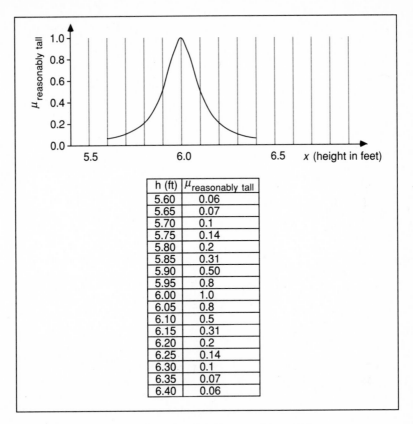

Figure 3.1 Membership function for "reasonably tall."

can be defined in terms of a continuous-valued function of height

$$\mu_{\tilde{A}}(x) = \begin{cases} 0, & x < 5.6 \\ (1 + 100(x - 6.0)^2)^{-1}, & 5.6 \leq x \leq 6.4 \\ 0, & x > 6.4 \end{cases} \qquad (3.1)$$

■

In the following pages, we provide definitions of several properties of fuzzy sets. We do not make explicit use of all these properties, but these definitions and examples do help to enhance our intuitive feeling of what constitutes a fuzzy-set.

Example 3.3 Vague Predicates.

In symbolic processing, in coping with uncertainty, assertions are often qualified by a certainty factor (CF). Predicates can then be defined in terms of their membership function in the domain of certainty factor. Thus, "definitely," "definitely not," and "not known" might be defined as follows:

$$\mu_{\text{definitely}} = \begin{cases} 0 & CF < 0.8 \\ 1 & 0.8 \leq CF \leq 1 \end{cases}$$

$$\mu_{\text{definitely not}} = \begin{cases} 0 & CF > -0.8 \\ 1 & -1.0 \leq CF \leq -0.8 \end{cases}$$

$$\mu_{\text{not known}} = \begin{cases} 0 & +0.2 < CF < -0.2 \\ 1 & -0.2 \leq CF \leq 0.2 \end{cases}$$

These definitions are illustrated in Figure 3.2.   ■

Definition 3.2 *The support of a fuzzy set $\tilde{A}$, $S(\tilde{A})$, is the crisp set of all $x \in X$ such that $\mu_{\tilde{A}}(x) > 0$.*

Example 3.4 The Support of the Concept of "Reasonably Tall." In Example 3.1, the support of $\tilde{A}$—that is, $S(\tilde{A})$—is {5.7, 5.8, 5.9, 6.0, 6.1, 6.2, 6.3}, which is to say that we know something about the concept of "reasonably tall" for those values of height that are in that indicated support set.   ■

Definition 3.3 *The (crisp) set of elements that belong to the fuzzy set $\tilde{A}$ at least to the degree α is called the α-level set:*

$$A_\alpha = \{x \in X | \mu_{\tilde{A}}(x) \geq \alpha\} \tag{3.2}$$

and $A'_\alpha = \{x \in X | \mu_{\tilde{A}}(x) > \alpha\}$ is called the strong α-level set.

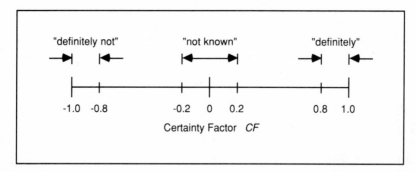

Figure 3.2 Definitions of predicates in terms of fuzzy sets in the domain of certainty factor.

Example 3.5 Describing a Fuzzy Set in Terms of α-level Sets. Referring again to Example 3.1, the possible α-level sets are

$$
\begin{aligned}
\tilde{A}_{0.36} &= \{5.7, 5.8, 5.9, 6.0, 6.1, 6.2, 6.3\} \\
\tilde{A}_{0.56} &= \{5.8, 5.9, 6.0, 6.1, 6.2\} \\
\tilde{A}_{0.83} &= \{5.9, 6.0, 6.1\} \\
\tilde{A}_{1.0} &= \{6.0\}
\end{aligned}
\tag{3.3}
$$

Convexity is sometimes a useful property when we carry out set-theoretic operations on a number of fuzzy sets. In contrast to classic set theory, we are interested in this case in convexity with reference to the membership function, rather than in the support of a fuzzy set. The convexity condition is stated in Definition 3.4, and is illustrated more intuitively by the curves shown in Figures 3.3(a) and 3.3(b). ■

Definition 3.4 *A fuzzy set $\tilde{A}$ is convex if*

$$
\mu_{\tilde{A}}(\lambda x_1 + (1 - \lambda)x_2) \geq \min(\mu_{\tilde{A}}(x_1), \mu_{\tilde{A}}(x_2)), \quad x_1, x_2 \in X, \quad \lambda \in [0, 1]
\tag{3.4}
$$

A fuzzy set is convex if all α-level sets are convex.

Although the example of "reasonably tall" (Example 3.1) deals with a linguistic variable serving as a feature name, linguistic variables are also to be found in decision functions and in decision rules. The second role—that of serving as a possibility distribution—manifests itself more in the classification act than in feature formation. The difference seems to be that, in the second role, the focus is the details of the membership function, and usually little needs to be done once that membership function has been obtained. This is in marked contrast with the circumstances of the first role, where the focus is the nature of operations that might be carried out on a set of membership functions.

The Possibility Distribution Role

In traditional pattern recognition, there are many different manifestations of the classification act. We might want to decide whether a pattern belongs to class c_i or to class c_j, or whether, in syntactic pattern recognition, in parsing, one production rule or another should be used, or whether in the process of cluster formation it should be decided that pattern $\underline{x}$ belongs to cluster i or to cluster j. These are but different manifestations of the same task.

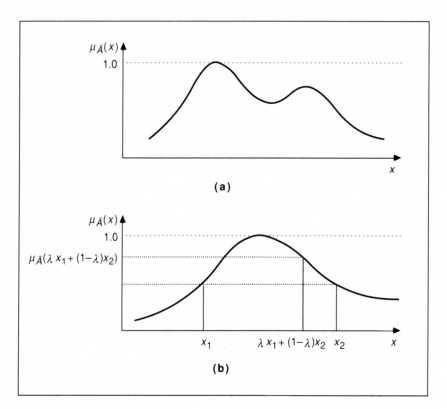

Figure 3.3   Illustration of convexity. (a) A nonconvex membership function.
(b) A convex membership function.

A well-understood and commonly used procedure is to use decision
functions $g_i(\underline{x})$ and to decide that $\underline{x}$ belongs to class c_i if and only if
$g_i(\underline{x}) > g_j(\underline{x})$ for all $j = 1, 2, \ldots, j \neq i$.

We can introduce the notion of possibility by modifying the concept
of class membership. The idea is not to ask whether $\underline{x}$ belongs to class c_i,
but rather to ask what is the degree of membership that $\underline{x}$ has relative
to class c_i, for all possible i. Class membership becomes a fuzzy set, the
support of which is the domain of all observable patterns. The value of
the membership function is numerically equal to the value of a possibility distribution function that expresses the *possibility* that the observed
pattern $\underline{x}$ might be an instance of class c_i.

Zadeh advocated the possibility-distribution point of view in [Zadeh
1978] and also discussed the difference between possibility and probability
distributions. In some respects, possibility constitutes the upper bound of

probability. What is impossible is also improbable, but what is possible may not always be probable.

There are also circumstances in which the two roles that we have discussed are essentially indistinguishable. For example, if classification is primarily the matter of estimating the possibility of belonging to the various classes, then emphasis is on the second role. However, if each of the "classes" constitutes a concept or equivalently is defined as a fuzzy set, then the first role is also involved. Consider the case when, in speech recognition, the relative volume of a vocalized segment needs to be classified as high, medium, or low. Each of these terms is more than just a class index. It is in turn a vaguely defined quantity, a fuzzy set defined in terms of a membership function. Therefore, we have the role of interfacing between linguistically expressed concepts and measurements, as well as the role of describing the different possibilities of belonging to the various classes.

3.3 Operations on Fuzzy Sets: The Extension Principle

The membership function is taken to be a crisp function defined in the space of nonnegative real numbers. If we perform set-theoretic operations on fuzzy sets to obtain yet other fuzzy sets, the question is what membership functions are induced as a result.

Some firm answers can be obtained in the case of the operations of intersection and union [Bellman and Giertz 1973; Fung and Fu 1975], and also of forming the complement. The matter is less well defined in the case of algebraic operations. For example, if the crisp concept is that of the Euclidean distance between two points (patterns), how is the *analogous* operation to be carried out for two points (patterns) that are defined only as fuzzy sets? Is it appropriate or useful to think of the interpattern distance as a fuzzy set? If so, how is that distance defined or inferred?

Zadeh [1975] proposed an extension principle that provides a general method for extending nonfuzzy mathematical concepts so that they apply to fuzzy sets. Jain [1976] and Dubois and Prade [1980] have proposed modifications and variations. Although the "original" general extension principle is quite specific in formulation and general in applicability, it is not clear that the results so obtained are always appropriate or useful.

The literature is not uniform in these matters. In addition, various researchers suggest operations that yield entities such as the mth power, the algebraic sum, the bounded sum, the bounded difference, and the algebraic product of fuzzy sets. In a sense, these operations and new entities were invented and defined because people thought that they were useful and captured some aspect of some properties of an aggregation of fuzzy sets. These operations do not always obey the extension principle, and it is expected that other operations of this type will continue to be proposed and defined heuristically in accordance with the needs of the problem and the intuition of the researcher. These matters are also discussed in Chapter 9, in the context of neural-net implementations of fuzzy logic.

In the following pages, we define and illustrate the intersection, union, and complement of fuzzy sets. We describe the general extension principle and then define several additional algebraic operations that do not correspond to any crisp procedure and are not obtained through the extension principle. We illustrate the use of some of these operations in applications.

Definition 3.5 *The membership function $\mu_{\tilde{A} \cap \tilde{B}}$ of the intersection $\tilde{C} = \tilde{A} \cap \tilde{B}$ is*

$$\mu_{\tilde{C}}(x) = \min\{\mu_{\tilde{A}}(x), \mu_{\tilde{B}}(x)\}, \qquad x \in X \tag{3.5}$$

Definition 3.6 *The membership function $\mu_{\tilde{A} \cup \tilde{B}}$ of the union $\tilde{C} = \tilde{A} \cup \tilde{B}$ is*

$$\mu_{\tilde{C}}(x) = \max\{\mu_{\tilde{A}}(x), \mu_{\tilde{B}}(x)\}, \qquad x \in X \tag{3.6}$$

Definition 3.7 *The membership function of the complement of a fuzzy set $\tilde{A}$, $\mu_{\not\subset \tilde{A}}(x)$ is defined by*

$$\mu_{\not\subset \tilde{A}}(x) = 1 - \mu_{\tilde{A}}(x), \qquad x \in X \tag{3.7}$$

Definition 3.8 *The cardinality or "power" of a finite fuzzy set is defined as*

$$|\tilde{A}| = \sum_{x \in X} \mu_{\tilde{A}}(x)$$

Also,

$$\|\tilde{A}\| = \frac{|\tilde{A}|}{|X|} \tag{3.8}$$

is called the relative cardinality of $\tilde{A}$. For infinite X, the cardinality is defined as

$$|\tilde{A}| = \int_x \mu_{\tilde{A}}(x)dx$$

and it is not true that it always exists.

Definition 3.9 *A general extension principle for finding fuzzy-set analogs of crisp procedures is defined as follows: Let X be a Cartesian product of universes $X_1, \ldots, X_r$, and let $\tilde{A}_1, \ldots, \tilde{A}_r$ be r fuzzy sets in $X_1, \ldots, X_r$, respectively. The function f is a mapping from X to a universe Y, $y = f(x_1, \ldots, x_r)$. Then a fuzzy set $\tilde{B}$ in Y is defined by*

$$\tilde{B} = \{(y, \mu_{\tilde{B}}(y)) | y = f(x_1, \ldots, x_r), (x_1, \ldots, x_r) \in X\} \qquad (3.9)$$

where

$$\mu_{\tilde{B}}(y) = \begin{cases} \sup \ \min\{\mu_{\tilde{A}_1}(x_1), \ldots, \mu_{\tilde{A}_r}(x_r)\} & \text{if } f^{-1}(y) \neq 0 \\ & \{(x_1, \ldots, x_r) \in f^{-1}(y)\} \\ 0 & \text{otherwise} \end{cases}$$

$$(3.10)$$

where f^{-1} is the inverse of f and "sup" denotes the least upper bound.

The physical meaning of $f^{-1}(y)$ is that it is that set of values of $(x_1, \ldots, x_r)$ for which $f(x_1, \ldots, x_r)$ would be y. There may be more than one such set for any value of y.

Example 3.6 Product of Two Fuzzy Sets.

Let us consider a simple operation—namely, that of forming a product. Let $\tilde{A}_1$ be a fuzzy set defined in the domain of x_1 and let $\tilde{A}_2$ be a fuzzy set defined in the domain of x_2. To fix ideas and to help us get an intuitive feeling for what we are trying to accomplish, let us understand $\tilde{A}_1(x_1)$ to mean (approximately 0.25) and $\tilde{A}_2(x_2)$ to be (approximately -1). Let us define $\tilde{B}(y)$ to represent the concept of the product of the two fuzzy sets. The question is, What is $\mu_{\tilde{B}}(y)$? Let

$$\tilde{A}_1 = \{(-1.0, 0.4), (0.25, 1.0), (1.0, 0.3)\}$$

and

$$\tilde{A}_2 = \{(-4.0, 0.2), (-1.0, 1.0), (1.0, 0.5)\}$$

Then, for

$$y = f(x_1, x_2) = x_1 x_2$$

we have by the extension principle that

$$\tilde{B}(y) = \{(-4.0, 0.2), (-1.0, 0.4), (-0.25, 1.0), (0.25, 0.5), (1.0, 0.3),$$
$$(4.0, 0.2)\}$$

In evaluating $\tilde{B}(y)$, we note that we obtain (-4.0) by forming the product of (1.0) and (-4.0). These numerical values for $\tilde{A}_1$ and $\tilde{A}_2$ have membership-function values of 0.3 and 0.2, respectively. The smaller value dominates, and we have the membership-function value of 0.2 for the product value of (-4.0). However, we can obtain the value of (-1.0) in two ways, either by $(-1.0)(1.0)$ or by $(-4.0)(0.25)$. The min operation is carried out for each product separately, and the larger of the two possibilities is then selected to yield the appropriate possibility value of (0.4).   ■

Example 3.7 Fuzzy Distance Between Fuzzy Sets.   As another example, we consider the matter of describing appropriately the concept of distance between two "points" that are defined in terms of fuzzy *spots*. Let x be a metric space with metric d; that is

1. d is a mapping from the metric space to the domain of nonnegative real numbers

2. $d(x, x) = 0$ for all x

3. $d(x_1, x_2) = d(x_2, x_1)$ for all x_1 and for all x_2

4. $d(x_1, x_3) \leq d(x_1, x_2) + d(x_2, x_3)$ for all $x_1, x_2,$ and x_3.

Then, if A and B are two fuzzy spots, $\tilde{d}(A, B)$ models a distance between these two fuzzy spots, and, according to the extension principle, for all δ in the domain of nonnegative real numbers,

$$\mu_{\tilde{d}(A,B)}(\delta) = \text{least upper bound of: } \min(\mu_A(u), \mu_B(v))$$
$$\delta = d(u, v)$$

For ordinary fuzzy sets—that is, fuzzy sets with crisp membership-functions—additional algebraic operations have been defined in the literature and have been found to be of use.   ■

Definition 3.10 *The algebraic sum (probabilistic sum) $\tilde{C} = \tilde{A} + \tilde{B}$ is defined as*

$$\tilde{C} = \{(x, \mu_{\tilde{A}+\tilde{B}}(x)) | x \in X\} \tag{3.11}$$

where

$$\mu_{\tilde{A}+\tilde{B}}(x) = \mu_{\tilde{A}}(x) + \mu_{\tilde{B}}(x) - \mu_{\tilde{A}}(x) \cdot \mu_{\tilde{B}}(x)$$

Definition 3.11   *The* *algebraic product of two fuzzy sets* $\tilde{C} = \tilde{A} \cdot \tilde{B}$ *is defined as*

$$\tilde{C} = \{(x, \mu_{\tilde{A}}(x) \cdot \mu_{\tilde{B}}(x)) | x \, \varepsilon \, X\} \qquad (3.12)$$

Definition 3.12   *As a special case of Definition 3.11, we find that the* mth *power of a fuzzy set* $\tilde{A}$ *is a fuzzy set with membership function*

$$\mu_{\tilde{A}^m}(x) = [\mu_{\tilde{A}}(x)]^m \qquad (3.13)$$

Definition 3.13   *The bounded sum* $\tilde{C} = \tilde{A} \oplus \tilde{B}$ *is defined as*

$$\tilde{C} = \{(x, \mu_{\tilde{A} \oplus \tilde{B}}(x))\} \qquad (3.14)$$

where

$$\mu_{\tilde{A} \oplus \tilde{B}}(x) = \min(1, \mu_{\tilde{A}}(x) + \mu_{\tilde{B}}(x))$$

Definition 3.14   *The bounded difference* $\tilde{C} = \tilde{A} \ominus \tilde{B}$ *is defined as*

$$\tilde{C} = \{(x, \mu_{\tilde{A} \ominus \tilde{B}}) | x \in X\} \qquad (3.15)$$

where

$$\mu_{\tilde{A} \ominus \tilde{B}}(x) = \max(0, \mu_{\tilde{A}}(x) + \mu_{\tilde{B}}(x) - 1)$$

We cite these few algebraic operations to show that, in addition to using the general extension principle, we can also invent and use ad hoc operations when common sense indicates that these would be useful and are needed. We shall encounter the mth-power operation and the concept of cardinality explicitly in the next section, but we shall not use the other operations.

3.4   Use of Fuzzy-Set Theory in Pattern Recognition

There are at least four circumstances in which the concepts and techniques of fuzzy-set theory are uniquely helpful in the practice of pattern recognition.

One is where a fuzzy set serves as an interface between a linguistically formatted feature (that is, a nonnumeric, symbolic feature) and quantitative measurements. This role of fuzzy sets is well understood, and evidence of its use is widespread, including in the medical diagnostic system, MYCIN [Shortliffe 1976]. In pattern recognition, there is an additional question of how to aggregate the evidence represented by an array of membership-function values. Different approaches are described in the literature. We call this interface role the *first circumstance of use* of fuzzy-set theory; we shall discuss it in the context of an example.

The *second circumstance of use* is at the class-membership level, rather than at the feature level. In the crisp case, classification consists of relegating a pattern to membership in one of the many possible classes. In the fuzzy-set approach, the class membership of a pattern itself is a fuzzy set, and the different class indices constitute the support for that fuzzy set. A pattern does not necessarily belong to just one class. There is a certain degree of possibility that the pattern might belong to each one of the classes, and membership functions supply values for these various possibilities. Nothing much is gained if information processing stops at that first step of classification, because ultimately one would have to decide in favor of one specific class, perhaps the one with the largest membership-function value. The different possibilities are of value, however, if the import of the decision propagates into a network of other related decisions. When we have knowledge of the other possibilities, we need not discard or forget meaningful options and alternatives. Fuzzy clustering or the fuzzy ISODATA procedure constitutes an instructive example of this *second circumstance of use*, as we shall also discuss in this section.

The *third circumstance of use* is where the membership-function values are used to help provide an estimate of missing or incomplete knowledge.

The *fourth circumstance of use* is similar to that of the second, but the context is that of structural rather than geometric pattern recognition. In the parsing of a structure such as a sentence, the fuzzy-set approach yields values for different possibilities of that structure being due to the action of various production rules. This circumstance of use has been discussed in the literature, but the results have often been cumbersome and are not generally extensible.

Examples of only the first three circumstances are discussed in the following pages.

Example 3.8 Use of Vague Features (Fuzzy-sets) in Speech Identification. The issue is, How are we to weight the total effect of an array of membership-function values? The material of Chapter 2 gives us some idea of how to cope with patterns consisting of an array of crisp numeric-valued components. But how are we to deal with patterns that seem to be similar in nature to crisp patterns but that actually differ in that the components of the pattern are membership-function values? The work by Pal and Majunder [1977,1978,1980] on vowel and speaker recognition forms the basis for the procedure described in this example. However, this method of aggregation is generally applicable.

Our purpose in citing this body of work and this approach is to suggest that, under quite general circumstances, a pattern consisting of an array of membership-function values might indeed be treated as any other "geometric" pattern of deterministic nature.

In the work on which this discussion is based, there is no appeal to any extension principle, neither in the agglomeration procedure nor in the decision procedure. Instead, classification is based on a similarity measure defined somewhat arbitrarily in terms of a ratio of the membership functions of a pattern and of cluster prototypes.

The pattern in question is in the form of an array of linguistically phrased features. Each of these features is a fuzzy-set, and the pattern with which we have to deal consists of an array of the membership-function values. That is,

$$\underline{x} = (p_1, p_2, \ldots, p_j, \ldots, p_n) \qquad (3.16)$$

where the values of p_i lie in the interval $[0,1]$. The membership-function values are obtained from the actual acoustic measurements, a_i, through the relationship

$$p_i = \left(1 + \left|\frac{\bar{a}_i - a_i}{E}\right|^F\right)^\alpha \qquad (3.17)$$

where $\alpha = -1$ and $\bar{a}_i$ is the ensemble average of the many values obtained for the ith feature. The constants E and F determine the shape of the membership function. The acoustic measurements could be the frequencies of the formants, or ratios of energies in various bands—depending on the objective of the task, different features were used. Our discussion is sufficiently general to cover all such circumstances.

There are m ill-defined pattern classes $c_1, c_2, \ldots, c_j, \ldots, c_m$, and there are h_j of prototypes in class c_j. Each of these prototype reference points can also be represented in terms of membership-function values; for example,

$$r_j^{(\ell)} = \left(p_{1j}^{(\ell)}, p_{2j}^{(\ell)}, \ldots, p_{ij}^{(\ell)}, \ldots, p_{nj}^{(\ell)}\right) \tag{3.18}$$

where $p_{ij}^{(\ell)}$ denotes the degree to which the property i is possessed by the ℓth prototype in c_j.

Instead of calculating a "distance" from pattern $\underline{x}$ to the prototypes, Pal and Majunder used the concept of a *similarity vector*. The similarity vector $s_j(\underline{x})$ for the pattern $\underline{x}$ with respect to the jth class is defined to be

$$s_j(x) = (s_{1j}, s_{2j}, \ldots, s_{ij}, \ldots, s_{nj}) \tag{3.19}$$

where

$$s_{ij} = \frac{1}{h_j} \sum_\ell s_{ij}^{(\ell)} \qquad \ell = 1, 2, \ldots, h_j \tag{3.20}$$

and

$$s_{ij}^{(\ell)} = \left(1 + W_i \left|1 - \frac{p_i}{p_{ij}^{(\ell)}}\right|\right)^{-2z} \tag{3.21}$$

The numerical value of s_{ij} denotes the grade of similarity of the ith property with that of c_j. The W_i are positive constants that can be individually tailored to indicate the relative sensitivity of the recognition process to deviations from the prototype values, z is an arbitrary positive integer.

With knowledge of all the similarity vectors, we can decide $\underline{x}$ belongs to class c_k if

$$|s_j(\underline{x})| < |s_k(\underline{x})|, \qquad k, j = 1, 2, \ldots, m; \qquad k \neq j \tag{3.22}$$

In this example, the voice pattern is described in terms of characteristics (or features), which are described linguistically and are defined as fuzzy-sets in the domain of acoustic measurements. Therefore, both a pattern and the cluster prototypes are defined in terms of membership-function values for each of the linguistically stated features. The manner in which $s_{ij}^{(\ell)}$ is calculated indicates that it is regarded as a membership function, but it is not derived from any extension principle. Because of this, this example is of interest principally because it illustrates what the interface role is and how descriptions in terms of membership-function values can be processed.

Pal and Majunder [1980] also used another approach in which they calculated Euclidean distances between pattern and prototypes in measurement space and then used fuzzy-set theory in the classification act. That procedure is less illustrative of the interface role of fuzzy sets.   ■

Example 3.9 Fuzzy Clustering.   Classical (crisp) clustering algorithms generate partitions such that each pattern is assigned to exactly one cluster. The ISODATA algorithm mentioned in Chapter 2 is one example of such algorithms. Often, however, a pattern is "between" clusters in the sense that it could have been classified as belonging to one cluster almost as well as to another. A crisp classification provides no hint of the details of that situation, but fuzzy clustering methods can yield more accurate representations of real data structures. The discussion of this example is based on the work of Bezdek [1976; 1980] and Ruspini [1970]. It has also been influenced by the discussions of Zimmermann [1985].

In this example we compare the partitioning of the set

$$X = \{\underline{x}_1, \underline{x}_2, \ldots, \underline{x}_n\}$$

into crisp versus fuzzy subsets (that is, clusters). Each partition into crisp or fuzzy subsets can be described by an indicator function u_{s_i} or a membership function $\mu_{\tilde{s}_i}$, respectively. These two functions can be considered to be mappings

$$u_{s_i} : X \rightarrow \{0, 1\} \qquad \text{for the crisp case} \tag{3.23}$$

and

$$\mu_{\tilde{s}_i} : X \rightarrow [0, 1] \qquad \text{for fuzzy cases} \tag{3.24}$$

Assignment of the patterns to the different clusters can be visualized in terms of a c-partition matrix, which might be crisp or fuzzy.

For a three-pattern, two-cluster case, the crisp two-partition matrices are

$$u_1 : \begin{array}{c} \\ c_1 \\ c_2 \end{array} \begin{pmatrix} \overset{\underline{x}_1}{1} & \overset{\underline{x}_2}{1} & \overset{\underline{x}_3}{0} \\ 0 & 0 & 1 \end{pmatrix} \tag{3.25}$$

$$u_2: \begin{array}{c} \\ c_1 \\ c_2 \end{array} \begin{array}{ccc} \underline{x}_1 & \underline{x}_2 & \underline{x}_3 \\ \left(\begin{array}{ccc} 1 & 0 & 0 \\ 0 & 1 & 1 \end{array} \right. & & \left. \right) \end{array} \tag{3.26}$$

$$u_3: \begin{array}{c} \\ c_1 \\ c_2 \end{array} \begin{array}{ccc} \underline{x}_1 & \underline{x}_2 & \underline{x}_3 \\ \left(\begin{array}{ccc} 1 & 0 & 1 \\ 0 & 1 & 0 \end{array} \right. & & \left. \right) \end{array} \tag{3.27}$$

The three other matrices are similar to these, but with $\underline{x}_1$ assigned to cluster c_2.

In contrast, a fuzzy clustering algorithm would yield fuzzy two-partition matrices of the nature of

$$\tilde{u}_1 = \begin{array}{c} \\ c_1 \\ c_2 \end{array} \begin{array}{ccc} \underline{x}_1 & \underline{x}_2 & \underline{x}_3 \\ \left(\begin{array}{ccc} 0.84 & 0.97 & 0.28 \\ 0.14 & 0.03 & 0.72 \end{array} \right. & & \left. \right) \end{array} \tag{3.28}$$

$$\tilde{u}_2 = \begin{array}{c} \\ c_1 \\ c_2 \end{array} \begin{array}{ccc} \underline{x}_1 & \underline{x}_2 & \underline{x}_3 \\ \left(\begin{array}{ccc} 0.56 & 0.72 & 0.31 \\ 0.44 & 0.28 & 0.69 \end{array} \right. & & \left. \right) \end{array} \tag{3.29}$$

and so on, and there exist infinitely many possible fuzzy two-partitions such as these.

More generally, in the crisp case, the element of the U matrix, u_{ik}, denotes the degree of membership of pattern $\underline{x}_k$ in the cluster or subset s_i; that is,

$$u_{ik} := u_{s_i}(\underline{x}_k) \tag{3.30}$$

and u_{ik} can have values of either 0 or 1.

In the fuzzy case, the elements of the $\tilde{U}$ matrix are μ_{ik}, and these entities also denote the degree of membership of pattern $\underline{x}_k$ to the cluster or subset $\tilde{s}_i$. Formally, the indicator function u_{s_i} and the membership function $\mu_{\tilde{s}_i}$ are subject to the following constraints:

1. $u_{ik} \in \{0, 1\}; \quad 1 \le i \le c, 1 \le k \le n$

2. $\sum_{i=1}^{c} u_{ik} = 1; \quad 1 \le k \le n$

3. $0 < \sum_{k=1}^{n} u_{ik} < n; \quad 1 \le i \le c$

and

1. $\mu_{ik} \in [0,1]; \quad 1 \le i \le c, 1 \le k \le n$ (3.31)

2. $\sum_{i=1}^{c} \mu_{ik} = 1; \quad 1 \le k \le n$ (3.32)

3. $0 < \sum_{k=1}^{n} u_{ik} < n; \quad 1 \le i \le c$ (3.33)

where i denotes category and k denotes pattern.

In the crisp case, patterns can belong to only one cluster. In contrast, in the fuzzy case, patterns can belong to several clusters, to different degrees. Constraints on $\mu_{\tilde{s}_i}(x_k)$ require that the "total membership" of a pattern x_k be normalized to 1 and that it not belong to more clusters than exist.

We shall now sketch one way of obtaining the quantities μ_{ik}, following the work of Bezdek [1976; 1980].

In the crisp ISODATA algorithm, the position of a cluster center is found to be the average of the positions of all the patterns in that cluster. That result is based on minimizing the sum of the variances of all variables j for each pattern in each cluster i. That is, for the crisp case, we vary the position of ν_i, the cluster center, to minimize

$$\sum_{i=1}^{N_C} \sum_{x_k \in c_i} \|x_k - \nu_i\|^2 = \sum_{i=1}^{N_C} \frac{1}{|c_i|} \sum_{x_k \in c_i} \sum_{j=1}^{D} (x_{kj} - \nu_{ij})^2 \qquad (3.34)$$

We find that

$$\nu_i = \frac{1}{|c_i|} \sum_{x_k \in s_i} x_k \qquad (3.35)$$

In (3.34), $|c_i|$ is the cardinality of the set of patterns in cluster i. For the crisp case, $|c_i| \equiv n_i$. Also for the crisp case, we can use the indicator-function values to remove the constraint $x_k \in c_i$ to yield a formulation of the problem as determining the minimum of the sum of the weighted variances,

$$\min z(u, \nu) = \sum_{i=1}^{N_C} \sum_{k=1}^{n} u_{ik} \|x_k - \nu_i\|^2 \qquad (3.36)$$

One of the ways to extend this problem to the fuzzy case is to draw an analogy between u_{ik} and μ_{ik}, and to define the problem of finding the fuzzy c-partitions as

$$\min z_m(\tilde{u}, \underline{\nu}) = \sum_{i=1}^{N_C} \sum_{k=1}^{n} (\mu_{ik})^m \|\underline{x}_k - \underline{\nu}_i\|^2 \qquad (3.37)$$

Differentiating the variance function with respect to $\underline{\nu}_i$ (for fixed $\tilde{u}$) and to μ_{ik} (for fixed $\underline{\nu}_i$) and applying the condition $\sum_i \mu_{ik} = 1$, we obtain

$$\underline{\nu}_i = \frac{1}{\sum\limits_{k=1}^{n} (\mu_{ik})^m} \sum_{k=1}^{n} (\mu_{ik})^m \underline{x}_k; \quad i = 1, \ldots, c \qquad (3.38)$$

and

$$\mu_{ik} = \frac{\left(\frac{1}{\|\underline{x}_k - \underline{\nu}_i\|^2}\right)^{1/(m-1)}}{\sum\limits_{j=1}^{N_C} \left(\frac{1}{\|\underline{x}_k - \underline{\nu}_j\|^2}\right)^{1/(m-1)}}; \quad i = 1, 2, \ldots, N_C; \, k = 1, \ldots, n \qquad (3.39)$$

The system of equations (3.38) and (3.39) cannot be solved analytically, but approximate solutions can be obtained using an iterative procedure similar to that of the crisp ISODATA algorithm.

Paraphrasing the work of Bezdek [1980], we describe the fuzzy clustering algorithm as

Step 1. *Initiate procedure.* Select number of current cluster centers, $2 \leq N \leq N_C$, where N_C is some preconceived, or expected, number. Choose a value for m, the exponential weight: $1 < m < \infty$. Select $\tilde{u}^{(0)}$. This value might be the crisp ISODATA solution, for example. Decide on termination criterion: Stop when $\delta = \|\tilde{u}^{(\ell+1)} - \tilde{u}^{(\ell)}\| \leq \varepsilon$.

Step 2. *Calculate cluster center positions.* Given $\tilde{u}^{(\ell)}$, calculate $\underline{\nu}_i^{(\ell)}$ using expression (3.38).

Step 3. *Calculate membership values.* Given $\underline{\nu}_i^{(\ell)}$, calculate $\tilde{u}^{(\ell+1)}$ using expression (3.39) if $\underline{x}_k \neq \nu_i^{(\ell)}$. Otherwise, set

$$\mu_{jk} = \begin{cases} 1 & \text{for } j = i \\ 0 & \text{for } j \neq i \end{cases}$$

Step 4. *Calculate δ.* Terminate if $\delta \leq \varepsilon$. Else return to step 2. ∎

Example 3.10 The Fuzzy Expected Value (FEV) and Its Use in Dealing with Incomplete Data.   It is a strong claim of fuzzy-set theory that the concept of a fuzzy-set is *not* merely a disguised form of subjective probability, and that it is suitable for dealing with problems in which the available information is incomplete, imprecise, or unreliable. In this example, we address these claims to see how fuzzy-set theory can be used in pattern recognition to fill in missing feature values.

The idea is that, once a membership function is known, there should be some way of estimating an average value of the membership function that is representative of that possibility distribution. Thus, if the possibility distribution is known for a feature, but the value of the membership function is missing for a specific pattern, we can use the estimated fuzzy expected value (FEV) in its stead. Often, this substitution is all that is required. If necessary, however, it would also be possible to determine the value of that element in the support set that has a membership-function value equal to or closest to the estimated FEV.

In this section, we give a nonformal definition of the FEV. Formal definitions may be found in a number of texts; see, for example, Kandel [1986]. First, we formulate preliminary definitions.

Let $\mu_{\tilde{A}}(x)$ be the membership function for a fuzzy-set $\tilde{A}$ defined in a universe of discourse x. For the present, we take x to be a continuous real-valued, positive, scalar variable. If $\tilde{A}$ is a finite set, we can delete the continuity requirements in this definition, and we need to make certain corresponding changes. $\mu_{\tilde{A}}(x)$ is normalized to have values in the interval [0, 1]. The function $\mu_{\tilde{A}}(x)$ is well behaved in the sense that it is piecewise continuous for the range of interest of x.

Let m be a measure function that provides a measure of subsets of the real line. In place of x, we define a variable ξ_T to represent $\{x|\mu_{\tilde{A}}(x) \geq T\}$. The quantity ξ_T is essentially the cardinality of the subset(s) with membership-function values equal to or greater than T.

For convenience, we can write $m\{x|\mu_{\tilde{A}}(x) \geq T\} \equiv m(\xi_T) = f_A(T)$, and we normalize $f_A(T) \to [0, 1]$. Then, it is clear that $f_A(T)$ is a monotonically decreasing function of T, going from $f_A(T) = 1$ when $T = 0$ to $f_A(T) = 0$ when $T = 1$, as shown in Figure 3.4.

We compare this quantity with another measure—the measure of the fraction of the universe of discourse available as the threshold T is increased. That is, we are interested in $m\{x|\mu_{\tilde{A}}(x) \leq T\}$, and we take this value to be equal to T.

The calculation of $\text{FEV}(\mu_{\tilde{A}})$ then consists of finding the intersection of the curves $f_A(T)$ and T. The intersection will be at a value $T = H$,

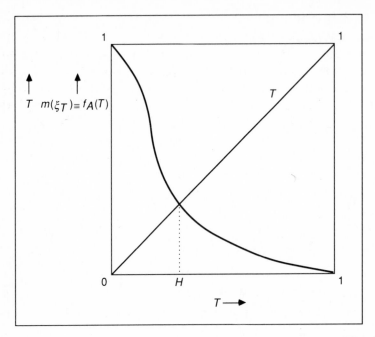

Figure 3.4   Graphic depiction of method for estimating value of $\text{FEV}(\mu_{\tilde{A}})$.

so $\text{FEV}(\mu_{\tilde{A}}) = H$. This definition is in accord with that of Kandel [1986] and with the standard definition found in the literature. It is an arbitrary definition, which may be interpreted in a number of ways—as it indeed has been. The present rationalization seems to be a reasonable and understandable one. Basically, in general, as T is increased, the measure of that fraction of the universe for which $\mu_{\tilde{A}}(x) \leq T$ increases. The FEV of $\mu_{\tilde{A}}(x)$ is therefore that value of $\mu_{\tilde{A}}$ for which the measure of the population having $\mu_{\tilde{A}}(x) \geq T$ is equal to that having $\mu_{\tilde{A}} \leq T$.

The procedure for finding the FEV of $\mu_{\tilde{A}}$ for a finite fuzzy-set $\tilde{A}$ can be obtained quite readily from this definition. We illustrate it by using an example similar to one given on page 77 of Kandel [1986]. ∎

Example 3.11 Obtaining the Fuzzy Expected Value for a Finite Fuzzy Set.

We consider again the concept $\tilde{A} \equiv$ "reasonably tall," which is defined as a fuzzy-set in the domain of height measurements. The membership function $\mu_{\tilde{A}}(h)$ is depicted in Figure 3.5(a).

Next, we synthesize $m\{x \mid \mu_{\tilde{A}}(x) \geq T\}$, where x is a normalized height variable and T is a normalized height threshold. For example, if we take 10 feet to be a convenient normalizing value, then $x = h/10$ and T is

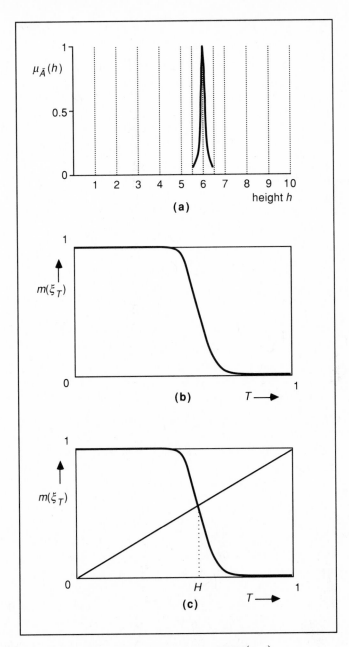

Figure 3.5 Illustration of determining the $\text{FEV}(\mu_{\tilde{A}})$.

height threshold/10. The function $m(\xi_T)$ is plotted in Figure 3.5(b); we see that $m(\xi_T)$ decreases as T increases.

Finally, in Figure 3.5(c) we illustrate the process of determining the fuzzy expected value of $\mu_{\tilde{A}}$—that is, $FEV(\mu_{\tilde{A}})$. From that value, we might draw conclusions about the expected values of height among the entire range of possible values.   ■

3.5 Comments and Bibliographical Remarks

There is a large body of literature on fuzzy-set theory and related work. The monograph *Fuzzy Sets and Systems: Theory and Applications* by Dubois and Prade [1980] is an eminently lucid account of the basic concepts of the field that covers almost all the important developments in the theory of fuzzy sets and in their applications up to 1979. Dubois and Prade reference approximately 550 publications appearing between 1965 and 1978; these citations represent about a thousand papers that existed on the subject at that time.

Kandel [1982], in his book *Fuzzy Techniques in Pattern Recognition*, also presents an introductory discussion of fuzzy-set theory and provides a bibliography of 3064 papers that deal with fuzzy-set theory or are at least peripherally related to that subject. His bibliography covers the period from 1961 to 1981.

Some interesting individual contributions are included in several edited volumes that appeared in between 1979 and 1982, including the texts by Gupta, Ragade, and Yager [1979], by Wang and Chang [1980], and by Mandani and Gaines [1981].

A more recent monograph by Kandel [1986], *Fuzzy Mathematical Techniques with Applications*, is also eminently readable and is useful in that it lists over 800 references, about one-third of which were published after 1981. Twenty-one journals and proceedings containing major papers on the theory of fuzzy-sets and its applications are listed. Two other monographs, one by Zimmerman [1985] and the other by Negoita [1985], are also noteworthy.

These publications bear testimony to the fact that the central tenets of fuzzy-set theory are perceived to be essentially correct and useful. Furthermore, these tenets capture the imagination of many researchers and give rise to attempts to formulate additional theories of general use. However, these more abstract results become less and less intuitively understandable and convincing as they leave physical interpretations behind.

Zadeh's highly readable but rather abstract discussion entitled "Fuzzy Logic" [1988] is an example of such discussions of fuzzy-set logic.

3.6 References and Bibliography

1. Bellman, R.E. and M. Giertz, 1973. On the analytic formalism of the theory of fuzzy sets, *Information Sciences*, Vol. 5, pp 149–156.

2. Bezdek, J.C., 1976. A physical interpretation of fuzzy ISODATA, *IEEE Transactions Systems, Man and Cybernetics*, Vol. 6, pp. 387–389.

3. Bezdek, J.C.,1980. A convergence theorem for the fuzzy ISODATA clustering algorithms, *IEEE Transactions on Pattern Analysis and Machine Intelligence*, Vol. 2, pp. 1–8.

4. Dubois, D. and H. Prade, 1980. *Fuzzy Sets and Systems: Theory and Applications*, Academic Press, New York.

5. Fung, L.W. and K.S. Fu, 1975. An axiomatic approach to rational decision making in a fuzzy environment. In L.A. Zadeh, K.S. Fu, R. Tanaka, and M. Shimura, (Eds.), *Fuzzy Sets and Their Applications to Cognitive and Decision Processes*, pp. 227–256, Academic Press, New York.

6. Gupta, M.M., R.,K. Ragade, and R.R. Yager, 1979. *Advances in Fuzzy Set Theory and Applications*, Elsevier North-Holland, New York.

7. Jain, R., 1976. Tolerance analysis using fuzzy sets, *International Journal of Systems Science*, Vol. 7, pp. 1393–1401.

8. Kandel, A., 1982.*Fuzzy Techniques in Pattern Recognition*, Wiley-Interscience, New York.

9. Kandel, A., 1986. *Fuzzy Mathematical Techniques with Applications*, Addison-Wesley, Reading, MA.

10. Mandani, E.H. and B., R. Gaines, 1981. *Fuzzy Reasoning and Its Applications*, Academic Press, New York.

11. Negoita, C.V., 1985. *Expert Systems and Fuzzy Systems*, Benjamin/Cummings, Menlo Park, CA.

12. Pal, S.K. and D.D. Majunder, 1977. Fuzzy sets and decision-making approaches in vowel and speaker recognition, *IEEE Transactions on Systems, Man and Cybernetics*, Vol. 7, pp. 625–629.

13. Pal, S.K. and D.D. Majunder, 1978. An automatic positive identification using fuzziness in property sets, *IEEE Transactions on Systems, Man and Cybernetics*, Vol. 8, pp. 302–307.

14. Pal, S.K. and D.D. Majunder, 1980. A self-adaptive fuzzy recognition system for speech sounds. In P.P. Wang and S.K. Chang (Eds.), *Fuzzy Sets: Theory and Applications to Policy Analysis and Information Systems*, Plenum Press, New York.

15. Ruspini, E., 1970. Numerical methods for fuzzy clustering, *Information Sciences*, Vol. 2, pp. 319–350.

16. Shortliffe, E.H., 1976. *Computer-based Medical Consultations:* MYCIN, Elsevier North-Holland, New York.

17. Wang, P.P. and S.K. Chang (Eds.), 1980. *Fuzzy Sets: Theory and Applications to Policy Analysis and Information Systems*, Plenum Press, New York.

18. Zadeh, L.A., 1975. The concept of a linguistic variable and its application to approximate reasoning. Parts 1, 2, and 3, *Information Sciences*, Vol. 8, pp. 199–249, pp. 301–357; Vol. 9, pp. 43–80.

19. Zadeh, L.A., 1978. Fuzzy sets as a basis for a theory of possibility, *Fuzzy Sets and Systems*, Vol. 1, pp. 3–28.

20. Zadeh, L.A., 1988. Fuzzy Logic, *Computer*, Vol. 21, pp. 83–92.

21. Zimmermann, H.J., 1984. *Fuzzy Set Theory and Its Applications*, Kluwer-Nijhoff, Hingham, MA.

CHAPTER 4

Patterns with Nonnumeric Feature Values

4.1 Introduction

We are accustomed to using linguistic symbols—that is, words—to represent feature *names*, but sometimes pattern feature *values* are also irreducibly nonnumeric. For example, we might have the following situation:

class of pattern : apple (namely the concept of "apple")

specific pattern : apple-1

name of nth feature : color

possible values of nth feature : red, green, yellow

As another example, a painter working on a specific assignment might be constrained to work with ready-mixed paints. In a pattern-formatted description of a room, one of the feature names might be "color-of-wood-trim," and the possible feature values might be "ivory," "beige," "yellow," "cream," and so on. These colors are identified by name by the vendor, and it is important to retain this representation in terms of these linguistic symbols. Furthermore, even if the vendor had associated numeric code indices with each of the colors—for example, 1410 for "ivory," 2012 for "beige," 1119 for "yellow," and so on—it would be difficult to make meaningful use of the numeric values in the manner of any conventional geometric pattern-recognition approach.

We could, of course, invent ways to convert linguistic-valued patterns into numeric-valued patterns. In one of these approaches, we might treat each of the linguistic values as a feature name. In the case of "apple," we would have three features—namely, "red-color," "green-color," and "yellow-color"—in place of the original feature "color." Each of these new features would need to be specified in terms of a value, which might be +1 or 0, representing true or false. Or the numeric value might be a subjectively specified belief value. Or each of the new features might be treated as a vague quantity, defined as a fuzzy set in the domain of some new variables, as described in Chapter 3.

These conversion methods are often impracticable, however, either because there is a very large increase in the number of features or because there is lack of knowledge for specifying the numeric values. For example, it is one thing to specify "beige" as a fuzzy set, but it is quite another thing to attempt to specify "beige" in terms of a membership function in the domain of the coordinates of a color map.

Because of these practical considerations and, perhaps more important, because of the intrinsic need sometimes to retain the representation in terms of linguistic symbols, we consider the task of classifying patterns that are irreducibly nonnumeric. *Specifically, and most important, we consider the task of learning discriminants for classifying such patterns.*

Three related approaches are described in this chapter. In the first approach, the task is simply that of determining the best discrimination tree, the measure of "best" being either in terms of the least number of features examined or in terms of some other measure of performance. The ID3 method as developed by Quinlan [1983] is a popular example of such an approach to learning a discrimination tree, and is closely related to the Concept Learning System (CLS) of Hunt [1962].

Generalization and specialization are important aspects of learning, and there are approaches other than ID3 that can accommodate those aspects of learning more readily. We describe two of these. One is procedure M described by Winston [1984] and similar in some respects to the approaches of AQVAL and INDUCE by Michalski [1973,1983]; the other is that introduced by Pao and Hu [1985] to provide another perspective on how discriminants or rules might be inferred inductively. Procedure M can build up or refine a structural, or semantic-net–like, description of the object (pattern), whereas the Pao–Hu approach treats all the attributes as a "flat" array and is suitable for parallel processing.

For purposes of comparison, we shall use the same problem to illustrate two or more different approaches.

4.2   The ID3 Approach

The ID3 approach to pattern recognition and classification consists of a procedure for synthesizing an efficient discrimination tree for classifying patterns that have nonnumeric attributes or feature values. The discrimination tree can also be expressed in the form of a body of rules and, because of this, ID3 is also often thought of as an inductive inference procedure for machine learning or rule acquisition.

ID3 can be very effective under certain conditions, but should not be used beyond its scope of validity. The approach is valid and useful when there is a body of data consisting of a large number of patterns, each of which is made up of a long list of non-numeric feature values—attribute values. The class memberships of some of these patterns are known. The task is to examine the bewilderingly large body of data and to find out what minimum combination of feature values suffices to determine class membership.

In the ID3 approach, we make use of the labeled examples and determine how features might be examined in sequence until all the labeled examples have been classified correctly. We might find, for example, that only a very small fraction of the features need be used for classification purposes. If this result, obtained for the labeled examples, is also representative of the much larger ensemble of patterns comprising the original body of data, then a very large gain will have been achieved through use of ID3. In addition, the fact that class membership depends on certain combinations of feature values, as discovered by the discrimination tree, might also provide insight into the basic mechanisms that determine the processes being examined.

We illustrate the procedure with an example from Quinlan [1983], then express the procedure more generally.

Example 4.1 Classifying Individuals on the Basis of Certain Physical Characteristics.   Consider I, a collection of patterns descriptive of the class membership of individuals on the basis of features such as "height" with values {short, tall}, "hair" with values {dark, red, blond}, and "eyes" with values {blue, brown}. The class membership is o or a. Thus, I is equal to

tall, dark, blue: a	tall, red, blue: o	short, blond, brown: a
short, dark, blue: a	tall, blond, brown: a	tall, dark, brown: a
tall, blond, blue: o	short, blond, blue: o	

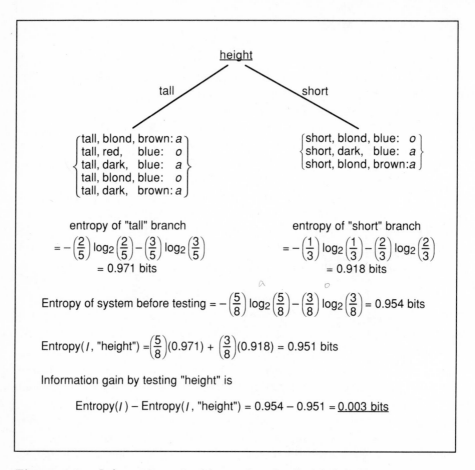

Figure 4.1   Information gained by testing the "height" feature.

You may have noticed that I does not represent all possible combinations of feature values. In fact, only eight out of 12 possible combinations are represented. The objective of the ID3 method is to be able to specify sequences of tests that will suffice to classify any and all patterns of I. It is also hoped that the same procedure would apply equally well to other patterns representative of the same problem or phenomenon but not captured in I.

ID3 uses an information-theoretic approach. The procedure is that at any point we examine the feature that provides the greatest gain in information or, equivalently, the greatest decrease in entropy. Entropy is defined as $-p \log_2 p$, where probability p is determined on the basis of frequency of occurrence.

Let us evaluate entropy at various stages of testing. Initially, in the absence of any information at all, if we are asked to guess the class membership of a pattern, we might be inclined to assign a probability of 0.5 to its being class a and an equal probability of 0.5 to its being class o. That is, we might assume the a priori probabilities to be equal, in the absence of any information to the contrary. The entropy is then

$$-p_a \log_2 p_a - p_o \log_2 p_o$$
$$= -0.5 \log_2 0.5 - 0.5 \log_2 0.5 = 1 \text{ bit}$$

However, if we know that there are five a-type patterns and only three o-type patterns, then the entropy is

$$-(5/8) \log_2(5/8) - (3/8) \log_2(3/8) = 0.954 \text{ bit}$$

In other words, there has been an increase of 0.046 bit in information content.

There is then the question of what feature is most effective in disentangling the class-membership relationships. We consider each of the three features height, color of hair, and color of eyes, and evaluate how much information is gained if we test on each of these features. It is important to realize that we are not looking for features that appear to be effective because they split off certain parts of I in a clean-cut fashion. Rather, we look for maximum gain in information content on a system basis.

The situations obtained on testing each of the three features are shown illustrated in Figures 4.1, 4.2 and 4.3. At this stage, all these data structures are one-level decision trees.

Testing on "height" divides the population into two categories, each of mixed class membership. As shown in Figure 4.1, the entropy of the "tall" branch is 0.971 bit, whereas the entropy of the "short" branch is 0.918 bit. Weighting the entropy of each branch by its population, we find that the entropy of the system, the entire population, is 0.951 bit. In other words, not much information is gained by testing on height. In contrast, as illustrated in Figures 4.2 and 4.3, the gains in information obtained by

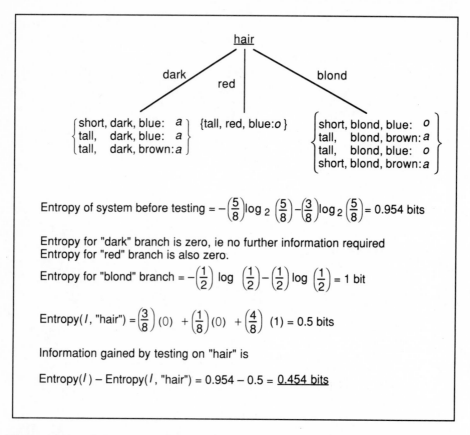

Figure 4.2   Information gained by testing the "hair" feature.

testing on the "hair" and "eyes" features are 0.454 bits and 0.347 bits, respectively. The ID3 mechanism specifies that we should test on "hair" because the corresponding gain in information content is the largest of the three possibilities.

Similarly, at the second level of the decision tree, testing on "eyes" yields the larger information-content gain. The resulting two-level decision tree is shown in Figure 4.4.

If, at the second level, more than one node (subpopulation) had to be expanded further, the same feature would have been used at all nodes at the same time to obtain an estimate of the information gained, systemwide, on testing with that feature.   ∎

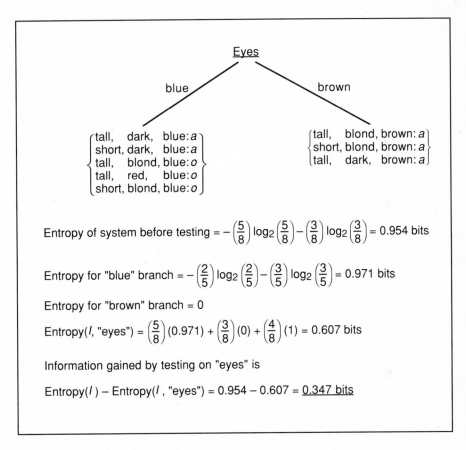

$$\text{Entropy of system before testing} = -\left(\frac{5}{8}\right)\log_2\left(\frac{5}{8}\right) - \left(\frac{3}{8}\right)\log_2\left(\frac{3}{8}\right) = 0.954 \text{ bits}$$

$$\text{Entropy for "blue" branch} = -\left(\frac{2}{5}\right)\log_2\left(\frac{2}{5}\right) - \left(\frac{3}{5}\right)\log_2\left(\frac{3}{5}\right) = 0.971 \text{ bits}$$

Entropy for "brown" branch = 0

$$\text{Entropy}(I, \text{"eyes"}) = \left(\frac{5}{8}\right)(0.971) + \left(\frac{3}{8}\right)(0) + \left(\frac{4}{8}\right)(1) = 0.607 \text{ bits}$$

Information gained by testing on "eyes" is

$$\text{Entropy}(I) - \text{Entropy}(I, \text{"eyes"}) = 0.954 - 0.607 = \underline{0.347 \text{ bits}}$$

Figure 4.3   Information gained by testing the "eyes" feature.

General Considerations

The general case is that of N labeled patterns partitioned into sets of patterns belonging to classes c_i, $i = 1, 2, 3, \ldots, C$. The population in class c_i is N_i. Each pattern has K features and each feature has J_k values. (For simplicity in the following discussion, we assume that all features have J values.) The ID3 prescription for synthesizing an efficient decision tree can be stated as follows:

Step 1. *Calculate initial value of entropy.* For the training set, class membership is known for all the patterns. Therefore, the initial en-

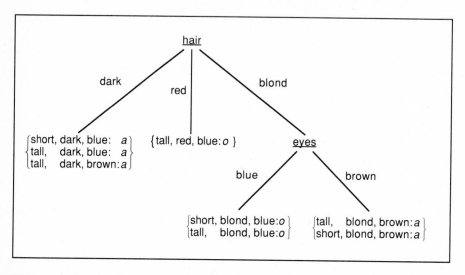

Figure 4.4   An ID3 two-level decision tree.

tropy for the system consisting of N labeled patterns is

$$\text{Entropy}(I) = \sum_{i=1}^{C} -(N_i/N)\log_2(N_i/N)$$

$$= \sum_{i=1}^{C} -p_i \log_2 p_i$$

Step 2. *Select a feature to serve as the root node of the decision tree.*

a. For each feature A_k, $k = 1, 2, 3, \ldots, K$, partition the original population into first-level populations according to the values a_{kj} of the J values of the feature A_k. There are n_{kj} patterns in the a_{kj} branch, but these patterns are not necessarily of any one single class.

b. For any branch population n_{kj}, the number of patterns belonging to class c_i is $n_{kj}(i)$. Evaluate the entropy of that branch using the relationship

$$\text{Entropy}(I, A_k, j) = \sum_{i=1}^{C} -n_{kj}(i)/n_{kj}\log_2 n_{kj}(i)/n_{kj}$$

The entropy of the system after testing on feature A_k is then

$$\text{Entropy}(I, A_k) = \sum_{j=1}^{J} \sum_{i=1}^{C} \left(n_{kj} / \sum_{j} n_{kj} \right)$$
$$[-n_{kj}(i)/n_{kj} \log_2 n_{kj}(i)/n_{kj}]$$

c. The decrease in entropy as a result of testing on feature A_k is

$$\text{Entropy}(I) - \text{Entropy}(I, A_k) = \Delta\text{Entropy}(k)$$

d. Select the feature A_{k_o} that yields the greatest decrease in entropy —that is, for which $\Delta Entropy(k_o) > \Delta Entropy(k)$ for all $k = 1, 2, 3, \ldots, K, \quad k \neq k_o$.

e. The feature A_{k_o} is then the root of the decision tree and the structure of the decision tree up to the first level is as shown in Figure 4.5.

Step 3. *Build the next level of the decision tree.* Select a feature $A_{k'}$ to serve as the level-1 node such that, after testing on $A_{k'}$ on *all* branches, we obtain the maximum gain in information content or the maximum decrease in entropy. The two-level decision tree at this point has a structure similar to that shown in Figure 4.6. (*Note that the same $A_{k'}$ is used at all the testing points, and the entropy of interest is the entire systemwide entropy.*)

Step 4. *Repeat steps 1 through 3.* Continue the procedure until all sub-populations are of a single class and the system entropy is zero.

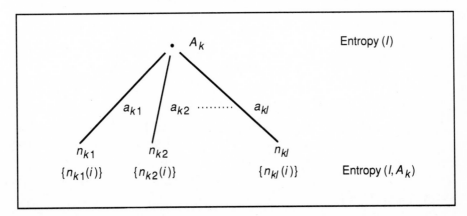

Figure 4.5   Structure of decision tree: root and level-1 populations.

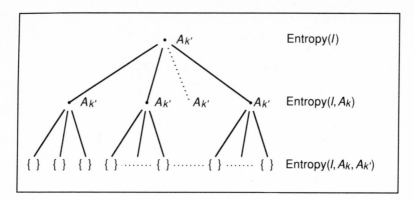

Figure 4.6   Buildup of decision tree on basis of steepest descent in entropy.

Complexity of ID3

In the ID3 method, the basic unit task is that of calculating the entropy for each branch. We have assumed for simplicity that there are J values for each of the K features. Then, at the root of the decision tree, there would be J such calculations for each of the K features. At the next level, there would be J nodes each with J branches. Therefore, at that level, there would be J^2 such calculations for each of the $(K - 1)$ features.

As the tree increases in levels, however, many of the branches will become of one class membership, and the computing burden will be decreased. For estimation purposes, it is reasonable to assume that a L-level tree is only about as complex as an $L/2$-level fully expanded decision tree. Therefore, the computing burden increases approximately as KJ^L; that is, it increases exponentially with respect to depth of the decision tree, but polynomially with respect to the number of features and to the number of values per feature. The quantity J^L is problem-dependent.

Advantages of ID3

The principal virtue of the ID3 procedure probably is the ease with which it can be automated. Experience indicates that ID3 can be of help in "discovering" what combination of features suffices to determine class membership. To that extent, ID3 discovers concepts.

Quinlan describes the computational burden somewhat differently. He states for example, that

ID3 was specifically designed to handle masses of objects, and in fact its computation time increases only linearly with difficulty of the problem as modeled by the product of:

- the number of exemplary objects [that is, our N],

- the number of attributes used to describe objects [that is, our K], and

- the complexity of the concept to be developed, measured by the number of nodes on the decision tree [that is, our J^L]. [Quinlan 1983, p. 464]

His and our descriptions of the computational requirements are essentially the same.

Disadvantages of ID3

The principal disadvantage of the ID3 method is that we cannot readily update the decision tree without having to rebuild the entire tree. That is, when a new pattern is classified incorrectly, we need to modify the tree so that the new pattern can be accommodated. We can do this modification by patchwork, in which case the tree gradually loses its role of being the most efficient and representative of some important concepts. Or we can start from the beginning to build a new tree. In the latter case, we need to retain in memory all the patterns we have ever encountered, an unattractive prospect.

Also, ID3 does not address issues of "generalization" and "specialization" easily. This drawback also is due to the fact that an ID3 tree is not easy to modify.

4.3 The Pao–Hu Method

Quinlan states that the ID3 method is a "descendant" of Hunt's Concept Learning System (CLS) [Hunt, 1962] and there is indeed room for many other variations on the same theme. The goal is the same—namely, to "discover" a set of necessary and sufficient conditions that describe class membership. There can be more than one such set, however, and the question of which set or which type of set is to be preferred depends on other subgoals and constraints.

The Pao and Hu [1985] method makes use of the background provided by the experiences of ID3, INDUCE [Michalski 1980], and the work of

Table 4.1   Describing Patterns In Terms of Descriptors (Pao–Hu Procedure)

Pattern Number	Pattern Description	Class Index
1	(height, short) and (hair, blond) and (eyes, blue) $D(1,1)$ and $D(2,1)$ and $D(3,1)$	o
2	(height, tall) and (hair, blond) and (eyes, brown) $D(1,2)$ and $D(2,1)$ and $D(3,2)$	a
3	(height, tall) and (hair, red) and (eyes, blue) $D(1,2)$ and $D(2,2)$ and $D(3,1)$	o
4	(height, short) and (hair, dark) and (eyes, blue) $D(1,1)$ and $D(2,3)$ and $D(3,1)$	a
5	(height, tall) and (hair, dark) and (eyes, blue) $D(1,2)$ and $D(2,3)$ and $D(3,1)$	a
6	(height, tall) and (hair, blond) and (eyes, blue) $D(1,2)$ and $D(2,1)$ and $D(3,1)$	o
7	(height, tall) and (hair, dark) and (eyes, brown) $D(1,2)$ and $D(2,3)$ and $D(3,2)$	a
8	(height, short) and (hair, blond) and (eyes, brown) $D(1,1)$ and $D(2,1)$ and $D(3,2)$	a

Winston on learning the concept of the ARCH from examples [Winston 1975], but it is different from each of these. In this method, we make use of a body of examples—that is, labeled patterns—and infer the required classification rules from it. Additional patterns can be accommodated readily, and both generalization and specialization can be scheduled as a matter of course.

A *pattern* is a conjunction of *descriptors*, with each descriptor comprising a feature name and at least one of the possible feature values. The "language" for describing the patterns can be more general, and a description might have a range of values and other associated information. We shall work through an example to illustrate the method.

Example 4.2 Inference of Classification Rules Using the Pao–Hu Method.   Using the same set of patterns as in Example 4.1, we proceed as follows.

Step 1. Number the patterns and rewrite them in terms of descriptors that also can be numbered for convenience. Retain class labels. The patterns and the corresponding descriptions in terms of descriptors are shown in Table 4.1. Thus, pattern 1 is described as $D(1,1) \wedge D(2,1) \wedge D(3,1)$, where D(1,1) denotes the first feature having the first of two possible values—namely, (height, short).

Step 2. Form the association table. If only one type of pattern is associated with a descriptor, change the designation of that descriptor to "distinct descriptor" abbreviated as DD(ij). These are the level-1 distinct descriptors, in contrast to the second-level distinct descriptors obtained subsequently. In the present example, we have the situation illustrated in Table 4.2.

At this stage we see immediately that any pattern that contains descriptor $D(2,2)$ is of class o, whereas any pattern that contains either $D(2,3)$ or $D(3,2)$ is of class a. We can state the findings in the form of rules, as described in step 3.

Step 3. Form rules by listing the first-level distinct descriptors; for example,

$$pattern \in class\ o\ if\ it\ contains\ D(2,2) \qquad (partial\ rule) \qquad (4.1)$$

Table 4.2 Descriptors and the Pattern Containing These Descriptors; Illustration of Distinct Descriptors

Descriptors	Associated Patterns	
Common descriptor	Class o	Class a
$D(1,1)$	(1,o)	(4,a), (8,a)
$D(1,2)$	(3,o), (6,o)	(2,a), (5,a), (7,a)
$D(2,1)$	(1,o), (6,o)	(2,a), (8,a)
$D(3,1)$	(1,o), (3,o), (6,o)	(4,a), (5,a)
1st-level distinct descriptors		
$D(2,2)$	(3,o)	
$D(2,3)$		(4,a), (5,a), (7,a)
$D(3,2)$		(2,a), (7,a), (8,a)

Table 4.3   Descriptors and Associated Patterns: Second-level Distinct Descriptors

Descriptors	Associated Patterns	
Second Level Distinct Descriptors with Negations	Class o	Class a
$D(3,1) \wedge \sim D(2,3)$ $\sim D(2,3) \wedge \sim D(3,2)$ $D(2,1) \wedge \sim D(3,2)$	$(1,o), (3,o), (6,o)$ $(1,o), (3,o), (6,o)$ $(1,o), (6,o)$	
Second-level distinct descriptor with conjunctions $D(2,1) \wedge D(3,1)$	$(1,o), (6,o)$	

(This is only a partial rule because there are other o class patterns not covered by this rule.)

> pattern $\in$ class a iff it contains $D(2,3)$ or $D(3,2)$ (complete rule)

$$(4.2)$$

(This is a complete rule because all class a patterns are covered by this rule.)

Step 4.   Continue to infer rules to cover remaining patterns. Two routes are possible.

     a. Form second-level distinct descriptors by forming conjunctions of a common descriptor and the negation of a first-level distinct descriptor contained in the patterns that we wish to eliminate, or by forming the conjunction of the negations of two first-level distinct descriptors.

         For example in Table 4.2, $D(3,1)$ is contained in patterns $(1,o), (3,o)$ and $(6,o)$ but it is also contained in patterns $(4,a)$ and $(5,a)$. Looking at the sixth line of Table 4.2; we see that the condition of $\sim D(2,3)$ would eliminate patterns $(4,a)$ and $(5,a)$, and $\sim D(3,2)$ would eliminate $(8,a)$. Therefore, the distinct descriptor of interest is $D(3,1) \wedge \sim D(2,3)$.

Proceeding in a similar manner, we would arrive at Table 4.3, which shows the level-two distinct descriptors obtained in this manner and the patterns associated with each such compound distinct descriptor.

In this case, all patterns have been separated in terms of first- or second-level distinct descriptors. From Tables 4.2 and 4.3, we have, for class-*a* patterns,

$$\text{pattern} \in \text{class } a \text{ iff } D(2,3) \lor D(3,2)$$

and for class-*o* patterns,

$$\text{pattern} \in \text{class } o \text{ if } D(2,2)$$
$$\text{if } D(3,1) \land \sim D(2,3)$$
$$\text{or } D(2,1) \land \sim D(3,2)$$
$$\text{or } \sim D(2,3) \land \sim D(3,2)$$

Stated in English, an individual is of class *a* iff

1. *(hair dark)* or *(eyes brown)*   (complete rule)

but is of class *o* if

2. *(hair red)*
3. or *(eyes blue)* and *(hair not dark)*   (complete rule)
4. or *(hair blond)* and *(eyes not brown)*
5. or *(hair not dark)* and *(eyes not brown)*

Comparing rules 3 and 4, we see that "short" and "tall" can be omitted because they form an exhaustive set. Of all the class *o* rules, rule 3 is the most powerful because it suffices to cover all class *o* patterns.

  b. If we wish to avoid the use of negations of descriptors we can synthesize second-level distinct descriptors in another way. For example, in the third line of Table 4.2, if we wish to eliminate patterns (2,*a*) and (8,*a*), we look for the *combination* of common descriptors that contains at least (1*o*) and (6,*o*), but is not contained in either (2,*a*) or (8,*a*). For example, $D(2,1) \land D(3,1)$ would be in neither (2,*a*) nor in (8,*a*). Proceeding in that manner, we obtain the alternate set of second-level distinct descriptors listed in Table 4.3.

The corresponding rules are an individual is of class o if

1. (*hair, red*)
2. or (*hair, blond*) and (*eyes, blue*)

In this example, we stop at this point, because all the associated pattern sets are of a single class. In this second instance the level-2 distinct descriptor is a conjunction of two first level common descriptors, $D(2, 1)$ and $D(3, 1)$. This is in contrast to the approach of step 4. We now can write the rules in many forms. This example suffices to explain the general method.

In the event that first-level and second-level distinct descriptors do not suffice to classify all patterns, we form third-level distinct descriptors using combinations of first-level descriptors and second-level distinct descriptors, and so on, to yet higher levels as required. ■

Complexity of the Pao–Hu Method

For comparison with the ID3 method, we consider a set of P patterns, each of which has K features. Each feature can take on any one of J values. These are JK descriptors, and the first task of this rule inference method consists of partitioning these descriptors into common descriptors and first-level distinct descriptors. The basic task is to prepare sets of associated-patterns for each of these descriptors. The task consists of taking each of the P patterns and making K entries in an array of possible JK sites. This subtask, therefore, consists of *making PK table-location entries* in an array of possible JK sites.

At the end of the table-entry task, the descriptors will have been divided into common descriptors and first-level distinct descriptors, each with an associated-pattern set. Each pattern serves as an inverted list of all the descriptors with which it is associated.

The next step consists of deleting all the patterns covered by the first-level distinct descriptors from the sets of patterns associated with the common descriptors. This is carried out for only one of the classes; for example, c_i. The residual set of patterns associated with the common descriptors are those for which classification rules need to be inferred with use of higher order, composite distinct descriptors.

Start with any common descriptor that has a relatively large number of c_i patterns in its associated-pattern set, then use these patterns as inverted lists and find which other common descriptor is shared by the largest number of such c_i patterns. A conjunctive statement of the two common descriptors is a second-level, distinct descriptor for the class in question *if* there are no patterns outside of that class that have both common descriptors in its' description. Such a conjunction of two common descriptors is found after comparing αJK lists with a specific list, where $\alpha \leq 1$, usually considerably less than unity. In addition, βJK of these conjunctive statements may have to be constructed if all possible forms of the classification rules are of interest.

If L-order distinct descriptors are required, the complexity of the method is on the order of $(\eta JK)^L$. However, the effective value of the parameter η is considerably less than one and exerts an attenuating effect on what might otherwise be a runaway exponential dependence on the order of difficulty of the problem.

Advantages of the Pao–Hu Method

The advantages of the Pao–Hu method are that only simple set operations and list processing are involved, and many different concepts can be discovered. Generalization and specialization, as well as updating, are achieved readily. In addition, much of the processing can be carried out in parallel.

Disadvantages of the Pao–Hu Method

There does not seem to be any real drawback to this method, except that it is not as readily automated as the ID3 method. Many different versions can be devised and there is opportunity for creativity. Of course, this flexibility might not be a disadvantage if proper use is made of it.

4.4 The Procedure M Approach

Procedure M, as articulated by Winston [1984], is another a procedure for learning class descriptions from samples that are representative of that class. It differs slightly from another procedure, called procedure W, also formulated by Winston [1984]. Whereas procedure W evolves a model description from a sequence of positive samples and near misses, procedure M learns a class description from sets of exemplars of objects that do belong to that class. In principle, procedure M does not request *near* misses, but it seems to require positive and negative examples and it is not clear when a negative example is or is not a near miss.

Procedures M and W differ from the ID3 and Pao–Hu approaches in that the primary emphasis in these procedures is on the use of *induction*

Table 4.4 Differences Between Positive Examples of A and Objects that are non-A.

	A	Ⱥ
P	A : straight long right side P : partial curved right side	Ⱥ : straight top link P : curved top link Ⱥ : straight long right side P : partial curved right side
M	A : left and right side connected directly at top M : left and right side are connected through link A : straight middle link M : no middle link	Ⱥ : straight top link M : bent top link Ⱥ : straight middle link M : no middle link
H	A : tops connected directly H : tops of sides are not connected	Ⱥ : straight top link H : no top link

heuristics for the *formation of features*. This focus is marked contrast to the concerns of the ID3 and Pao–Hu methods, which are primarily concerned with attaining the most efficient or the least complex way of using existing attributes or descriptions for discriminating between patterns that belong or do not belong to a certain class.

There are also similarities among these approaches. Procedure M starts with parts of an object and uses links to describe relationships between their parts. These links are similar to the attributes of ID3 and to the descriptors of the Pao–Hu method. To differentiate between the positive examples of objects and others that do not belong to the class, procedure M modifies links to be MUST and MUST NOT links. In the Pao–Hu method, similar effects are achieved through scanning the descriptors and labeling them as DISTINCT or COMMON descriptors.

Also, procedure M ultimately does build up a decision tree, which is the basis for inferred class descriptions. This tree is similar in appearance to that produced by the ID3 method, but the issue of processing efficiency is ignored in procedure M, and the primary concern is to find out how to incorporate the significant MUST and MUST NOT links in the class descriptions. In this respect, the Pao–Hu method is more akin to procedure M, but it differs in that it does not build up a decision tree in a beam-search manner, as advocated by procedure M. Also, the Pao–Hu method not only emphasizes the DISTINCT descriptors, but also makes use of conjunctions of COMMON descriptors.

Procedure M is described briefly in this section. We follow the exposition by Winston [1984] but use our own example, rather than his ARCH example, to explain and illustrate the use of the procedure.

In our example, we examine the process of learning what constitutes a legitimate representation of the first letter of the alphabet of the English language. We are shown two positive examples of A and also three examples of what constitutes non-A, and we follow the method of procedure M to learn what is important and what is irrelevant in describing A. In this procedure, we start with a "neutral" semantic-net–like description of a positive example, and then we compare that example with negative examples and note the differences between two. In this way, we learn what is important and what is not, and we build up a more relevant description of a positive example in terms of meaningful features. The positive examples consist of the letter A written in two different ways and the letters P, M, and H constitute the negative examples.

The two positive and three negative examples of As are illustrated in Table 4.4, as are the differences between pairs of examples. The elemental components of A and the links between these elements are shown in Figure 4.7.

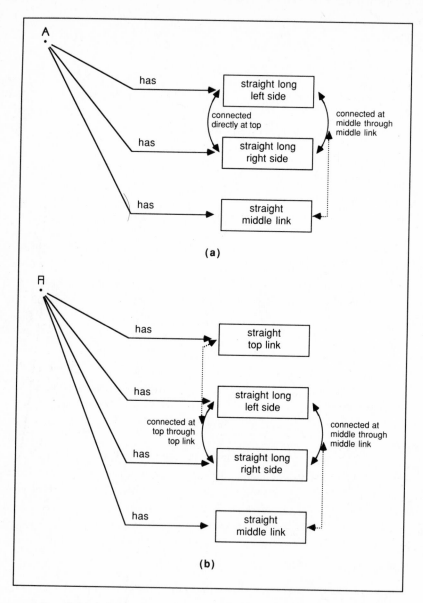

Figure 4.7   Initial description of two positive examples of A.

Part of the work of procedure M is to discuss the differences shown in Figure 4.8 and to express them in terms of MUST and MUST NOT links between the elements of A. In this way, we build up the features of the patterns that represent these examples.

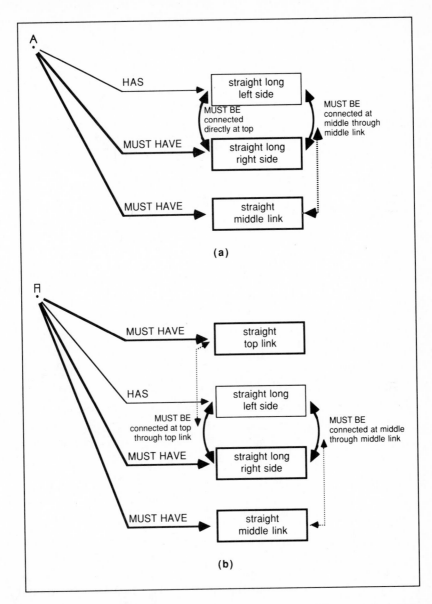

Figure 4.8   Learned descriptions after comparisons with examples of Non-*A* objects.

In Figure 4.9, we see the same differences expressed explicitly in terms of MUST links referred to the elements of the positive example. In other cases, MUST NOT links might be more descriptive and are used accordingly.

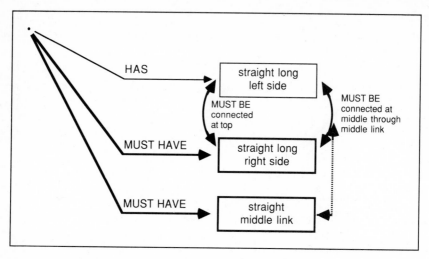

Figure 4.9   Generalized description of positive examples of A.

More generally, use of procedure M involves the following steps.

Step 1. Select a class member with which to work.

    a. Select a nonmember to be excluded by an addition to the class descriptions under construction.

    b. Select a difference with which to work with, using a MUST link or a MUST NOT link. These links are built using SPECIALIZE and corresponding heuristics, such as the *require-link* heuristic or the *forbid-link* heuristic.

    c. Repeat the nonmember selection and description organization until all nonmembers are excluded. (Note that one addition to the class description may, fortuitously, exclude more than one nonmember and may, unfortunately, exclude one or more members.)

Step 2. Use the description obtained with step 1 with other, unmatched class members to drive the generalization heuristics. That is, we use GENERALIZE and associated heuristics, such as *climb tree, enlarge set, close interval,* and *drop link* to include additional members. However, no GENERALIZE heuristic is allowed if it would generalize the description such that a nonmember would start matching again.

Step 3. Continue applying steps 1 and 2 until all class members have been described. The result may be several descriptions for any one class.

The advantages of this procedure are that relevant features are "discovered" and incorporated, and are used as we go along. Also, all alternative descriptions are explored.

Next, we shall describe the procedures for the SPECIALIZE and GENERALIZE heuristics. Except for minor changes, the wording is essentially the same as that of Winston [1984].

The steps of the SPECIALIZE procedure are as follows.

Step 1. Match the evolving class description to the sample (generally a nonmember) to establish correspondence among parts.

Step 2. Determine whether there is a single, most important difference between the evolving description and the sample.

    a. If there is a single, most important difference, determine whether the class description or the sample has a link that is not in the other:

        i. If the evolving class description has a link that is not in the sample, use the *require-link* heuristic.

        ii. If the sample has a link that is not in the description, use the *forbid-link* heuristic.

    b. Otherwise, ignore the sample.

The steps of the GENERALIZE procedure are as follows.

Step 1. Match the evolving class description to the sample to establish correspondences among parts.

Step 2. For each difference, determine the different type.

    a. If the difference is that the link points to a different class in the evolving description from the class to which the link points in the sample, determine whether the classes are part of a classification tree.

        i. If the classes are part of a classification tree, use the *climb-tree* heuristic.

     ii. If the classes form an exhaustive set, use the *drop-link* heuristic.

     iii. Otherwise, use the *enlarge-set* heuristic.

  b. If the difference is that a link is missing in either the evolving description or the example, use the *drop-link* heuristic.

  c. If the difference is that different numbers, or an interval and a number outside the interval, are involved, use the *close-interval* heuristic.

  d. Otherwise, ignore the difference.

The heuristics referred to in the SPECIALIZE and GENERALIZE procedures are listed next; these descriptions also follow those of Winston [1984], except for minor changes.

- The *require-link* heuristic is used when an evolving description has a link in a place and a negative example does not. The description link is converted from a neutral statement to a MUST form.

- The *forbid-link* heuristic is used when a negative example has a link in a place and an evolving description does not. A MUST NOT link form is installed in the evolving description.

- The *climb-tree* heuristic is used when some feature in an evolving description corresponds to a different feature in an example. MUST BE A links are routed to the most specific shared class in a data structure (a classification tree) which includes both the feature in the evolving description and the feature in the example. The name of the feature in the description is that of the shared class in the classification tree.

- The *enlarge-set* heuristic is used when some feature in an evolving description corresponds to a different feature in an example. MUST BE A links are routed to a new class composed of the union of the features' classes.

- The *drop-link* heuristic is used when the features that are different in an evolving description and in an example form an exhaustive set. The *drop-link* heuristic also is used when an evolving description has a link that is not in the example. That link is dropped from the description.

- The *close-interval* heuristic is used when a number or interval in an evolving description corresponds to a number in an example. If the description uses a number, the number is replaced by an interval spanning the description's number and the example's number. If the description uses an interval, the interval is enlarged to include the example's number.

Continuing with the examples of the two *A*s, we illustrate the use of procedure *M* by showing that we might be tempted to GENERALIZE by indicating that the two sides be linked with MUST BE CONNECTED, meaning that the manner of the connection is not important. Such a description is shown in Figure 4.9. If we did that, however, we would find that *M* would be accepted as a positive example on that basis, and we would need to SPECIALIZE again, perhaps by adding a link such as MUST NOT HAVE BENT TOP.

Procedure *M* differs from the ID3 and Pao–Hu methods in how features are formed or selected. Both the ID3 and Pao–Hu methods implicitly assume that there is a *large* number of features or attributes, each with a number of possible values. The principal concern, under those circumstances, is to devise a systematic method for "discovering" which combination of these numerous attributes suffices to determine class membership. Specialization and generalization are essentially secondary matters, taken care of as a matter of course. In contrast, procedure *M* starts with a description of an object in terms of the latter's *parts*, then examines the relationships between those parts. These relationships, or *links*, are considered to be significant if they distinguish between objects that belong to a specific class and those that do not. Class descriptions are built up from these links or features.

4.5 Comments and Bibliographical Remarks

Pattern recognition by humans is of two different types. In one type, the essential nature of the act is that of rapid access to an appropriate content-addressable memory. Recognition, identification, classification, and associative recall all seem to be consequences of that associative access to the correct memory state. A related aspect of that action is the degree to which omissions and distortions are tolerated in the processing of a pattern. The other type of pattern recognition is a more complex mode. It involves accessing bodies of knowledge that might seem to be remote from the context of the patterns in question, and reasoning across contexts. The second type of pattern recognition proceeds at a slower pace.

Both types (if there indeed are two, or only two) are of practical importance and are of interest to any theory that aspires to serve as the basis for computer-based pattern-recognition technology.

The material of this chapter is interesting and important because it plays a useful role in linking concepts in the technical areas of symbolic-processing, adaptive pattern recognition, fuzzy-set theory, and neural-net computing, and because it may be helpful when we perform the second type of pattern recognition.

In the past two decades or so, the artificial-intelligence research community has evolved a powerful and useful *symbolic-processing* technology in which knowledge representation and reasoning all depend on the use of symbols, the names and values of which are *linguistic*. This practice has driven a wedge between symbolic processing and that of pattern recognition, in which the values of the pattern features are usually numeric and processing is parallel in nature. As described in Chapter 3, fuzzy-set theory, the membership function, and the use of possibility distributions combine to provide a bridge between the one style of processing and the other. In Chapter 9, we also describe how neural-net computing can accommodate the incorporation of fuzzy-set theory. This chapter has provided reference points from the symbolic-processing perspective.

More generally, in symbolic processing, there is a great deal of activity in the study of machine learning. Beside the two edited volumes of Michalski, Carbonell, and Mitchell [1973; 1983] there are a journal (*Machine Learning*) and conferences devoted to that activity. In this field, learning by example is closest in spirit to geometric pattern recognition; Michalski's work over the years [1973; 1980] has helped to establish this link. Procedure M [Winston 1984] is an amalgamation of Michalski's work and Winston's work on building a symbolic representation of what constitutes an ARCH [Winston 1975]. It provides a useful description of how a structured pattern might be synthesized with symbolic processing and yet be available for further processing as a pattern.

The Pao and Hu [1985; 1987] method approaches the task from the other direction: Given a set of labeled patterns of linguistic symbols, how do we infer symbolically formatted statements about these patterns? The approach is powerful, but, to date, it has not been widely practiced, perhaps because the symbolic-processing community traditionally has felt little need to view knowledge in terms of patterns, except in terms of matching of rule antecedents.

This latter viewpoint has been changing, a trend that has given rise to the connectionist-net adjunct to symbolic processing. Two issues are involved. In the one case, we recognize that neural nets or connectionist nets are excellent for examining many options in parallel and therefore should be used in symbolic processing. Use of such networks, however, involves representing knowledge in the form of patterns or arrays. How should—or would—this representation be carried out in the case of strings of linguistic symbols of list structures of such symbols? The second, related issue is the matter of representation or coding. Neural nets work most effectively with numeric values, so we must determine how to code linguistic symbols numerically in a robust manner, so that small errors in the input would cause only corresponding small changes in the output consequences. The latter issue has been most frequently addressed by use of a highly redundant distributed representation; for example, a symbol such as "apple" would be represented by an array of numeric values distributed across a field of memory units. A particular pattern of such values would represent the presence of the symbol "apple." This concept of *coarse-coding* is used in many of the connectionist-net publications [Touretzky and Hinton 1985; Touretzky and Geva 1987]. Use of such representations in structures of nets has been considered by several researchers and is still an active research issue. NETL, as proposed by Fahlman [1979], is an early example of such a system. The effort to merge symbolic processing and connectionist-net computing continues [Fahlman and Hinton, 1987; Gallant, 1988]; inevitably, pattern-formatted knowledge representation and processing also become involved.

The ID3 approach to pattern classification is well suited to dealing with patterns that have nonnumeric feature values. Although it uses sequential rather than parallel processing, it is useful for sorting large bodies of nonnumeric valued pattern—otherwise a tiresome and numbing task.

4.6   References and Bibliography

1. Fahlman, S.E., 1979. *NETL: A System for Representing and Using Real-World Knowledge*, MIT Press, Cambridge, MA.

2. Fahlman, S.E. and G.E. Hinton, 1987. Connectionist architectures for Artificial Intelligence, *Computer*, Vol. 20, pp. 100–108.

3. Gallant, S.I., 1988. Connectionist expert systems, *Communications of the ACM*, Vol. 31, No. 2, pp. 152–169.

4. Hunt, E.B., 1962. *Concept Learning: An Information Processing Problem*, Wiley, New York.

5. Michlalski, R.S., 1980. Pattern recognition as rule-guided inductive inference, *IEEE Transactions on Pattern Analysis and Machine Intelligence*, Vol. 2, No. 4, pp. 349–361.

6. Michlalski, R.S., 1973. AQVAL/1–Computer implementation of variable valued logic system VL1 and examples of its application to pattern recognition, *Proceedings of the First International Joint Conference on Pattern Recognition*, Washington, D.C., pp. 3–17.

7. Michlalski, R.S., J.G. Carbonell, and T. M. Mitchell, 1983. *Machine Learning: An Artificial Intelligence Approach*, Tioga, Palo Alto, CA.

8. Pao, Y.H. and C.H. Hu, 1985. Processing of pattern based information, Part 1: Inductive methods suitable for use in pattern recognition and artificial intellignce. In J.T. Tou, (Ed.), *Advances in Information Systems Science*, Vol. 9, Plenum Press, New York.

9. Pao, Y.H. and C.H. Hu, 1982. A systematic procedure for inductive inference of decision rules applicable to certain instances of pattern recognition, *Proceedings of the International Conference on Pattern Recognition*, Munich, October.

10. Quinlan, J.R., 1979. Discovering rules from large collections of examples: A case study. In D. Michie (Ed.), *Expert Systems in the Micro Electronic Age*, Edinburgh University Press, Edinburgh.

11. Quinlan, J.R., 1983. Learning efficient classification procedures and their application to chess end-games. In R.S. Michalski, J.G. Carbonell and T.M. Mitchell (Eds.), *Machine Learning*, Tioga, Palo Alto, CA.

12. Touretzky, D.S. and S. Geva, 1987. A distributed connectionist representation for concept structures, *Proceedings of the Ninth Annual Conference of the Cognitive Science Society*, Seattle, WA, July.

13. Touretzky, D.S. and G.E. Hinton, 1985. Symbols among the neurons: Details of a connectionist inference architecture, *Proceedings of the International Joint Conference on Artificial Intelligence*, Vol. 9, pp. 238–243, Morgan Kaufmann, Los Alto, CA.

14. Winston, P.H., 1975. Learning structural descriptions from examples. In P.H. Winston, (Ed.), *The Psychology of Computer Vision*, McGraw-Hill, New York.

15. Winston, P.H., 1984. *Artificial Intelligence*, 2d ed, Addison-Wesley, Reading, MA. Reprinted with permission.

PART 2

Neural-Net Implementations

CHAPTER 5

Learning Discriminants: The Generalized Perceptron

5.1 Introduction

A concept central to the practice of pattern recognition is that of *discriminants*. The idea is that a pattern-recognition system learns adaptively from experience and distills various discriminants, each appropriate for its purpose. For example, if only class membership is of interest, the system learns from observations of patterns that are identified by class and infers a discriminant for classification.

When functioning as a pattern classifier, the system exercises that discriminant in a straightforward efficient manner. (The theoretical basis for the existence of such discriminants, even in the case of stochastic pattern recognition, was explored in Chapter 2.)

In pattern recognition's quintessential form, both the learning and recognition phases would be achieved with concurrent distributed processing and the entire procedure would be powerful and rapid. This seems to be the case in biological neural systems and should also be the case for computer-based adaptive pattern-recognition systems.

In this part of this book, we address the issue of how adaptive pattern recognition might be implemented with use of algorithms and system architectures based on parallel distributed processing. These algorithms and system architectures are strongly influenced by the results of neurobiology research.

One of the most exciting developments during of the early days of pattern recognition was the Perceptron, the idea that a network of elemental processors arrayed in a manner reminiscent of biological neural nets might be able to learn how to recognize and classify patterns in an autonomous manner. Correspondingly, one of the severe setbacks of early pattern recognition was the realization that simple linear networks were inadequate for that purpose, and that nonlinear nets based on threshold-logic units (TLUs) lacked effective learning algorithms. Nevertheless, the α-Perceptron and the layered machine provided a solid conceptual base for further work. In the interim, work on linear and piecewise linear machines laid the mathematical groundwork for further progress [Widrow 1962; Sklansky and Wassel 1981].

Recent research results have changed the situation drastically. The generalized delta rule of Rumelhart, Hinton, and Williams [1986] constitutes one practicable way of implementing a Perceptronlike system, and other generalizations of that approach are being explored. These matters are described in this chapter.

Section 5.2 is devoted to a brief review of some approaches to learning linear discriminants for pattern recognition. The fault of inadequacy did not lie with the particular details of any of these approaches, but rather with the intrinsic limitation associated with the use of any linear discriminant. The generalized delta rule (GDR) for use in semilinear nets with hidden units transcends some of these limitations; it is described in Section 5.3. Issues regarding the degree of connectivity required for such nets are examined in Section 5.4.

In pattern recognition and in learning, the twin processes of generalization and specialization are all-important. Generalization enables a pattern-recognition system to function competently throughout pattern space, even though it has learned from observing only a limited body of examples. Specialization allows such a system to recover from error and to improve itself. These matters are described in Section 5.5 from the perspectives of mapping and metric synthesis.

The GDR is far from perfect or even perfectly understood. Extensions of GDR are described in Section 5.6; an alternate, simpler, approach to the learning of discriminants is described in Chapter 8.

5.2 Linear Discriminants: The Precursors

It is wisely stated that the most valuable knowledge that a person— or machine—can acquire is the knowledge of how to learn. In pattern recognition, it is essential that the system be able to learn from experience and to infer discriminants autonomously.

In Chapter 2, we saw how a stochastic pattern-recogniton situation described in terms of class conditional probability densities and Bayesian statistics could in fact be described equally well in terms of discriminants, and in some cases even in terms of linear discriminants. Given that perspective, the more cogent concern is how we might learn discriminants directly, without going through lengthy and largely inconsequential steps.

In this connection, the facts concerning the Perceptron are well known and well documented. Rosenblatt [1959, 1962] envisaged the Perceptron to be a parallel distributed-processing system made up of a network of multipliers and summing functions. His linear two-layer version of the Perceptron was inadequate for the tasks envisioned for it. The accurate and insightful—but terribly discouraging—analysis of the limitations of that simple Perceptron by Minsky and Papert [1969] is also well known. Nilsson's description of the layered machine [Nilsson, 1965] showed that the concept of a generalized Perceptron with "hidden" layers was already well understood. Unfortunately, no practicable learning algorithm was available for such machines at that time.

In this section, we revisit the linear Perceptron algorithm in the form in which it has been taught in pattern recognition for decades [Duda and Hart, 1973]. For all purposes, it is the same as the iterative form of the Widrow–Hoff algorithm [Widrow and Hoff, 1960], and can be expressed in the form of a *delta rule* for learning the value of *weights*. In the next section, we describe the extension of this learning procedure to yield the generalized delta rule as formulated by Rumelhart, Hinton, and Williams [1986].

A linear discriminant can be represented schematically in the form of an array of multipliers and summing junctions, as shown in Figure 5.1. In that illustration, pattern feature values are the inputs to a "black box," the discriminant. We can peer into that box and we see that each input is connected to the output by a link containing a multiplier, such that the input to the output node is the sum of all the appropriately weighted inputs. In the case of a two-class classification problem, only one output would be required and the two values of the output might be 1 and -1, corresponding to the two classes c_1 and $\sim c_1$, respectively. The task is to learn a set of weight values so that all patterns can be classified correctly using a single set of weights.

A multiclass classification task would require several outputs, as shown in Figure 5.2. The notation is made more elaborate than in the two-class problem, so that we can express the linear-discriminant procedure in terms of a simple delta rule and then pass to the generalized delta rule (GDR).

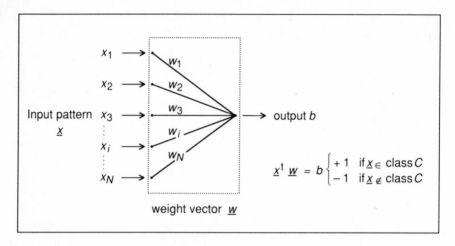

Figure 5.1   Schematic representation of a linear discriminant.

Note that the nodes in Figure 5.2 are "placeholders" in that the input is equal to the output at all nodes. Therefore, in network implementation of a linear discriminant, all the nodes are linear, as are the links. As we shall see, this is not so in the case of networks based on the generalized delta rule.

In the following problem, first we determine the discriminant in terms of an exact analytical task and learn that there may be difficulties that would preclude our obtaining a solution. Therefore, we then use an iterative approach for the linear Perceptron algorithm, which leads to the delta rule. This approach also has an easily understood graphical interpretation.

In the analytical approach, we describe patterns in terms of column vectors $\underline{x}$, so that $\underline{x}^t = \{x_1, x_2, \ldots, x_N\}$, and group the training-set patterns, row-wise, in the form of a matrix X. Solving for the linear discriminant consists of looking for a column vector $\underline{w}$ such that

$$X\underline{w} = \underline{b}, \qquad (5.1)$$

where the elements of $\underline{b}$ are the "output" values specified by the training-set example.

In a binary-classification problem, the values of $\underline{b}$ might be specified to be positive if $\underline{x}$ belongs to class c_1 and negative if $\underline{x}$ belongs to $\sim$ class $\underline{c}_1$. In terms of networks, this circumstance corresponds to having a single scalar output b that can have different values.

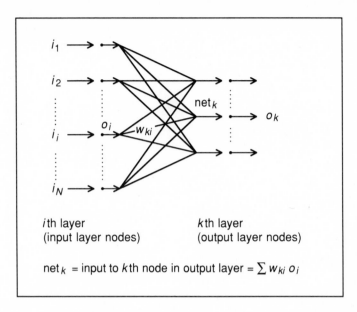

Figure 5.2 A more elaborate network representation of a multioutput linear discriminant.

For M patterns in N-dimensional space, we can write expression (5.1) in expanded form as

$$\begin{bmatrix} x_{11} & x_{12} & x_{13} & \cdots & x_{1N} \\ x_{21} & x_{22} & x_{23} & \cdots & x_{2N} \\ \vdots & \vdots & \vdots & \ddots & \vdots \\ x_{M1} & x_{M2} & x_{M3} & \cdots & x_{MN} \end{bmatrix} \begin{bmatrix} w_1 \\ w_2 \\ \vdots \\ w_N \end{bmatrix} = \begin{bmatrix} b_1 \\ b_2 \\ \vdots \\ b_M \end{bmatrix} \tag{5.2}$$

and specify that $\underline{x}_i \in c_1$, if b_i is positive, and that $\underline{x}_i \in \sim c_1$, if b_i is negative. We know that we can solve equation (5.1) in terms of the pseudoinverse of X; that is,

$$X^t X \, \underline{w} = X^t \underline{b} \tag{5.3}$$

and

$$\underline{w} = (X^t X)^{-1} X^t \underline{b} \tag{5.4}$$

or

$$\underline{w} = X^\dagger \underline{b} \tag{5.5}$$

where $X^\dagger$ is the pseudoinverse and, in principle, can also be obtained as the limiting value of the process

$$X^\dagger = \lim_{\varepsilon \to 0}(X^t X + \varepsilon I)^{-1} X^t \qquad (5.6)$$

In practice, however, nonsensical values are obtained if the determinant of $X^t X$ is vanishingly small.

The exact analytical procedure is impractical not only because of analytical difficulties, but also because it does not seem to correspond to circumstances encountered in real situations. From a formal pattern recognition perspective, we can envision having a fixed "set" of training-set patterns. However, the circumstances encountered by a biological neural net might be different; patterns might be encountered sequentially, one at a time. This is often true of real pattern recognition tasks. In the more realistic case, the appropriate discriminant equations would be

$$\underline{x}_p \underline{w} = \underline{b} \qquad p = 1, 2, \ldots \qquad (5.7)$$

and the requirement would be that a single set of weights $\underline{w}$ suffice to yield the correct set of outputs $\underline{b}$ for all patterns $\underline{x}_p, p = 1, 2, 3, \ldots$. The linear Perceptron algorithm and the iterative version of the Widrow–Hoff procedure both advocate finding $\underline{w}$ through the following rules:

Let

$$\underline{w}_1 = \text{arbitrary}$$

and

$$\underline{w}_{k+1} = \underline{w}_k + \rho(b^k - \underline{w}_k^t \cdot \underline{x}^k)\underline{x}^k \qquad (5.8)$$

where b^k is the appropriate value of b for pattern $\underline{x}^k$ and might be $+1$ for c_1 patterns and -1 for $\sim c_1$ patterns, and $\underline{x}^k$ is the pattern being considered at step k.

Expression (5.8) is a rule for updating the weight vector until all pattern vectors are classified correctly. The procedure is to add a certain amount of $\underline{x}^k$ to $\underline{w}_k$ if $\underline{x}^k$ is not classified correctly. The proportionality factor is $\rho(b^k - \underline{w}_k^t \underline{x}^k)$, which is zero or vanishingly small if $\underline{x}^k$ is classified correctly. In most cases of interest, it is impossible to satisfy all the equations $\underline{w}^t \underline{x}^k = b^k$, so the corrections never stop. Convergence can be ensured if ρ is decreased with k; that is, let $\rho \to 0$ as iteration proceeds. However, the convergence so obtained is artificial and does not necessarily yield a valid $\underline{w}$ that will classify all patterns correctly.

Expression (5.8) can be rewritten as

$$\Delta \underline{w} = \eta \delta \underline{x} \qquad (5.9)$$

where the quantity δ in expression (5.8) is equal to $(b - \underline{w}^t \underline{x})$, the difference between the desired output (b) and the actual output produced by the net, that is, $\underline{w}^t \underline{x}$. In expression (5.9), $\underline{x}$ is the input pattern.

Therefore, the simple delta rule of expression (5.9) states that the change in the weight vector should be proportional to δ and to the input pattern. This is the delta rule that is generalized to yield the GDR.

From a graphical point of view, both the linear Perceptron algorithm and the iterative Widrow–Hoff procedure consist of updating the weight vector by considering each misclassified pattern in turn and by adding a fraction of each misclassified pattern to the weight vector. This practice is continued until all patterns are classified correctly or until it is clear that the procedure will fail to converge to a satisfactory solution.

If more than one output is involved, then the solution is a weight matrix rather than a weight vector, and the required outputs also form a matrix. The procedure remains the same.

In the linear case, there is no advantage to having more than one layer of nodes in the Perceptron structure illustrated in Figure 5.2. That is, the complication of an internal layer is not useful. The matrix product of two linear matrices is still but a matrix, and the nature of the solution is the same as before. That is,

$$X W_1 W_2 = B \qquad (5.10)$$

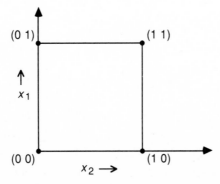

Figure 5.3   Patterns of even and odd parity.

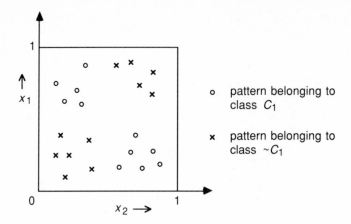

Figure 5.4   Another pattern-recognition problem that cannot be handled by a linear classifier.

might as well have been written as

$$XW = B \qquad (5.11)$$

and solving iteratively for a single W is easier than is cycling through the two successive steps of solving for W_1 and W_2.

A linear Perceptron with no internal layer is incapable of yielding a discriminant that will solve the EXCLUSIVE-OR or parity problem. That is, the linear Perceptron cannot automatically learn the discriminant that will classify correctly the even and odd parity patterns shown in Figure 5.3, or the clusters of c_1 and $\sim c_1$ patterns shown in Figure 5.4.

5.3 The Generalized Delta Rule for the Semilinear Feedforward Net with Backpropagation of Error

The semilinear feedforward net as reported by Rumelhart, Hinton, and Williams [1986] has been found to be an effective system for learning discriminants for patterns from a body of examples. The system architecture of such a net is identical to that of the layered machine shown in Figure 6.2 of Nilsson's *Learning Machines* [1965, p. 96] except that the activation function for the nodes of the otherwise linear net is an analytic function. It is also similar to the architecture of the α-Perceptron proposed by Rosenblatt [1961] except that there are hidden layers of nodes.

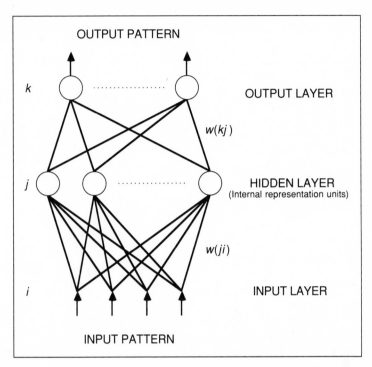

Figure 5.5   A schematic depiction of a semilinear feedforward connectionist net.

The system architecture for such a net is illustrated schematically in Figure 5.5.

In general, such a net is made up of sets of nodes arranged in layers. The outputs of nodes in one layer are transmitted to nodes in another layer through links that amplify or attenuate or inhibit such outputs through weighting factors. Except for the input layer nodes, the net input to each node is the sum of the weighted outputs of the nodes in the prior layer. Each node is activated in accordance with the input to the node, the activation function of the node, and the bias of the node.

Thus, in Figure 5.5, the components of an input pattern constitute the inputs to the nodes in layer i. The outputs of the nodes in that layer may be taken to be equal to the inputs, or we can take the opportunity to normalize those inputs in the sense that they can be scaled to fall between the values of -1 and $+1$.

The net input to a node in layer j is

$$\text{net}_j = \sum w_{ji} o_i \tag{5.12}$$

The output of node j is

$$o_j = f(\text{net}_j) \tag{5.13}$$

where f is the activation function.

For a sigmoidal activation function, we have

$$o_j = \frac{1}{1 + e^{-(\text{net}_j + \theta_j)/\theta_o}} \tag{5.14}$$

In expression (5.14) the parameter θ_j serves as a threshold or bias. The effect of a positive θ_j is to shift the activation function to the left along the horizontal axis, and the effect of θ_o is to modify the shape of the sigmoid. A low value of θ_o tends to make the sigmoid take on the characteristics of a *threshold-logic unit (TLU)*, whereas a high value of θ_o results in a more gently varying function. These effects are illustrated in Figure 5.6.

Continuing our description of the computational processes, we have for the nodes in layer k the input

$$\text{net}_k = \sum w_{kj} o_j \tag{5.15}$$

and the corresponding outputs

$$o_k = f(\text{net}_k) \tag{5.16}$$

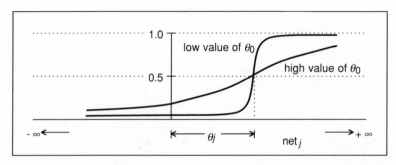

Figure 5.6   The sigmoidal activation function, with bias and shape modification.

In the learning phase of training such a net, we present the pattern $\underline{x}_p = \{i_{pi}\}$ as input and ask that the net adjust the set of weights in all the connecting links and also all the thresholds in the nodes such that the desired outputs t_{pk} are obtained at the output nodes. Once this adjustment has been accomplished by the net, we present another pair of $\underline{x}_p$ and $\{t_{pk}\}$, and ask that the net learn that association also. In fact, we ask that the net find a single set of weights and biases that will satisfy *all* the (input, output) pairs presented to it. This process can pose a very strenuous learning task and is not always readily accomplished.

In general, the outputs $\{o_{pk}\}$ will not be the same as the target or desired values $\{t_{pk}\}$. For each pattern, the square of the error is

$$E_p = \frac{1}{2} \sum_k (t_{pk} - o_{pk})^2 \tag{5.17}$$

and the average system error is

$$E = \frac{1}{2P} \sum_p \sum_k (t_{pk} - o_{pk})^2 \tag{5.18}$$

where the factor of one-half is inserted for mathematical convenience at some later stage in our discussion.

In the generalized delta rule formulated by Rumelhart, Hinton, and Williams [1986] for learning the weights and biases, the procedure for learning the correct set of weights is to vary the weights in a manner calculated to reduce the error E_p as rapidly as possible. In general, different results are obtained depending on whether one carries out the gradient search in weight space on the basis of E_p or of E. In the former case, the corrections to the weights are made sequentially, on the basis of the learning to be carried out for the sequence of the patterns, one at a time. A true gradient search for minimum system error should be based on the minimization of expression (5.18). This latter procedure is feasible for adaptive pattern recognition, but is unlikely to correspond to processes carried out in biological neural nets. We shall say more about this matter after we consider the generalized delta rule.

Omitting the p subscript for convenience, we write expression (5.17) as

$$E = \frac{1}{2} \sum_k (t_k - o_k)^2 \tag{5.19}$$

We achieve convergence toward improved values for the weights and thresholds by taking incremental changes Δw_{kj} proportional to $-\partial E/\partial w_{kj}$;

that is,

$$\Delta w_{kj} = -\eta \frac{\partial E}{\partial w_{kj}} \tag{5.20}$$

However, E, the error, is expressed in terms of the outputs o_k, each of which is the nonlinear output of the node k. That is,

$$o_k = f(\text{net}_k) \tag{5.21}$$

where net_k is the input to the kth node and by definition is the weighted linear sum of all the outputs from the previous layer:

$$\text{net}_k = \sum w_{kj}\, o_j \tag{5.22}$$

The partial derivative $\partial E/\partial w_{kj}$ can be evaluated using the chain rule

$$\frac{\partial E}{\partial w_{kj}} = \frac{\partial E}{\partial \text{net}_k} \frac{\partial \text{net}_k}{\partial w_{kj}} \tag{5.23}$$

Using expression (5.22), we obtain

$$\frac{\partial \text{net}_k}{\partial w_{kj}} = \frac{\partial}{\partial w_{kj}} \sum w_{kj}\, o_j = o_j \tag{5.24}$$

We now define

$$\delta_k = -\frac{\partial E}{\partial \text{net}_k} \tag{5.25}$$

and write

$$\Delta w_{kj} = \eta \delta_k\, o_j \tag{5.26}$$

an expression similar in form to the delta rule of expression (5.9).

To compute $\delta_k = -\partial E/\partial \text{net}_k$, we use the chain rule to express the partial derivative in terms of two factors, one expressing the rate of change of error with respect to the output o_k, and the other expressing the rate of change of the output of the node k with respect to the input to that same node. That is, we have

$$\delta_k = -\frac{\partial E}{\partial \text{net}_k} = -\frac{\partial E}{\partial o_k} \frac{\partial o_k}{\partial \text{net}_k} \tag{5.27}$$

The two factors are obtained as follows:

$$\frac{\partial E}{\partial o_k} = -(t_k - o_k) \tag{5.28}$$

and

$$\frac{\partial o_k}{\partial \text{net}_k} = f_k'(\text{net}_k) \tag{5.29}$$

From which we obtain

$$\delta_k = (t_k - o_k)f_k'(\text{net}_k) \tag{5.30}$$

for *any output-layer* node k, and we have

$$\Delta w_{kj} = \eta(t_k - o_k)f_k'(\text{net}_k)o_j = \eta\delta_k\, o_j \tag{5.31}$$

Circumstances are different if the weights do not affect output nodes directly. We still write

$$\begin{aligned}
\Delta w_{ji} &= -\eta\frac{\partial E}{\partial w_{ji}}\\
&= -\eta\frac{\partial E}{\partial \text{net}_j}\frac{\partial \text{net}_j}{\partial w_{ji}}\\
&= -\eta\frac{\partial E}{\partial \text{net}_j}o_i\\
&= \eta\left(-\frac{\partial E}{\partial o_j}\frac{\partial o_j}{\partial \text{net}_j}\right)o_i = \eta\left(-\frac{\partial E}{\partial o_j}\right)f_j'(\text{net}_j)o_i\\
&= \eta\delta_j\, o_i
\end{aligned} \tag{5.32}$$

However, the factor $\partial E/\partial o_j$ cannot be evaluated directly. Instead, we write it in terms of quantities that are known and other quantities that can be evaluated. Specifically, we write

$$\begin{aligned}
-\frac{\partial E}{\partial o_j} &= -\sum_k\frac{\partial E}{\partial \text{net}_k}\frac{\partial \text{net}_k}{\partial o_j} = \sum_k\left(-\frac{\partial E}{\partial \text{net}_k}\right)\frac{\partial}{\partial o_j}\sum_m w_{km}\, o_m\\
&= \sum_k\left(-\frac{\partial E}{\partial \text{net}_k}\right)w_{kj} = \sum_k\delta_k\, w_{kj}
\end{aligned} \tag{5.33}$$

We see that, in this case,

$$\delta_j = f'_j(\text{net}_j) \sum_k \delta_k \, w_{kj} \tag{5.34}$$

That is, the deltas at an internal node can be evaluated in terms of the deltas at an upper layer. Thus, starting at the highest layer—the output layer—we can evaluate δ_k using expression (5.30), and we can then propagate the "errors" backward to lower layers. Summarizing, and using the additional subscript p to denote the pattern number, we have

$$\Delta_p w_{ji} = \eta \delta_{pj} \, o_{pi} \tag{5.35}$$

If the j nodes are output-layer nodes, we have

$$\delta_{pj} = (t_{pj} - o_{pj}) \, f'_j(\text{net}_{pj}) \tag{5.36}$$

However, if the j nodes are internal nodes, then we need to evaluate δ_{pj} in terms of δs at a higher layer; that is,

$$\delta_{pj} = f'_j(\text{net}_{pj}) \sum_k \delta_{pk} \, w_{kj} \tag{5.37}$$

In particular, if

$$o_j = \frac{1}{1 + \exp\left[-\left(\sum_i w_{ji} o_i + \theta_j\right)\right]} \tag{5.38}$$

then

$$\frac{\partial o_j}{\partial \text{net}_j} = o_j(1 - o_j) \tag{5.39}$$

and the deltas are given by the following two expressions:

$$\delta_{pk} = (t_{pk} - o_{pk}) \, o_{pk}(1 - o_{pk}) \tag{5.40}$$

$$\delta_{pj} = o_{pj}(1 - o_{pj}) \sum_k \delta_{pk} \, w_{kj} \tag{5.41}$$

for the output-layer and hidden-layer units, respectively.

Note that the thresholds θ_j are learned in the same manner as are the other weights. We simply imagine that θ_j is the weight from a unit that always has an output value of unity. Also note that the derivative

$\partial o_j/\partial \text{net}_j$, equal to $o_j(1 - o_j)$, reaches its maximum for $o_j = 0.5$ and, since $o \leq o_j \leq 1$, approaches its minima as o_j approaches zero or one. Since the change in weight is proportional to this quantity, it is clear that weights that are connected to units in their midrange are changed the most. In some sense, these units are still uncommitted and are not certain whether to "turn on" or "turn off." The weights change rapidly under those conditions, and this feature probably contributes to the stability of the learning procedure.

It is important to note that, for the activation function given by expression (5.38), a node cannot have output values of 1 or 0 without infinitely large positive or negative weights. Therefore, in learning mode, the values of 0.9 and 0.1 might suffice for specifying binary target output values.

In learning w_{ji}, it is good practice to calculate $\Delta_p w_{ji}$ for each pattern in the training set of patterns, and to take

$$\Delta w_{ji} = \sum_p \Delta_p w_{ji} \tag{5.42}$$

The learning procedure therefore consists of the net starting off with a random set of weight values, choosing one of the training-set patterns, and, using that pattern as input, evaluating the output(s) in a feedforward manner. The errors at the output(s) generally will be quite large, which necessitates changes in the weights. Using the backpropagation procedure, the net calculates $\Delta_p w_{ji}$ for all the w_{ji} in the net for that particular p. This procedure is repeated for all the patterns in the training set to yield the resulting Δw_{ji} for all the weights for that one *presentation*. The corrections to the weights are made and the output(s) are again evaluated in feedforward manner. Discrepancies between actual and target output values again result in evaluation of weight changes. After complete presentation of all patterns in the training set, a new set of weights is obtained and new outputs are again evaluated in a feedfoward manner.

The net can be made to track the system error and also the errors for individual patterns. In a successful learning exercise, the system error will decrease with the number of iterations, and the procedure will converge to a stable set of weights, which will exhibit only small fluctuations in value as further learning is attempted.

There are several other issues we need to keep in mind when we implement such nets. There is, for example, the question of how the value of η is to be chosen. This is not a new or unusual problem; it is common to all steepest-descent methods of locating minima of functions. As might be expected, a large η corresponds to rapid learning but might also result in oscillations. Rumelhart, Hinton, and Williams [1986] suggest that expressions (5.31) and (5.35) might be modified to include a sort of *momentum* term. That is, we write

$$\Delta w_{ji}(n+1) = \eta(\delta_j\, o_i) + \alpha\Delta\, w_{ji}(n) \qquad (5.43)$$

where the quantity $(n+1)$ is used to indicate the $(n+1)$th step, and α is a proportionality constant. The second term in expression (5.43) is used to specify that the change in w_{ji} at the $(n+1)$th step should be somewhat similar to the change undertaken at the nth step. In this way, some inertia is built in, and momentum in the rate of change is conserved to some degree. Examination of the system error E over a large number of steps in the iterative approach to a solution will generally show that a finite α tends to dampen the oscillations but can also serve to slow the rate of learning.

If weight corrections are carried out after presentation of each pattern, the method is not truly a gradient search procedure. In addition, the value of η needs to be small; otherwise, large excursions can take place in weight space.

Note that the net must not be allowed to start off with a set of equal weights. It has been shown that it is not possible to proceed from such a configuration to one of unequal weights, even if the latter corresponds to smaller system error [Rumelhart, Hinton, and Williams 1986].

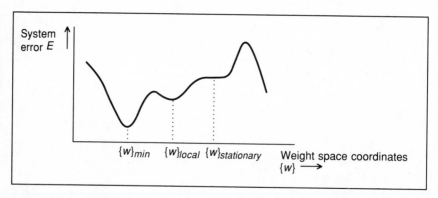

Figure 5.7   Illustration of the possibility of the learning procedure being trapped at nonoptimum values.

Another issue concerns the question of whether the system might get trapped in some local minimum or even at some stationary point, or perhaps oscillate between such points. Under such circumstances, the system error remains large regardless of how many iterations are carried out. This situation is depicted schematically in Figure 5.7. In that figure, we show the system error as a function in weight space. We hope to learn the weights $\{w\}_{min}$ but might get trapped at point $\{w\}_{local}$ or even at point $\{w\}_{stationary}$.

5.4   Complexity Requirements of the Feedforward Multilayer Machine

In a connectionist net that learns discriminants for pattern classification, it is natural to ask how many layers are required for the learning and discrimination task, and how many nodes are required in each layer. A simple argument provides insight [Lippman, 1987]. Complications aside, we can argue that a three-layer machine can form arbitrarily complex decision regions and can therefore separate populations of patterns even though such distributions might be intermeshed spatially in pattern space.

Each first-layer node forms a hyperplane in pattern space, because the input to the node is the linear sum of the inputs. As the inputs change in value, the linear sum traces a line in two-dimensional space, a plane in three-dimensional space, and hyperplanes in N-dimensional space.

As we saw from the discussion of Chapter 2, boundaries between distributions can often be represented approximately by hyperplanes. Consequently, in the use of connectionist nets for learning discriminants, we can think in terms of partitioning the different populations into small hyperregions. Once we have accomplished this partitioning, we can classify the various decision regions appropriately.

This view indicates that each hyperregion requires $2N$ nodes in the first hidden layer, one node for each of the sides of the hyperregion. At the next layer, a node is needed to carry out an AND operation on that collection of hyperplanes. Thus, whereas a node in the first internal layer forms a hyperplane, a node in the second internal layer forms a hyperregion from the outputs from the first layer nodes. The outputs of second-layer nodes will be "high" only for patterns within each such hyperregion. These matters are illustrated in Figure 5.8. Consider the case where patterns of a single class c_i are in several disconnected regions in N-dimensional pattern

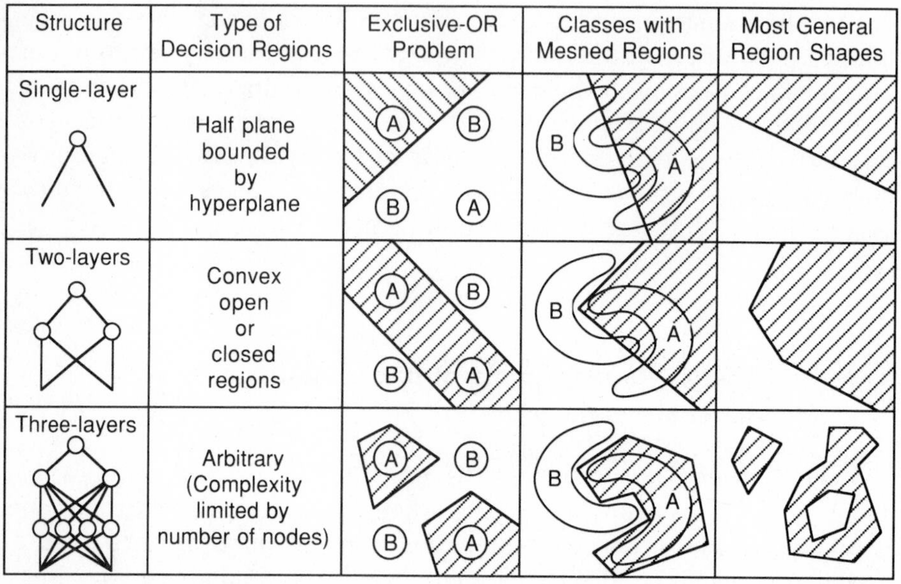

Structure	Type of Decision Regions	Exclusive-OR Problem	Classes with Mesned Regions	Most General Region Shapes
Single-layer	Half plane bounded by hyperplane			
Two-layers	Convex open or closed regions			
Three-layers	Arbitrary (Complexity limited by number of nodes)			

Figure 5.8   A simple view of the role of hidden units in multilayer perceptrons, for two inputs and the hard-limiting case. (Lippman, R.P., 1987. An introduction to computing with neural nets, *IEEE ASSP Magazine,* Vol. 4, p. 14, ©1987, IEEE. Adapted from and reprinted with permission.)

space. Each such region is covered by a second-layer node. If an output-layer node can be arranged to perform an OR operation on all the second layer c_i nodes, then any c_i pattern will be recognized and classified correctly regardless of in which region it is located. We can implement the OR function by arranging the weights to be equal to and less than 1 and the threshold of the output node to be sufficiently low that, if any *one* of the connected second-layer nodes were to go "high," the output node would be triggered.

In principle, the hyperregions need not even be convex and could be complex in shape. In practice, the actual situations are not always as simple as described. There is often a high degree of redundacy in hyperplanes. In many cases, if not all, there will be class c_i patterns on both sides of any hyperplane, and it may be difficult if not well-nigh impossible for the second-layer nodes to know which hyperplanes to incorporate into the AND operation.

In practice, an excessive number of nodes in any one layer can generate noise. On the other hand, fault tolerance can be obtained with such redundancy in the number of nodes.

Sometimes, we can simplfy difficult learning tasks by increasing the number of internal layers. We can certainly do so when there are three to four internal layers. Rumelhart, Hinton, and Williams [1986], however, found that exponential increases in the number of hidden units were necessary to produce a linear increase in learning speed on the EXCLUSIVE-OR problem. Other researchers have found that increasing the number of hidden layers actually *decreased* the rate of learning in the random vector-pairing problem. The tendency is to try to expedite the learning process by increasing the extent of nonlinearity, rather than by increasing the complexity of the semilinear net. We shall say more about this subject in Section 5.6 and in Chapter 8.

5.5 The Mapping Perspective

With a perspective slightly different from that described in the previous sections, the action of a neural net may be viewed principally as a mapping through which points in the input space (that is, pattern space) are transformed into corresponding points in an output space on the basis of designated attribute values, of which class membership might be one [Pao and Sobajic 1987].

The input space is generally an N-dimensional Euclidean space. We know how to calculate the Euclidean distance between points, and therefore we know which patterns are close to each other and what others are far apart. That is, we have a metric for the input space. However, the mapping effected by the connectionist net distorts and transforms that space, so not only is the dimensionality of the output space generally different from that of the input space, but also patterns are rearranged in accordance with their class membership index values or in accordance with their designated attribute values, rather than according to their positions in the original input space.

A question of interest is whether points that are close to each other in input space are also close to each other in output space. This generalization property is of considerable theoretical and practical interest and consequence. This issue is also related to the question of "topologically correct" mappings in unsupervised learning [Kohonen 1982].

We shall find that the mapping learned by the net synthesizes a new metric for the input space for use in estimating "distances" between points, no longer on the basis of original distances in Euclidean space, but rather on the basis of similarity in output space. We shall also find that this new metric is a spatially varying quantity, which implies that

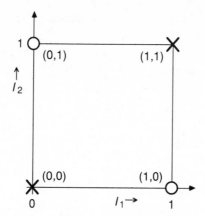

Figure 5.9   Pattern representaton for the parity problem in the two-dimensional input space I.

generalization can be carried out with confidence locally rather than globally.

In this section, we examine the details of some input–output mappings in order to introduce the metric synthesis viewpoint.

The two-dimensional parity problem—that is, the EXCLUSIVE-OR problem—is illustrated in Figure 5.9 in terms of the four two-dimensional binary-valued patterns that are located at the four vertices of a unit square. A neural net with one hidden layer, with two nodes in the layer, and with a single node in the output layer was allowed to train itself so that both the even-parity patterns had the value of (nearly) 0 and the odd-parity patterns had the value of (nearly) 1 at the output node. The details of how this was achieved are very interesting.

The action of the first-stage of linear transformation achieved through weighting and summing is illustrated in Figure 5.10. The transformation is from I space to T space. We see that the two even-parity patterns are brought together. The action of nonlinear activation of the two intermediate nodes transforms the T_1 and T_2 coordinate values into the O_1 and O_2 node outputs, as shown in Figure 5.11. The action of the final output node can be summarized as being equivalent to placing a line to separate the two types of patterns, those with even parity and those with odd parity. This line is shown in Figure 5.12.

When a sigmoidal activation function is used, it is possible to view this transformation from a different perspective. Not only are these four patterns classified correctly in the final representation, but also all points

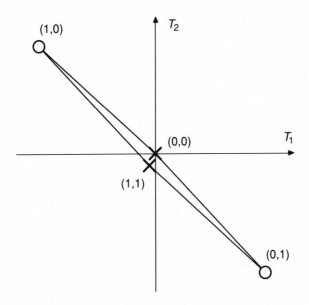

Figure 5.10   Effect of the linear transformation $T = WI$.

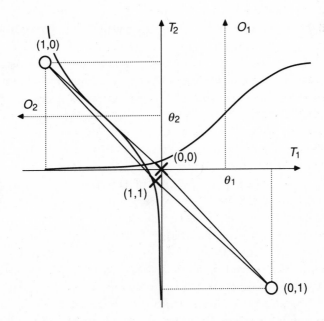

Figure 5.11   The character of the nonlinear mapping by activation functions of the hidden units.

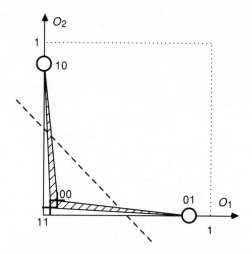

Figure 5.12   The linear-pattern separability in the space of hidden-unit outputs.

in the input space are assigned a value ranging from (nearly) 0 to (nearly) 1. Moreover, two induced understandings of the input space are possible; these are shown in Figures 5.13(a) and 5.13(b). If an extra point of one type or the other is inserted in the center of the input space, then unambiguous mappings can be obtained.

We now use a somewhat more complicated case to illustrate what we mean by *metric synthesis*. Consider the arbitrarily designated seven-point problem shown in Figure 5.14. The neural net used to learn how to separate the x patterns (nearly 0 in designated value) and the o patterns (nearly 1 in designated value) had three nodes in the hidden layer. As mentioned previously, the action of nodes in the first hidden layer is to synthesize lines; these lines are indicated in Figure 5.14. A three-dimensional depiction of the positions of the seven points in the space of the three intermediate nodes indicates that the two sets of points are indeed separated by one hyperplane (Figure 5.15).

Of equal interest is the mapping shown in Figure 5.16, where the output-space coordinate values of various selected points are listed for points shown in their input space position. We see that the action of the neural net forces a metric on the input space different from the usual metric of Euclidean space. Points that are nearby in the Euclidean space may or may not be that nearly alike in terms of the induced coordinate values(s). The induced metric is more suggestive of Riemmanian geometry

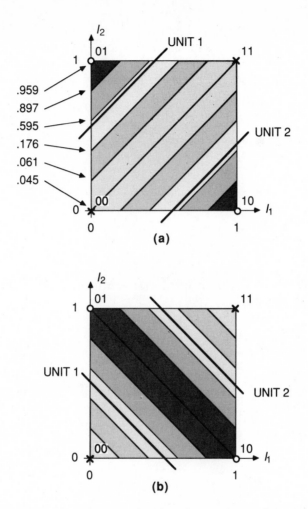

Figure 5.13   Two possible generalized understandings of the input space. (a) Valley induced in input space. (b) Ridge induced in input space.

rather than of Euclidean geometry, in the sense that the metric not only is a function of space but also is generally a tensor rather than a scalar quantity.

This action of metric induction is a valuable characteristic of the generalized Perceptron neural-net approach. It is clear that strategically placed examples can influence that metric-synthesis procedure to a considerable extent.

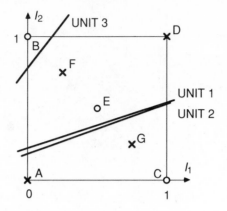

Figure 5.14   Patterns for the seven-points problem.

5.6 Comments and Bibliographical Remarks

In Chapter 2, we showed how statistical pattern classification by the criterion of maximum decision-function value or minimum risk could be cast into a form of determining discriminants for achieving such classification. In other words, the learning and use of discriminants for the purpose of pattern classification is a universally valid approach, regardless of whether we are dealing with deterministic or statistical data. The material in this

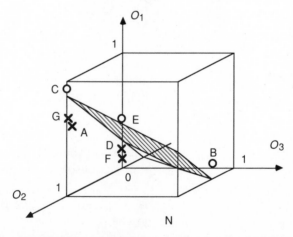

Figure 5.15   Separating hyperplanes in the space of hidden-units outputs. Location of the seven patterns in space of the three intermediate nodes.

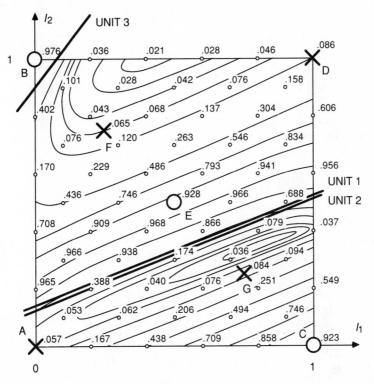

Figure 5.16 Illustration of metric for determining whether nearby points are also close to each other in output space.

chapter is important because the use of an analytic function for the activation function and the generalized delta rule serve to give us, for the first time, a simple, valid procedure for learning discriminants. Similar procedures had been proposed and practised by a few other contemporary researchers; Rumelhart, Hinton, and Williams [1986] were successful in articulating their views and communicating their results to the benefit of all.

The generalized delta rule (GDR), however, does not scale well, and neither the addition of more nodes in a hidden layer nor of more layers seem to be of much help after a certain point. The learning rate can become impractically slow, or learning may not be achieved at all. We can look at this situation from two viewpoints.

In GDR, all the links are linear, and the entire network computation can be visualized in terms of synthesizing hyperplanes and forming linear combinations of these and hypervolumes. It is often said that the first-layer nodes form hyperplanes and the second-layer nodes use these hyperplanes to form hypervolumes that partition pattern space into regions of different class memberships. The basic problem is that this qualitative understanding is misleading and is essentially wrong. In actuality, hyperplanes do not stop neatly at the boundaries of hypervolumes, but rather extend through all space. Therefore, a hyperplane might serve well in defining the boundary of one hypervolume, but extend to intrude into the interior of another hypervolume. Confronted with a wealth of hyperplanes, the second-level nodes sometimes cannot decide what combination of hyperplanes should be chosen to form the optimum set of hypervolumes.

An alternate view of the network-formation process is provided by the detailed discussion of Nilsson [1965]. From his viewpoint, the network-computation procedure is transformation of coordinates, or mapping of the patterns from the original pattern space successively into other more appropriate space until linear discrimination can be achieved. That is probably the more legitimate viewpoint; thus, there is no reason to suppose that only two hidden layers will be required at the most. Nor is there any reason why even two such layers would be required.

In Chapter 8, we show that the requisite mapping can be carried out more directly on the input patterns without getting that process mixed up with the learning of the final discriminant.

Also, as far as classification is concerned, there is probably no reason why the generalized Perceptron approach needs to be used at all. Unsupervised learning or clustering, structured hierarchically if necessary, would seem to be sufficient for all conceivable classification tasks. It is the task of estimation that requires the synthesis of a new metric for the original pattern space and the use of the Perceptron approach. We discussed this matter in Chapters 1 and 2, as well as in this chapter.

Although the GDR provides a method for the training set of multilayered nets, the learning rate often can be very slow, and it seems that the net does not scale well as the size of the patterns are increased. Several researchers have sought to improve the power of such nets by incorporating "higher-order" terms into the net. The sigma-pi units discussed by Rumelhart, Hinton, and Williams [1986] amount to making joint activations explicitly available to the net, whereas the meta–generalized delta rule approach of Pomerleau [1987] is viewed as making the weight of a link joining two nodes susceptible to influence by other nodes. It is clear that incorporation of higher-order terms does indeed help to increase the learning. We discuss these matters in more generalized terms in Chapter 8, in the context of the functional-link net. Giles and Maxwell [1987] offered an appealing and insightful discussion of the nature of the learning task—namely, that single feedforward slabs of first-order threshold logic units (TLUs) can implement only linearly separable mappings. Since most problems of interest are not linearly separable, this is a serious limitation. The GDR approach amounts to constructing a cascade of layers or slabs of first-order TLUs. However, training in cascades is difficult, because there is no simple way to provide the hidden units with a training signal. In the view of Giles and Maxwell, these problems can be overcome by use of slabs of higher-order TLUs. The high-order terms are equivalent to previously specified hidden units.

We agree with this view and find it helpful and appealing. The functional-link net described in Chapter 8 was developed independently of the work of Giles and Maxwell, but is entirely in consonance with the conceptual view of dealing with slabs of previously specified units derived from the original inputs.

5.7   References and Bibliography

1. Duda, R.O. and P.E. Hart, 1973. *Pattern Classification and Scene Analysis*, Wiley, New York.

2. Giles, C.L. and T. Maxwell, 1987. Learning, invariance, and generalization in high-order neural networks, *Applied Optics*, Vol. 26, pp. 4972–4978.

3. Kohonen, T., 1982. Self-organized formation of topologically correct maps, *Biological Cybernetics*, Vol. 43, pp. 59–69.

4. Lippman, R.P., 1987. An introduction to computing with neural nets, *IEEE ASSP Magazine*, Vol. 4, pp. 4–22.

5. Minsky, M. and S. Papert, 1969. *Perceptron: An Introduction to Computational Geometry*, MIT Press, Cambridge, MA.

6. Nilsson, N.J., 1965. *Learning Machines: Foundations of Trainable Pattern Classifying Systems*, McGraw-Hill, New York.

7. Pao, Y.H., and D.J. Sobajic, 1987. Metric synthesis and concept discovery with connectionist networks, *Proceedings of the IEEE Systems, Man and Cybernectics Conference*, Alexandria, VA, October.

8. Pomerleau, D.A., 1987. The meta-generalized delta rule: A new algorithm for learning in connectionist networks. Carnegie-Mellon University, Computer Science Dept. report, CMU-CS-87-185, Pittsburgh, PA.

9. Rosenblatt, F., 1959. Two theorems of statistical separability in the Perceptron. In *Mechanisation of Thought Processess*, Proceedings of symposium No. 10 held at the National Physical Laboratory, Nov. 1958, Vol. 1, pp. 421–456, H.M. Stationery Office, London.

10. Rosenblatt, F., 1962. *Principles of Neurodynamics: Perceptrons and The Theory of Brain Mechanisms*, Spartan, New York.

11. Sklansky, J. and G.N. Wassel, 1981. *Pattern Classifiers and Trainable Machines*, Springer-Verlag, New York.

12. Rumelhart, D.E., G.E. Hinton, and R.J. Williams, 1986. Learning internal representations by error propagation. In D.E. Rumelhart and J.L. McClelland (Eds.), *Parallel Distributed Processing: Explorations in the Microstructures of Cognition.* Vol. 1: *Foundations,* pp. 318–362, MIT Press, Cambridge, MA.

13. Widrow, B., 1962. Generalization and information storage in networks of Adaline "Neurons." In M.C. Yovits, G.T. Jacobi, and G.D. Goldstein (Eds.), *Self-Organizing Systems*, pp. 435–461, Spartan Books, Washington, D.C.

14. Widrow, B., 1960. *Western Electric Show and Conventions Record,* Part 4, pp. 96–104, Institute of Radio Engineers.

CHAPTER 6

Recognition and Recall on the Basis of Partial Cues: Associative Memories

6.1 Introduction

Through the years, two human traits have continued to elicit great interest among philosophers and researchers.

One of these is the ability of humans to retrieve information on the basis of associated cues. For example, a few bars of a tune can evoke memory of the entire tune; a glimpse of the back of a head in a crowd can be sufficient basis for thinking of an old friend. Such powers and other related phenomena have fueled a continuing interest of philosphers and psychologists in the "human associative memory," even from as early as the days of Aristotle. With the advent of the electronic digital computers, information-processing scientists and engineers have sought to understand how such powers might be simulated with and implemented in computers.

A related trait is the ability of humans to recognize speech utterances and handwriting in a very robust manner despite major variations, distortions, or omissions.

Since these are human traits, researchers have looked to their limited knowledge of human neural nets for inspiration and guidance in computer simulation model building. Therefore many computer associative-memory models also tend to be nets of neuronlike nodes functioning on the basis of distributed processing and storage. However, not all associative-memory models have been of neural-net nature, not all computer neural-net models are intended to function as associative memories.

The primary function of this chapter is to provide an account of several approaches to the implementation of the combined functions of pattern recognition and automatic associative recall.

There are many ways of accomplishing pattern recognition *and* recall of a previously associated pattern. However, some of these systems do not have characteristics similar to those of the human associative memory and therefore are not considered to be associative memories.

The general characteristics required of an associative memory include the abilities

1. To store many associated (stimulus, response) pattern pairs

2. To accomplish this storage through a self-organizing process

3. To store this information in a distributed, robust (possibly highly redundant manner)

4. To generate and output the appropriate response pattern on receipt of the associated stimulus pattern

5. To regenerate the correct response pattern even though the input stimulus pattern is distorted or incomplete

6. To add to existing memory

Deviations from some of these capabilities are also of concern because they are indications of possible deficiencies in the overall robustness of the system. For example, "overlapping" of the memory should bring about increasingly less faithful regeneration of the output patterns, rather than any abrupt indication of limit of capacity. Ideally, damage to part of the internal structure of the memory might cause decreased accuracy in the responses, but not a total breakdown. Similarly, limited amounts of distortion or omissions in a stimulus pattern should cause little or no distortion in the associated response pattern, and increasing amounts of distortion in the input should cause correspondingly larger distortions in the output with no abrupt breakdown of recall.

Although these stringent expectations tend to place associative memories into a specialized category of pattern-recognition activity, this topic is nevertheless strongly related to many other areas of pattern recognition. In particular, Chapter 5 has to do with recognition of stimuli and Chapter 7 relates to self-organization of memory.

Figure 6.1 shows how associative recall can be accomplished through non–associative-memory means. Although valid, those implementations would not have the same degree of robustness and plasticity (to borrow

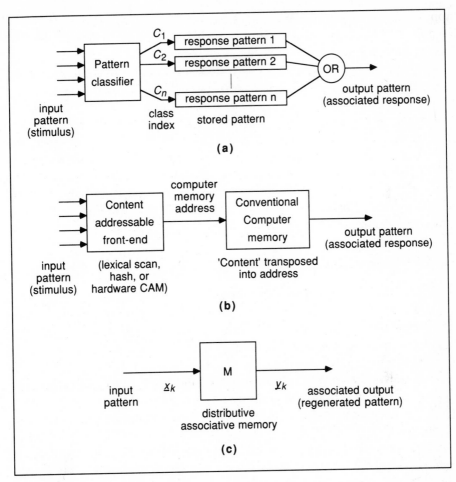

Figure 6.1 Comparison of different approaches to achieving associative recall. (a) Classification followed by read out of stored response pattern. (b) Specialization of (a) through use of content addressable memory as front-end. (c) Schematic illustration of distributed associative memory. Only (c) is considered to be an associative memory.

a term from behavioral science) expected of humanlike associative memories.

In Figure 6.1(a), *classification* through any suitable pattern recognition means (not excluding a neural-net Perceptronlike front end) is followed by accessing of a computer memory from which the entire correct response pattern is read out. This implementation of associative recall may be quite robust in the recognition aspect, but is brittle, in the sense of producing all or nothing, in the response aspect. It is certainly not distributed and can never be adequately redundant.

In some sense, the schemes illustrated in Figure 6.1(b) represent a specialization of the more general description of Figure 6.1(a). Figure 6.1(b) makes the point that the concept of *content addressability* is not necessarily the same as that of associative recall of the type we are discussing. A content-addressable front end, regardless of the nature of the enability process, can indeed transform the "content" to an address, whereupon the appropriate response pattern can be read out. But the entire procedure is still brittle as far as response generation is concerned. As indicated, the content addressability can be achieved variously through lexical scanning, software pattern matching, hashing, or a hardware content addressable memory (CAM).

In contrast, the preferred associative memory illustrated schematically in Figure 6.1(c) is of distributed architecture and has all the characteristics 1 through 6 listed previously in this section.

Details of several representative associative memories are discussed in the following two sections. Section 6.2 is concerned with earlier work, with matrix memories, and with holographic memories, all of essentially linear nature. Section 6.3 deals with the Hopfield type of algorithm and with neural-net implementations of that type of memory. Such algorithms can be cast in the form of minimizing the value of some criterion function and, in that form, become suited to iterative processing and to implementation with neural nets.

Unsupervised learning or clustering may be an important part of the self-organizing function of associative memories, and it may eventually develop that the neural-net structures currently being developed for unsupervised learning can indeed serve as the principal component of an associative memory. That subject matter is an interesting and important topic all in itself, and its role as a component in an associative memory might be a secondary matter. For this reason, cluster formation, discovery of structure, and unsupervised learning are not included in this chapter, but are discussed in Chapter 7. That collection of strongly related topics constitutes an important aspect of adaptive pattern recognition.

6.2 Matrix Associative Memories

Given an associated pair of pattern $(\underline{x}_k, \underline{y}_k)$ where $\underline{x}_k$ is a vector in M-dimensional space and $\underline{y}_k$ is a vector in N-dimensional space, we can form a direct product—that is, a dyadic product—of the nature of $M = \underline{y}_k \underline{x}_k^t$, and the matrix M serves as an associative memory with many of the six desired characteristics listed in Section 6.1.

Specifically, if $\underline{x}_k$ and y_k are column vectors, then storage is achieved through formation of

$$M = \underline{y}_k \underline{x}_k^t \tag{6.1}$$

and retrieval is attained through the linear algebraic operation of

$$M\underline{x}_k = \underline{y}_k \underline{x}_k^t \underline{x}_k = \langle \underline{x}_k^t \underline{x}_k \rangle \underline{y}_k$$

or

$$= \underline{y}_k \quad \text{if the value of the scalar product } \langle \underline{x}_k^t \underline{x}_k \rangle \text{ is unity} \tag{6.2}$$

In equation (6.1) we use the angular brackets to emphasize the scalar-product nature of the operation $\underline{x}_k^t \underline{x}_k$, in contrast to the dyadic nature of the product $\underline{y}_k \underline{x}_k^t$.

To illustrate the characteristics of the direct product, we consider two column vectors $\underline{x}_k$ and $\underline{y}_k$, each with three components, and form

$$M = \underline{y}_k \underline{x}_k^t \equiv \begin{bmatrix} y_{k1}x_{k1} & y_{k1}x_{k2} & y_{k1}x_{k3} \\ y_{k2}x_{k1} & y_{k2}x_{k2} & y_{k2}x_{k3} \\ y_{k3}x_{k1} & y_{k3}x_{k2} & y_{k3}x_{k3} \end{bmatrix} \tag{6.3}$$

Retrieval is attained as shown by

$$M\underline{x}_k = \underline{y}_k \underline{x}_k^t \underline{x}_k \equiv \begin{bmatrix} y_{k1}x_{k1} & y_{k1}x_{k2} & y_{k1}x_{k3} \\ y_{k2}x_{k1} & y_{k2}x_{k2} & y_{k2}x_{k3} \\ y_{k3}x_{k1} & y_{k3}x_{k2} & y_{k3}x_{k3} \end{bmatrix} \begin{bmatrix} x_{k1} \\ x_{k2} \\ x_{k3} \end{bmatrix}$$

$$= (x_{k1}^2 + x_{k2}^2 + x_{k3}^2) \begin{bmatrix} y_{k1} \\ y_{k2} \\ y_{k3} \end{bmatrix} \tag{6.4}$$

$$= \begin{bmatrix} y_{k1} \\ y_{k2} \\ y_{k3} \end{bmatrix} \quad \text{that is, if } \underline{x}_k \text{ is normalized,}$$

$$= \underline{y}_k \quad \text{perfect recall!}$$

Interestingly enough, if the stimulus is not $\underline{x}_k$, but is $\underline{x}'_k$, a distorted form of $\underline{x}_k$, then the response is

$$M = \underline{y}_k \underline{x}_k^t \underline{x}'_k = \langle \underline{x}_k^t \underline{x}'_k \rangle \underline{y}_k \tag{6.5}$$

Thus, in this simple case of a single associated pair, $\underline{y}_k$ would still be recovered in undistorted form, but with a smaller amplitude, if $\langle \underline{x}^t_k \underline{x}'_k \rangle < \langle \underline{x}^t_k \underline{x}_k \rangle$.

In the case of many associated pairs, we form the associative memory simply enough, by superimposing all the pairs in the following manner:

$$M = \sum_k \underline{y}_k \underline{x}^t_k \tag{6.6}$$

Associative recall of response y_m, on presentation of stimulus $\underline{x}_m$, is again achieved by simple linear-matrix muplication, but perfect recall is not always possible because of interference, or "cross-talk," between the different pairs.

Thus, in general

$$M\underline{x}_m = \left(\sum_k \underline{y}_k \underline{x}^t_k \right) \underline{x}_m$$

$$= \langle \underline{x}^t_m \underline{x}_m \rangle \underline{y}_m + \sum_{k \neq m} \langle \underline{x}^t_k \underline{x}_m \rangle \underline{y}_k \tag{6.7}$$

but

$$M\underline{x}_m = \underline{y}_m \qquad \text{if } \langle \underline{x}^t_k \underline{x}_m \rangle = \delta_{km} \tag{6.8}$$

Equation (6.6) indicates that perfect recall is possible if the stored patterns $\underline{x}_k$ constitute a set of orthonormal basis vectors spanning the M-dimensional space. For such patterns, $\langle \underline{x}^t_k \underline{x}_m \rangle = 0$ for all $k \neq m$, and $\langle \underline{x}^t_m \underline{x}_m \rangle = 1$, and recall is perfect, as indicated.

If the actual stimulus is a distorted version of the originally stored pattern—that is, if we have $\underline{x}'_m$ instead of $\underline{x}_m$—then the regenerated response will be a degraded version of $\underline{y}_m$.

A distorted $\underline{x}_m$ can be expressed in general as a combination of a change in the amplitude of $\underline{x}_m$ and the incorporation of an additional component $\underline{\delta}$, orthogonal to the original $\underline{x}_m$. The regenerated response is then

$$M\underline{x}'_m = M(\alpha \underline{x}_m + \underline{\delta}) \qquad \text{where } \alpha \leq 1 \text{ and } \langle \underline{x}^t_m \underline{\delta} \rangle = 0$$

$$= \alpha \langle \underline{x}^t_m \underline{x}_m \rangle \underline{y}_m + \sum_{k \neq m} \langle \underline{x}^t_k \underline{x}_m \rangle \underline{y}_k + \sum_{k \neq m} \langle \underline{x}^t_k \underline{\delta} \rangle \underline{y}_k \tag{6.9}$$

Thus, in the case of a nonorthornormal set of $\underline{x}_k$ vectors, there would be three sources of degradation in response. The term $\alpha\langle \underline{x}^t_m \underline{x}_m \rangle \underline{y}_m$ in (6.7) indicates that there could be a decrease in the amplitude of the correct response, accompanied perhaps by two noise terms, one being the normally present cross-talk and the other being that introduced by the distortion $\underline{\delta}$. In the case of an orthonormal set of $\underline{x}_k$, the $\sum_{k \neq m} \langle \underline{x}_k \underline{x}_m \rangle \underline{y}_k$ term of equation (6.7) remains as degradation caused by distortion in the input pattern.

In connection with the occurence of cross-talk and with the likelihood of distorted stimuli, the question of what constitutes *optimal performance* arises. In the general case, optimal performance might be defined on the basis of least mean-square error for the entire set of stored pairs or, alternatively, on the basis of minimum system error for properly weighted performance of the memory over the likely ensemble of distorted stimuli. Less is known of the latter matter than of the former, but it is clear that additional parameters can be introduced in the memory-formation procedure and that the least mean-square system error can be minimized with respect to these parameters. Although this additional step might be bothersome, it does provide means for ensuring that no one response is uniquely exceptionally bad. The error is simply spread over all patterns, and the square of a large number of small deviations is nevertheless smaller than the square of a single very large deviation.

Specifically, if we write

$$M = \sum \underline{y}_k (\alpha_k \underline{x}^t_k) \tag{6.10}$$

then we can vary the parameters α_k so as to ensure that the system error

$$E = \left(\sum_m \left\| \left(\underline{y}_m - \underline{y}'_m \right) \right\|^2 \right)^{1/2} \tag{6.11}$$

is as small as possible.

In equation (6.9), $\underline{y}_m$ is the expected response and $\underline{y}'_m$ is the actual response. Thus, the actual response is

$$M x_m = \underline{y}'_m = \sum_k y_k (\alpha_k \underline{x}^t_k) \underline{x}_m \tag{6.12}$$

and optimizing the memory consists of varying the α_ks until a set of α_k values is obtained for which E, as given by (6.9), has the lowest of all possible values. This process can be carried out readily through gradient search in α_k space.

In practice, nature is not always considerate and, accordingly, the $\underline{x}_k$ vectors do not always form an orthonormal set. The question is then whether the $\underline{y}_k$ might not be more usefully "associated" with an internal intermediate set of othornormal functions. These functions would in turn be "associated" with the requisite outputs. The intermediate step serves as a filter to remove the cross-talk. This alternate form of associativity might be possible, but the "association" might not necessarily be through the form of a correlation matrix. The latter is indeed possible, and this qualitative idea is the basis of holographic associative memories.

6.3 Holographic Memories

Let us retain, at first, the correlation-matrix format of an association. Let $\underline{z}_k$ be an orthonormal set of vectors that span an Euclidean L-dimensional space, and let us form two correlation matrices,

$$M_1 = \sum_j \underline{z}_j \underline{x}_j^t \tag{6.13}$$

and

$$M_2 = \sum_k \underline{y}_k \underline{z}_k^t \tag{6.14}$$

As before, the associated pairs are $(\underline{x}_k, \underline{y}_k)$. To achieve recall on presentation of the stimulus $\underline{x}_m$, we form the product

$$M_1 \underline{x}_m \equiv \underline{z}_m \langle \underline{x}_m^t \underline{x}_m \rangle + \sum_j \underline{z}_j \langle \underline{x}_j^t \underline{x}_m \rangle \tag{6.15}$$

To proceed further, we need to form a filtering or projection operation that decomposes $M_1 \underline{x}_m$ into its components along the $\underline{z}_j$ axes and retains the identity of only the largest component. That is, we carry out the operation

$$\max_\ell \{ \langle \underline{z}_\ell^t \underline{z}_m \rangle \langle \underline{x}_m^t \underline{x}_m \rangle + \sum_j \langle \underline{z}_\ell \underline{z}_j \rangle \langle \underline{x}_j^t \underline{x}_m \rangle \} \tag{6.16}$$

and retain the identity of the ℓ that yields the largest term in (6.14).

If we assume that $\langle \underline{x}_m^t \underline{x}_m \rangle > \langle \underline{x}_j^t \underline{x}_m \rangle$ for $j \neq m$, then we recover the correct value of the index m and go on to generate the vector $\underline{z}_m$. Only the single vector $\underline{z}_m$ is presented to M_2, to yield

$$M_2\underline{z}_m \equiv \sum_k \underline{y}_k \underline{z}_k^t \underline{z}_m = \langle \underline{z}_m^t \underline{z}_m \rangle \underline{y}_m = \underline{y}_m \qquad \text{a perfect recall!} \qquad (6.17)$$

This type of approach is called *holographic* because the information is distributed, there is a "recording" as achieved through the process of formation of M_1, and there is a "playback" as achieved through presentation of $\underline{x}_m$ to M_2.

If there is no filtering, then the "noise" can be quite excessive and storage capacity may be substantially degraded. On the other hand, as we see with filtering, excellent recall can be achieved.

The optical holographic realization of such concepts also serves to remind us that association need not always be implemented in correlation-matrix form.

The principal ideas underlying an optical holographic associative memory are illustrated schematically in Figures 6.2, 6.3, and 6.4. Fig-

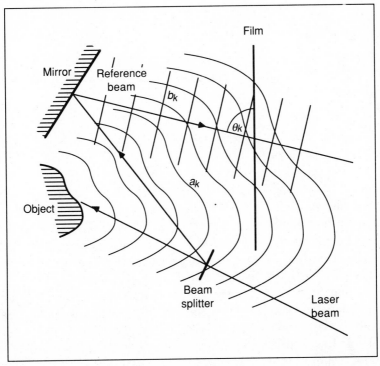

Figure 6.2 Recording of associated fields, (a_k, b_k); a_k is object field and b_k is reference field, a plane wave.

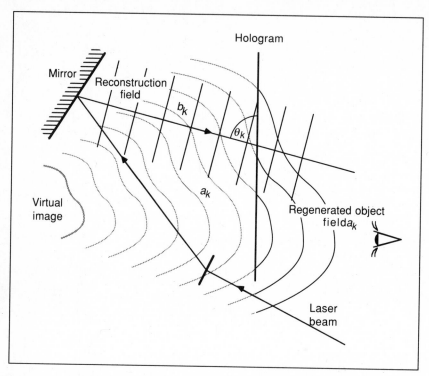

Figure 6.3   Circumstances of conventional holography; reference beam b_k and hologram regenerate field a_k and virtual image.

ure 6.2 shows how the interference between a reference field $\underline{b}$ and an object $\underline{a}$ is recorded on a film. Actually, many different object fields a_k are recorded, each with its own reference field $\underline{b}_k$. In the geometry shown in Figure 6.2, the fields $\underline{b}_k$ are all plane waves of the same optical wavelength, but they differ in their angle of incidence relative to the recording plane. The "spatial frequencies" are accordingly different. The fields in all cases are spatially coherent; that is, the relative phases are stable. The pairs (a_k, b_k) are recorded singly, one pair at a time, and the film is developed only after all pairs have been recorded.

In ordinary holography, we know that, if the hologram is illuminated with the reference beam b_k, then the field a_k is generated from the hologram and a virtual image is seen, as illustrated in Figure 6.3.

What is less well known is that, if the hologram is illuminated with the field a_k, then the reference field b_k is generated. If, as they do in the present case, the reference fields differ only in their incidence angle, a lens

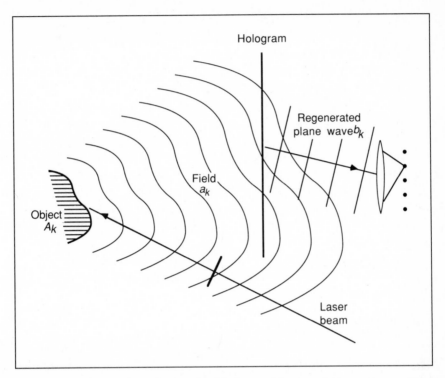

Figure 6.4   Operation of an optical holographic associative memory. Regeneration of the response b_k by stimulus a_k.

can be used to identify which of the reference fields have been generated by an incident object field. This aspect of holography is shown schematically in Figure 6.4.

We thus construct an optical holographic associative memory by illuminating an object A_k to form the field a_k, then mixing a_k with the reference b_k. The intensity of the combined field $(a_k + b_k)$ is recorded on a film in the plane of the hologram. This recording results in a spatial variation in the optical density of the film proportional to $(a_k^t a_k + b_k^t b_k + a_k^t b_k + b_k^t a_k)$. Only one of these terms is of interest, however, and the effects of the other three have to be ameliorated. The film is not developed and fixed until *all* the associated pairs have been recorded and the hologram so formed contains the optical density variation proportional to $\Sigma_k a_k^t b_k$, as well as other undesired terms.

The optical transmission of the hologram is made proportional to this optical density; thus, when the hologram is subsequently illuminated with the field a_m, we obtain the transmitted field $(\Sigma_k a_k^t b_k) a_m$. This expression indicates that the reference beam b_m is regenerated with constant amplitude $a_m^t a_m$ and remains a plane wave. There is a multitude of other miscellaneous beams of nonuniform amplitude. As noted previously, we can detect the constant-amplitude plan wave b_m by focusing with a lens. The other reconstructed plan waves, b_k $(k \neq m)$, would be weaker, of nonuniform amplitude, and scattered in direction. They would not focus well.

From this discussion, we see that, in principle, the optical holography associative memory functions quite well in that, when presented with the stimulus a_m, it generates the response b_m quite readily. In practice, the optical holographic memory will not be a viable device until a robust real-time optical recording medium with read–write capability becomes commonly available.

Note that our discussion has been theoretical and schematic. Figures 6.2, 6.3, and 6.4 are not intended to illustrate accurate positioning of experimental components, and we have not wished to describe the details of actual holography procedures.

6.4 Walsh Associative Memories

Holographic associative memories can be implemented with Walsh functions. These functions are the discrete binary analogs of sine and cosine functions and have interesting characteristics particularly convenient for the needs of associative processing. The associate memory so formed is similar in action to that of an optical holographic associative memory, except that there are no undesired intensity terms and conjugate field terms to be eliminated.

Briefly, the Walsh functions form a set of orthonormal functions in 2^m-dimensional space. That is, the Walsh functions span two-dimensional space, four-dimensional space, eight-dimensional space, and so on; related orthonormal sets can be generated for in-between–dimensional spaces also.

The Walsh functions can be generated recursively through substitution of the array H into itself:

$$H = \begin{pmatrix} 1 & 1 \\ 1 & -1 \end{pmatrix} \qquad (6.18)$$

Thus, if the two basis functions in two-dimensional space are

$$\underline{W}^{(2)}{}_0 = \frac{1}{\sqrt{2}}[1, 1]$$
$$\underline{W}^{(2)}{}_1 = \frac{1}{\sqrt{2}}[1, -1]$$

(6.19)

then the four basic functions in four-dimensional space are obtained through substitution of H into itself to yield

$$\underline{W}^{(4)}_0 = \frac{1}{\sqrt{4}}[1, 1, 1, 1]$$
$$\underline{W}^{(4)}_1 = \frac{1}{\sqrt{4}}[1, -1, 1, -1]$$
$$\underline{W}^{(4)}_2 = \frac{1}{\sqrt{4}}[1, 1, -1, -1]$$
$$\underline{W}^{(4)}_3 = \frac{1}{\sqrt{4}}[1, -1, -1, 1]$$

(6.20)

There are several ways of indexing the Walsh functions, but we shall not delve into those details. It suffices for the present purposes to note that $\langle \underline{W}_i * \underline{W}_j \rangle = \delta_{ij}$, where the asterick $(*)$ indicates element-by-element multiplication, and the angular brackets indicate summation of all the element-by-elements products so formed.

The Walsh functions can serve as the set of orthonormal vectors $\underline{z}_k$ of equations (6.12) through (6.15). They are eminently suitable for that purpose. They also can be used to implement yet another type of associative memory which is more economical in memory requirements but not as robust as in direct use of Walsh functions as internal references.

The steps of storage and associative response for such a memory are as follows:

Step 1. *Storage.* For associated pairs $(\underline{x}_k, \underline{y}_k)$, form products $\underline{x}_k * \underline{W}_{(k)}$ and superimpose them to form the memories

$$M_1 = \sum_k \underline{x}_k * \underline{W}_{(k)}$$
$$M_2 = \sum_k \underline{y}_k * \underline{W}_{(k)}$$

(6.21)

where $\underline{W}_{(k)}$ donates the Walsh function associated with the kth pattern.

Step 2. *Associative Retrieval of Walsh Function Index.* For stimulus pattern $\underline{x}_m$, form the element-by-element product

$$M_1 * \underline{x}_m = (\underline{x}_m * \underline{x}_m) * W_{(m)} + \sum_{k \neq m} (\underline{x}_m * \underline{x}_k) * W_{(k)} \quad (6.22)$$

Now form the Walsh transform of expression (6.22) to obtain the quantities

$$\langle (M_1 * \underline{x}_m) * W_{(m)} \rangle = \langle \underline{x}_m * \underline{x}_m * \underline{W}_{(m)} * \underline{W}_{(m)} \rangle$$
$$+ \left\langle \sum_{k \neq m} (\underline{x}_m * \underline{x}_k) * \underline{W}_{(k)} * \underline{W}_{(m)} \right\rangle (6.23)$$

for the Walsh component associated with the mth stored pattern, and

$$\langle (M_1 * \underline{x}_m) * W_{(j)} \rangle = \left\langle \sum_{\substack{k \nmid m \\ j \nmid m}} \langle \underline{x}_m * \underline{x}_k \rangle * \underline{W}_{(k)} * \underline{W}_{(j)} \right\rangle \quad (6.24)$$

for the Walsh components associated with patterns $\underline{x}_j, j \neq m$.

If the elements of the vectors $\underline{x}_k$ are restricted to values of $+1$ and -1, then the first term of the right hand side of (6.23) is much larger than is the second term of that same right hand side, and is also larger then the right hand side of expression (6.24) for all $j \neq m$. Thus, retrieval consists at first of identifying the index (m) associated with the stimulus $\underline{x}_m$.

Step 3. *Retrieval of Associated Patterns.* The associated response $\underline{y}_m$ can be generated in a variety of ways once the index (m) is known. Depending on the precise mechanism adopted, however, this entire scheme is or is not a true associative memory.

One straightforward way is to multiply M_2 by $\underline{W}_{(m)}$, element by element, to yield

$$M_2 * \underline{W}_{(m)} = \sum_k \underline{y}_k * \underline{W}_{(k)} * \underline{W}_{(m)}$$

$$= \underline{y}_m * \underline{W}_{(m)} * \underline{W}_{(m)} + \sum_{k \neq m} \underline{y}_k * W_{(k)} * \underline{W}_{(m)}$$

$$= \underline{y}_m + \sum_{k \neq m} \underline{y}_k * \underline{W}_{(k)} * \underline{W}^*_{(m)} \quad (6.25)$$

The first term in (6.23) is identical to $\underline{y}_m$ and the second term in (6.23) is smaller than $\underline{x}_m$ as long as the memory is not overburdened and an acceptable version of y_m is retrieved.

6.5 Network Associative Memories

Theoretical models consisting of connected nets of idealized neurons also may act as associative memories. In this section, we describe a simple version of one principle type of such neural-net model. It is a binary, discrete-time, additive model, aspects of which have been studied since 1943 by a number of researchers, including Hebb [1949] and McCulloch and Pitts [1943]. More recently, it has received considerably increased attention because of Hopfield's detailed exposition of its characteristics Hopfield [1982; 1984] and also because of interesting applications of this type of memory by Hopfield and Tank [1985] and by other researchers.

In one sense, the Hopfield net is similar to the matrix associative memory. As we know, if we represent a pattern in the form of a vector and form the outerproduct of that vector with *itself*, we obtain an autoassociative matrix memory, as has been described in Section 6.2. If we superimpose many such arrays on top of one another, we obtain a memory with a capability of storing several patterns and providing autoassociative recall. This memory would be a special case of the matrix memories described in Section 6.2.

In the matrix memory, the cross-products obtained in formation of the outerproduct becomes the elements of the matrix. In this network perspective, the cross-products becomes the value of the weights linking the two respective nodes.

Kohonen understood well the two diferent but related perspectives and described the relation in his book on associative memory [Kohonen 1977, p. 148]. Hopfield's contribution lies in the elaboration of the network perspective. Understanding the memory in terms of a Liapunov function and in terms of asynchronous processing at individual nodes all constitute important new advances that will influence the course of future developments in these matters. That is why we consider network associative memories independently of matrix associative memories, despite the close connections of the two developments. The renewed attention to this model is also due in part to the increasing availability of hardware suitable for realization of models such as this in a net of connected, but independent, concurrent, elemental processors.

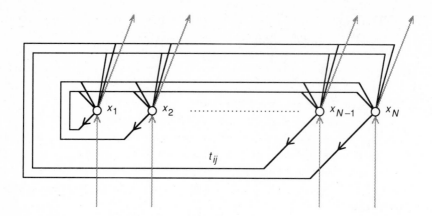

Figure 6.5   Connectivity of a Hopfield net. $x_1, x_2, \ldots, x_N$ are values of outputs of nodes (neurons), t_{ij} are the strengths of interaction between nodes, and the dotted lines indicate that it is possible to input and output the values of x_i.

The architecture of the Hopfield net is illustrated schematically in Figure 6.5. All neurons are connected to all other neurons. We consider the case where the value of x_i can be 1 or 0.

The N discrete binary x_i values constitute a pattern that can also be considered to be the state vector of the system.

One of the characteristics of such a net is that it can function as an autoassociative memory. That is, a number of different patterns (state vectors) can be "stored" in such a memory. If any one of the stored patterns is presented to the memory—that is, if the memory is set in one of the stored states—then the memory will remain in that state. That is, the memory will be *stable*. If a distorted version of any stored pattern is presented to the memory, the memory will evolve from that state to the stable state that is nearest to the distorted state.

Such a memory is indeed content addressable, and it is more than that. When functioning properly, it can regenerate the original prototype—the stable state in terms of which the distorted input had been recognized. It is therefore autoassociative, in contrast to the correlation matrix associative memories discussed previously, which are heteroassociative and can regenerate any pattern associated with the input pattern.

Regardless of our depth of interest in neurobiological matters or in psychology research, it is interesting to note that the quantities x_i may be considered to be *short-term memory*, whereas the t_{ij} can be thought of as being *long-term memory*. A memory *learns* by modifying the values of t_{ij}, the internode weightings, but it can record and retain any pattern for a short while by modifying x_i, the node outputs.

Matters of interest include the issues of global stability and local stability, learning modes, storage capacity, and procedures for attaining optimal performance.

In the following pages, we describe a Hopfield net, first for a binary output net, and subsequently for continuous valued outputs. After that, we address the issue of allowing the system state to wander stochastically in state space, with a bias for the low-energy stable stables in accordance with a temperature of the system. We can "anneal" a system by lowering the temperature gradually, with the expectation that undesired local minima can be avoided through that means.

The input to the ith node comes from two sources: external inputs I_i and inputs from other nodes. The total *input* to node i is then

$$\text{Input to } i = H_i = \sum_{j \neq i} t_{ij} x_j + I_i \tag{6.26}$$

The output of node i is x_i, and, at update time, the values of x_i are updated in accordance with the algorithm

$$
\begin{aligned}
x_i &\to V_i^0 \quad \text{if } \left(\sum t_{ij} x_j + I_i\right) < U_i \\
x_i &\to V_i^1 \quad \text{if } \left(\sum t_{ij} x_j + I_i\right) > U_i
\end{aligned}
\tag{6.27}
$$

In (6.27), the binary levels V_i^0 and V_i^1 may be 0 and 1 or -1 and $+1$, or any other desired pair of values, and U_i is a threshold value at node i.

In the Hopfield net, the nodes are interrogated and updated in value in a stochastic manner, asynchronously, taking place at a mean rate W for each node. The times of interrogation of each node are independent of those of other nodes. Because of this independency, the system vector as it evolves through state space will display a combination of propagation delays, jitter, and noise. Thus, asynchronous processing may be of interest because it might be representative of some real neural system; it is also of interest from an information-processing-system point of view, because it avoids the difficulties of propagating sychronization signals throughout large networks, and of requiring that each node have global knowledge of the net at all times.

Given the equations of motion for the system, or, equivalently, given the updating rules, we can investigate the matter of stability. For a content-addressable memory such as the Hopfield net, it is important to know how the memory responds to an arbitrary but sustained input pattern. For example, does the memory evolve toward an equilibrium state representing a stored pattern that resembles the input pattern to some considerable extent? If so, how is that equilibrium state reached and how many such states can exist or can be created in that memory? These questions address the matter of the *global* behaviour of the memory. There is also the more specific question of *local stability*, which is often stated as stability *in the sense of Liapunov*. The question is whether the system will migrate toward a local equilibrium point (or state) if placed near that point or if displaced from that point by a small extent by some perturbation. In both the global and the local cases, the practice is to describe the system in an abbreviated manner in terms of a Liapunov, or energy, function. The system is fully described in state space, but is characterized in terms of a single scalar quantity, the "energy," or, equivalently, the value of a suitable Liapunov function.

In the language of such an approach, a system could hold n patterns in memory if it could be shown that these n pattern states correspond to local minima, and if it could be shown that each of the minima is locally stable in the sense of Liapunov. In such a memory, the storage of the $(n+1)$th pattern must not distort the previous n equilibria; memory capacity is determined by this criterion.

Now we construct a Liapunov function:

$$E = -\frac{1}{2}\sum_{i \neq j}\sum t_{ij}x_i x_j - \sum I_i x_i + \sum U_i x_i \qquad (6.28)$$

We see that, for any specific net, the value of E is determined by the value of the state vector $\underline{x}$. As the x_i values evolve, E also will evolve.

The change ΔE in E due to changing the state of node i by Δx_i is

$$\Delta E = -\left[\sum_{j \neq i} t_{ij}x_j + I_i - U_i\right]\Delta x_i \qquad (6.29)$$

where we have made use of the conditions that

$$t_{ij} = t_{ji} \qquad \text{and} \qquad t_{ii} = 0 \qquad (6.30)$$

According to (6.27), however, Δx_i is positive only when the bracketed term is positive, and is negative only when the bracketed term is negative. Thus, any change in E under the algorithm is negative. E is bounded, so the iteration of the algorithm must lead to stable states that do not further change with time. This conclusion addresses the issue of *global stability*.

Concerning *local stability*, if we regard the location of a particular stable point in the state space of the memory as one of the stored patterns, then states near that particular stable point contain partial information about that memory. Global-stability considerations mandate that at least one stable state will be attained. Local-stability considerations include the issue of whether an initial state of *partial* information about a stored pattern will evolve toward the nearby final state with *all* the information in the pattern. Although it is difficult to say many precise things about likely trajectories, we can see whether states which are memorized patterns are stable against further evolution. To do this, we examine how patterns are to be stored.

The Information-Storage Algorithm

To store the set of patterns *stable states* $\underline{x}^s$, $s = 1, 2, \ldots, m$, we set

$$t_{ij} = \sum_s (2x_i^s - 1)(2x_j^s - 1)$$

$$t_{ii} = 0 \tag{6.31}$$

In particular, if we store only a single pattern $\underline{x}^s$, then

$$t_{ij} = (2x_i^s - 1)(2x_j^s - 1) \tag{6.32}$$

If we then present a new pattern $\underline{x}^{s'}$ to the memory, we see that the input at node i is

$$H_i^{s'} = \sum_j t_{ij}(2x_j^{s'} - 1) = \sum (2x_i^s - 1)(2x_j^s - 1)(2x_j^{s'} - 1)$$

$$= (2x_i^s - 1)\left[\sum_j (2x_j^s - 1)(2x_j^{s'} - 1)\right] \tag{6.33}$$

For all input $I_i = 0$, the value of the term within the brackets is nearly zero if $\underline{x}^{s'}$ differs significantly from $\underline{x}^s$, and averages to $N/2$ if $\underline{x}^{s'} \cong \underline{x}^s$ or is very similar to $\underline{x}^s$, where N is the dimension of the pattern.

Thus, if x_i^s is 1 and $\underline{x}^{s'} \cong \underline{x}^s$, then $H_i^{s'}$ is positive and $x_i^{s'}$ remains 1 or is set to 1, the result being $x_i^{s'} = x_i^s$. On the other hand, if $x_i^s = 0$ and $\underline{x}^{s'} \cong \underline{x}^s$, then $H_i^{s'}$ is negative and $x_i^{s'}$ remains 0 or is set to 0, the result again being

$$x_i^{s'} = x_i^s \tag{6.34}$$

This result indicates that a stable point $\underline{x}^s$ is stable against small deviations from $\underline{x}^s$.

In the event that many patterns are stored, we know from (6.28) that

$$H_i^{s'} = \sum_j t_{ij} x_j^{s'} = \sum_s (2x_i^s - 1)\left[\sum_j (2x_j^s - 1)(2x_j^{s'} - 1)\right] \tag{6.35}$$

and we have a situation similar to that of (6.30). Summation over j within the brackets yields a small quantity, nearly zero, for all values of s except for $s = s'$, for which the value is approximately $N/2$. Thus, the summation over j serves as $\frac{N}{2}\delta_{ss'}$ and the input to the ith node is

$$H_i^{s'} \simeq (2x_s - 1)\frac{N}{2} \tag{6.36}$$

Again, we see that if $x_s = 1$ then $H_i^{s'}$ is positive and x_s' remains 1 or is set to 1, or, if $x_s = 0$, then $H_i^{s'}$ is negative and x_s' remains 0 or is set to 0. Except for the noise arising from the $s \neq s'$ terms, the stored state $\underline{x}_s$ is stable against small deviations from $\underline{x}_s$.

We can summarize the binary Hopfield algorithm as follows:

For *storage*, to store m patterns $\underline{x}^s$, $s = 1, 2, \ldots, m$, set

$$t_{ij} = \sum_{s=1}^m (2x_i^s - 1)(2x_j^s - 1) \tag{6.37}$$

For *recall*, for input pattern $\underline{x}^{s'} = \{x_1^{s'}, x_2^{s'}, x_3^{s'}, \ldots, x_N^{s'}\}$, evaluate

$$x_i^{s'} = \sum_j t_{ij}(2x_j^{s'} - 1)$$

Update $x_i^{s'}$

$$x_i^{s'} \to 1 \quad \text{if} \quad \left(\sum_j t_{ij}(2x_j^{s'} - 1)\right) > U_i$$

$$x_i^{s'} \to 0 \quad \text{if} \quad \left(\sum_j t_{ij}(2x_j^{s'} - 1)\right) < U_i$$

Repeat until

$$\Delta x_i^{s'} = 0 \quad \text{for all } i \tag{6.38}$$

Continuous Model

Hopfield has also described a continuous-variable version of the binary-valued associative memory.

In this model, the output node, or "neuron," is uniquely determined by the instantaneous input to the node; that is,

$$x_i = g_i(u_i) \tag{6.39}$$

where the output x_i, for node i has the range $V_i^0 \leq x_i \leq V_i^1$ and is a continuous and monotonically increasing function of the instantaneous input U_i to the node i.

Typically, the input–output relation $g_i(u_i)$, shown in Figure 6.6(a), is a sigmoidal curve with asymptotic V_i^0 and V_i^1. For example, $g(u_i)$ might be

$$g_i(u_i) = \frac{1}{1 + \exp[-(u_i + \theta_i)/\theta_t]} \tag{6.40}$$

where θ_i would be the threshold of the node and θ_t is a parameter that renders the sigmoid more gradual or abrupt. The asymptote values in the case of (6.39) are 0 and 1, and the function is the same as that used in the generalized delta rule net of Chapter 5. The manner in which the shape of $g_i(u_i)$ changes with (u_i) is illustrated in Figure 6.6(b).

For neurons exhibiting action potentials, u_i could be thought of as the near-soma potential of a neuron from the total affect of the latter's excitation and inhibiting inputs. In terms of a node, it is reasonable to think of u_i as serving the role of an effective "net" input similar to the "net" of the Rumelhart semilinear feedforward model. It is also reasonable to think of the output as being deterministically related to the input in the manner of (6.39). For neurons, in some instances, the output x_i might represent the short-term average of the firing rate of the cell i.

In the Hopfield model, u_i lags behind the instantaneous outputs x_j of the nodes to which it is connected. Thus, $t_{ij}x_j$ will serve to charge up u_i, but u_i will tend to leak off, at a certain rate.

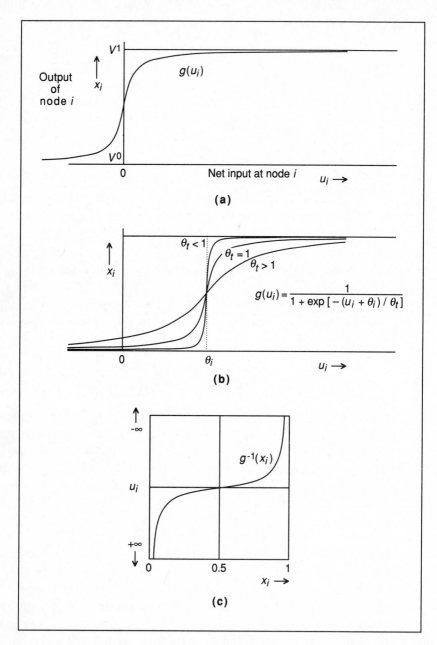

Figure 6.6   Input–output and output–input relations for a "neuron" or node. (a) Typical sigmoidal input–output relation. (b) Variation of shape of $g(u_i)$ with "temperature". (c) The output–input relation $u_i = g_i^{-1}(x_i)$ for the $g(u_i)$ shown in (a).

With some inspiration from the terminology of electrical circuits, we write

$$C_i\left(\frac{du_i}{dt}\right) = \sum_j t_{ij}x_j - u_i/R_i + I_i \tag{6.41}$$

$$u_i = g_i^{-1}(x_i) \tag{6.42}$$

Electrically, $t_{ij}x_j$ might be understood to represent the electrical current input to cell i due to the present potential of cell j. The quantity t_{ij}^{-1} represents the finite impedance between the output x_j and the body of cell i. It would also be considered to represent the synapse efficacy. The term $-u_i/R$ is the current flow due to finite transmembrane resistance R_i, and it causes a decrease in u_i. I_i is any other (fixed) input current to neuron i. Thus, according to (6.38), the change in u_i is due to the charging action of all the $t_{ij}x_j$ terms, balanced by the decrease due to $-u_i/R$, with a bias set by I_i.

The inverse relationship $u_i = g_i^{-1}(x_i)$ is a one-to-one relationship, as shown in Figure 6.6(c).

The Liapunov function of interest for this situation is

$$E = -\frac{1}{2}\sum_{ij}\sum_j t_{ij}x_i x_j$$

$$+ \sum_i (1/R_i)\int_0^{x_i} g_i^{-1}(x)dx + \sum_i I_i V_i \tag{6.43}$$

For symmetric t_{ij}, the time derivative is

$$\frac{dE}{dt} = -\sum_i (dx_i/dt)\left[\sum_i t_{ij}x_j - u_i/R_i + I_i\right] \tag{6.44}$$

The quantity in square brackets is the right hand side of (6.38), so

$$\frac{dE}{dt} = -\sum_i \frac{dx_i}{dt}C_i\frac{du_i}{dt} \tag{6.45}$$

or

$$\frac{dE}{dt} = -\sum_i C_i g_i^{-1'}(x_i)\left(\frac{dx_i}{dt}\right)^2 \tag{6.46}$$

We note that $g_i^{-1'}(x_i) \equiv \frac{\partial g_i^{-1}}{\partial x_i}$ is nonnegative, and so are C_i and

$(dx_i/dt)^2$. Accordingly,

$$\frac{dE}{dt} \leq 0, \quad \text{and} \quad \frac{dE}{dt} = 0 \quad \text{implies} \quad \frac{dx_i}{dt} = 0 \quad \text{for all } i. \quad (6.47)$$

Since E is bounded, equation (6.46) shows that the system moves in state space toward lower and lower values of E, and comes to rest at one of the minima. The continuous-valued Hopfield net is thus shown to be globally stable. The memorization of patterns, however, is more complex than in the case of the binary-valued model. The stable points—that is, the memorized patterns—are determined not only by the prescription

$$t_{ij} = x_i x_j \quad (6.48)$$

but also by the shape of $g(u)$ and by the value of R_i.

6.6 Comments and Bibliographical Remarks

The term *associative memory* is used by different people to denote different entities and capabilities. At one extreme, the term is essentially synonymous with *content-addressable memory*. Given a massive store of unstructured data items, each of which is in the form of a pattern, how might we go about achieving a rapid scan of the stored data to locate the pattern that matches the search pattern exactly or partially, if the latter mode is prescribed? Of course, once that stored pattern is identified, associated pointers may be used to retrieve other "associated" information. Nevertheless, the principal act is that of achieving content addressability. The monograph by Kohonen [1980] contains a good bibliography on this subject. In addition, there exists a large body of literature on database machines designed to search massive disk memories.

The memories described in this chapter differ from purely content-addressable memories in some clearly identifiable aspects. In the matrix and holographic memories, for example, pattern information is stored in distributed form, so local damage to any small part of the memory does not result in total loss of any one aspect of the stored information, but rather result in only an overall distributed degradation of the stored patterns.

The matrix associative memory is described well in the text by Kohonen [1977]. Holographic memories are considered in detail by Willshaw

[1971]. An early discussion of the principal underlying concepts was published by Willshaw, Buneman, and Longuet-Higgins [1969]. Both the matrix and the holographic associative memories are linear devices and are readily implementable in heteroassociative form. That is, input pattern $\underline{y}_k$ can evoke the associated pattern $\underline{x}_k$ as output. This heterassociativity is in contrast to the Hopfield model, which is essentially autoassociative. Despite these differences, the essence of the act is that a distorted version of the appropriate cue can evoke a correct, noncorrupted response, which is the principal function of this type of memory.

Pao approached the same task also from the viewpoint of multiply stored holograms, but used Walsh functions as reference beams [Pao and Merat 1975; Pao, Schultz, and Altman 1976; Pao and Hartoch 1982]. These functions are their own conjugate and also have other properties that endow such memories with interesting characteristics.

Hardware realizations of multiply recorded optical holographic associative memories are difficult to attain, and each case would be an experimental tour de force. Recently, however, Abu-Mostafa and Psaltis [1987] reported such implementations, and we can expect further progress with advances in optical computing.

The Associatron proposed by Nakano [1972] is worthy of remembrance as an early hardware model of an associative memory. The autoassociativity aspect of the Hopfield net is circumvented if "time" is incorporated into the process. The idea is that an input pattern puts the memory in one of the local minima, the autoassociative response to the stimulus, at which point the energy surface of the system automatically begins to "relax" into another predetermined conformation. The system evolves along the surface into a new local minimum, which is therefore heteroassociatively related to the original input.

Once "time" is incorporated in some such manner, together with the concept of cooperative relaxation of the energy surface, the Hopfield net can be used to model a wide range of temporal phenomena. Tank and Hopfield [1987] discuss tasks similar to those of recognition of words in a continuous stream of speech, and Kleinfeld [1986] and Sompolinsky and Kanter [1986] use that approach for modeling of the generation of temporal patterns by neural central-pattern generators.

The concept of time is used in a different manner in Klopf's [1987] studies of conditioning involving a natural time scale of events, and *chan ges* before and after events. With regard to global and local characteristics of content-addressable memories, Grossberg [1988], in his review article of nonlinear neural networks, discussed the questions of stability and the Liapunov method. That article also contains a good bibliography of related earier work by Grossberg and other researchers, including the important paper by Cohen and Grossberg [1983] on global stability.

To some extent, the memories discussed in this chapter are only content-addressable memories and are not associative memories in the sense of human associative memories; the latter deal with higher-order, more complex associations of direct concern to psychology or cognitive science [Anderson and Bower 1987; Schank 1982]. These diverse matters are not unrelated, but the relationships are certainly indirect and not understood.

The capacity of the Hopfield associative memory has been studied by McEliece, Posner, and Rodemich [1987]. They find that, for n binary-valued nodes, the number of stored patterns that can be recovered exactly can be no more than $n/(4 \log n)$ asymptotically as n approaches infinity. In a neural-network model, however, the basic memory-storage element is the connection weight between neurons (synapses). As the number of connections increases, the capacity increases dramatically. For example, in the case of 100 nodes, $n = 100$, the ordinary Hebbian model can store about five patterns. Chen and colleagues [1986] report that the number increased to ~ 500 for a triple-correlation model. Of course, the number of connections can also be enormous. It is worth noting that the greater storage capacity obtained in this manner also can be used to provide het-eroassociativity. Thus, the letters AB can be stored as one pattern, and A can be used as a partial cue to recover B as well. This approach is in contrast to making the correlation matrix asymmetric or to incorporat-ing cooperative relaxation of the energy surface with "time." Peretto and Niez [1986] have also studied the question of storage capacity of multicon-nected neural networks. They report a thought-provoking result; namely, within the framework of Hebb's laws, the number of stored bits is pro-portional to the number of synapses. However, the proportionality factor decreases when the order of involved synaptic contact increases. They suggest that this characteristic tends to favor neural architectures with low-order synaptic connectivities. They show that memory storage can be optimized through partitioning of networks.

Kosko [1987] reports on an associative-memory system that is tan-talizing in that it incorporates the concepts of a "conventional" matrix associative memory within that of the Hebbian learning rule. In effect, Kosko's work confirms Kohonen's view that the matrix associative mem-ories reported previously may also be understood from the neural net point of view [Kohonen 1977, p. 148]. The retrieval procedures are different. Kosko extends this approach to the study of the structure for an adaptive bidirectional associative memory.

Other researchers have also considered the matter of adaptation in networks similar to that of Hopfield nets. Almeida [1987] and Pineda [1987] consider the Hopfield network with graded neurons (nodes with analog values) and use a recurrent generalization of the delta rule of Rumelhart, Hinton, and Williams [1986] to modify the synaptic weights, adaptively.

6.7 References and Bibliography

1. Abu-Mostafa, Y.S. and D. Psaltis, 1987. Optical neural computers, *Scientific American*, Vol. 256, pp. 88–95, March.

2. Almeida, L.B., 1987. A learning rule for asynchronous perceptrons with feedback in a combinational environment. *Proceedings of the IEEE First International Conference on Neural Networks*, San Diego, CA., June.

3. Anderson, J.R. and G.H. Bower, 1973. *Human Associative Memory*, V.H. Winston, Washington, D.C.

4. Chen, H.H., Y.C. Lee, G.Z. Sun, H.Y. Lee, T. Maxwell, and C.L. Giles, 1986. High order correlation model for associative memory. *American Institute of Physics Conference Proceedings, No. 151: Neural Networks for Computing*, Snowbird, Utah.

5. Cohen, M.A. and S. Grossberg, 1983. Absolute stability of global pattern formation and parallel memory storage by competitive neural networks, *IEEE Transactions on Systems, Man and Cybernetics*, Vol. 13, pp. 815–826.

6. Grossberg, S., 1988. Nonlinear neural networks: Principles, mechanisms and architectures. In *Neural Networks*, Vol. 1, pp. 17–61, Pergamon Press, New York.

7. Hebb, D.O., 1949. *The Organization of Behaviour*. Wiley, New York.

8. Hopfield, J.J., 1982. Neural networks and physical systems with emergent collective computational abilities. *Proceedings of the National Academy of Sciences*, Vol. 74, pp. 2554–2558.

9. Hopfield, J.J., 1984. Neurons with graded response have collective computational properties like those of two-state neurons. *Proceedings of the National Academy of Sciences*, Vol. 81, pp. 3088-3092.

10. Hopfield, J.J., 1985. "Neuron" computation decisions in optimizating problems, *Biological Cybneretics*, Vol. 52, pp. 141–151.

11. Kleinfeld, D., 1986. Sequential state generation by model neural networks, *Proceedings of the National Academy of Sciences*, Vol. 83, pp. 9469–9473.

12. Klopf, H.A., 1987. *A Neuronal Model of Classical Cconditioning.* U.S. Air Force Avionics Laboratory Technical Report, AFWAL-TR-87-1139, Wright-Patterson Air Force Base, Dayton, OH.

13. Kohonen, T., 1977. *Associative Memory: A System-Theoretical Approach,* Springer-Verlag, New York.

14. Kohonen, T., 1980. *Content-Addressable Memories*, Springer-Verlag, New York.

15. Kosko, B., 1987. Adaptive bidirectional associative memories, *Applied Optics*, Vol. 26, pp. 4947–4960.

16. McClulloch, W.S. and W. Pitts, 1943. A logical calculus of the ideas immanent in nervous activity. *Bulletin of Mathematical Biophysics*, Vol. 5, pp. 115–133.

17. McEliece, R.J., E.C. Posner, and E.R. Rodemich, 1987. The capacity of the Hopfield associative memory, *IEEE Tranactions on Information Theory*, Vol. 33, pp. 461–482.

18. Nakano, K., 1972. Associatron - A model of associative memory. *IEEE Transaction Systems, Man and Cybernetics*, pp. 380-388.

19. Pao, Y.H. and G.P. Hartoch, 1982. Fast memory access by similarity measure. In J. Hayes, D. Michie, and Y.H. Pao (Eds.), *Machine Intelligence 10,* Wiley, New York.

20. Pao, Y.H. and F.L. Merat, 1975. Distributed associative memory for patterns, *IEEE Transaction Systems, Man and Cybernetics*, 5, pp. 620–625.

21. Pao, Y.H., W.L. Schultz, and J.F. Altman, 1976. Implementation of human judgement and 'experience' in computer aided interpretation of medical images, *Proceedings Third International Joint Conference on Pattern Recognition,* Del Coronada, CA., November.

22. Peretto, P. and J.J. Niez, 1968. Long term memory storage capacity of multiconnected neural networks, *Biological Cybernetics*, Vol. 54, pp. 53–63.

23. Pineda, F.J., 1987. Generalization of backpropagation to recurrent neural networks., John Hopkins University, Applied Physics Laboratory, Memo SIA-63-87, Baltimore, MD.

24. Schank, R.C., 1982. *Dynamic Memory: A Theory of Reminding and Learning in Computers and People*, Cambridge University Press, New York.

25. Sompolinsky, H. and I. Kanter, 1986. Temporal association in asymmetric neural networks, *Physical Review Letters*, Vol. 57, pp. 2861–2864.

26. Tank, D.W. and J.J. Hopfield, 1987. Neural computation by concentrating information in time, *Proceedings of the National Academy of Sciences*, Vol. 84, pp. 1896–1900.

27. Willshaw, D.J., 1971. Model of distributed associative memory, unpublished doctoral dissertation, Department of Machine Intelligence, University of Edinburgh, Edinburgh.

28. Willshaw, D.J., O.P. Buneman, and H.C. Longuet-Higgins, 1969. Nonholographic associative memory, *Nature*, Vol. 222, p. 960–962.

CHAPTER 7

Self-Organizing Nets for Pattern Recognition

7.1 Introduction

In one sense, it could be said that the network-related materials in Chapters 5 and 6 are connected quite directly to prior work developed previously in pattern recognition, the only difference being that now the emphasis is on the computations being carried out concurrently in networks of elemental processors. There is much truth in that viewpoint, and it is helpful to recognize and make use of both the similarities and differences between well-established procedures and the newly proposed neural-net approaches.

For example, the Rumelhart, Hinton, and Williams algorithm was the first widely disseminated account of how a multilayered Perceptron network can be trained to accommodate the knowledge contained in a training set of patterns. Prior to that, although the basis for the inherent power of Perceptronlike devices was well understood [Nilsson 1965], there was no practicable way to train such devices. Use of the sigmoidal activation function and the generalized delta rule yielded, for the first time, a method for inferring classification rules from sets of labeled patterns—a method that was free from the difficulties of explicit synthesis of decision functions and also was different from the approach of "nearest-neighbors." The algorithm brought new insight and a new learning procedure to pattern recognition. Perhaps the fact that it was proposed in terms of a network architecture is almost incidental. Yet it was the context of neural-net computing that occasioned the proposal of this procedure, so network considerations are not incidental at all.

The constraint that pattern-information processing be carried out in a self-consistent manner, with feedback, in a network of processors forces us to think of pattern recognition in ways that are significantly different from those into which we had settled comfortably previously. Also, in this new mode, we can more easily receive and make use of hints inferred from neurobiology and psychology researchers. Thus, in the case of associative memories and especially of the linear holographic and matrix associative memories, previous investigations had concentrated on what was stored at the "nodes" or the elements of the matrix. It turns out that, in a structure such as the Hopfield net, it is the links that serve as the memory. That is, information is stored in the synapses and in a sense the nodes are merely the registers for input and output. This insight can be traced to Hebb [1949], and illustrates again the importance for interdisciplinary interaction.

The Rumelhart, Hinton, and Williams and the Hopfield neural-net computational approaches differ in several significant ways. The essence of the former is that it includes a feedbackward phase, and, because of that, the learning procedure is robust and self-consistent. As presently formulated, the Hopfield algorithm is a purely feedforward method and is "open-ended," so to speak. Yet the idea of some memory structure being able to reconstruct the correct associated pattern even when stimulated with a distorted cue is undoubtedly a valid one, and perhaps further research will shed light on how the Hopfield structure might be used in larger multifunctional networks. This will come about when we evolve beyond considerations of extremely small unifunction fragments of neural nets. We address some of these issues in Chapter 8.

It is in this context that we present material in this chapter that, although related to conventional pattern recognition, is aimed ambitiously at understanding pattern-information processing at more complex levels. We touch on only one aspect of these ambitious goals.

The specific topic of interest is to determine what configuration of cell automata and what autonomous functionalities are required if we ask that a collection of automata be able to organize itself to learn categories of patterns, and be able to recognize subsequent patterns in terms of learned categories.

We could say that we are interested in determining how unsupervised learning algorithms of the K-means or ISODATA types might be implemented in distributed processing form. That view is correct and appropriate to some extent. Again, however, new insights are forced on us when we have to implement such algorithms with distributed control instead of relying on central control and on conventional sequential-computing paradigms.

In Section 7.3, we describe a net that is influenced by an amalgamation of ideas from Carpenter and Grossberg [1985; 1987], Kohonen [1987], Amari [1977], and Fukushima [1980], but follows most closely the ART1 and ART2 architectures of Carpenter and Grossberg [1985, 1987]. Basically, we describe a generic "follow the leader" type of prototype-synthesis procedure. Depending on the metric used to measure similarity, we would be implementing a neural-net version of the K-means or ISO-DATA algorithms or some other clustering procedure.

In that section, we also consider what functionalities are required at the node or cell level if such nets are indeed to be capable of functioning in a truly stable autonomous manner with distributed processing and distributed control. Much of this material is based on the work of Grossberg and Carpenter.

In Section 7.4, we discuss an aspect of self-organization that transcends those covered in Section 7.3, namely that of topological relationships between patterns and whether these patterns can be reflected in corresponding relationships amongst the images created by self-organized mapping.

Lateral inhibition is a network characteristic needed in self-organizing nets. As a preliminary to Section 7.3, we describe in the next section a subnet, called MAXNET, that uses lateral inhibition to accentuate and select the one node, among a set of nodes, that has the greatest output. This same mechanism is used in the net descriptions of Section 7.3. In Section 7.2, we first describe it in the context of a feedforward Hamming net maximum-likelihood classifier for patterns of binary inputs, corrupted by noise.

7.2 MAXNET

When presented with a pattern $\underline{x}$ with binary-valued features, MAXNET classifies that pattern as belonging to class c_j on the basis of the Hamming distance between the class exemplar and the input pattern $\underline{x}$; that is, decide $\underline{x} \in c_j$

$$\begin{aligned} &\textit{iff}\ \text{Hamming distance}\ (\underline{u}_j, \underline{x}) < \text{Hamming distance}\ (\underline{u}_k, \underline{x}) \\ &\quad \text{for all}\ k = 1, 2, \ldots, M \quad k \neq j \end{aligned} \tag{7.1}$$

where $\underline{u}_j$ is the exemplar or class prototype for class j. The feature values of pattern $\underline{u}_j$ are also binary valued.

In other words, $\underline{x}$ is classified as belonging to class j if the Hamming distance between $\underline{x}$ and the class exemplar for class c_j is smaller than the distance from $\underline{x}$ to any of the other class exemplars.

The Hamming distance between $\underline{x}$ and exemplar u_j is simply N minus the sum of the product of the corresponding pairs of feature values; that is,

$$\text{Hamming distance } (\underline{x}, \underline{u}_j) = N - \sum_i (u_{ji} x_i) \tag{7.2}$$

where N is the number of features in the pattern. This quantity is precisely the number of instances in which the corresponding feature values in $\underline{u}_j$ and $\underline{x}$ do not agree.

The architecture of a MAXNET is shown schematically in Figure 7.1. The feature values of the class exemplars are encoded in the weights u_{ji}. For any pattern $\underline{x}$, the feature values x_i are made available to the input nodes. These values are weighted and summed, and the net input to the node j at the next layer is simply the numerical value of the number of instances for which the input value agreed with value of the weight on the connecting link.

These matching scores are presented as inputs to the MAXNET subnet

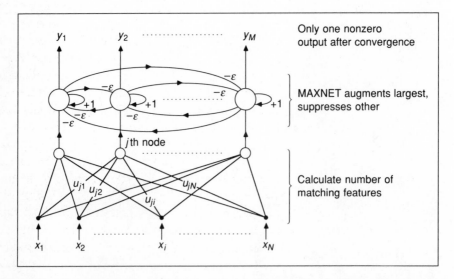

Figure 7.1   Architecture of MAXNET in the context of a Hamming net classifier.

nodes. Each of these nodes is weighted and interconnected so as to maintain its own value and to attempt to suppress the others. That is, MAXNET eventually picks that node for which the matching score is the largest. This action is equivalent to MAXNET picking that node for which the Hamming distance between $\underline{x}$ and the class exemplar is least.

In the MAXNET subnet, let t_{jk} be the connection weight from node j to node k. We take

$$t_{jk} = \begin{cases} 1 & \text{for } j = k \\ -\varepsilon & \text{for } j \neq k \quad \varepsilon < \frac{1}{M} \\ & k, \ j = 1, 2, \ldots, M \end{cases} \tag{7.3}$$

where M is number of possible classes, and also is the number of nodes in the subset.

In the subnet, processing proceeds iteratively on the basis that the value of the output of node j at "time" $t + 1$ is given in terms of the output values at time t, by the relationship

$$\mu_j(t + 1) = f_t\Big(\mu_j(t) - \varepsilon \sum_{k \neq j} \mu_k(t)\Big) \qquad j, k = 1, 2, \ldots, M \tag{7.4}$$

where

$$\begin{aligned} f_t(\alpha) &\propto \alpha \quad \text{for } \alpha > 0 \\ f_t(\alpha) &= 0 \quad \text{for } \alpha < 0 \end{aligned} \tag{7.5}$$

In expression (7.4), we see that the output $\mu_j(t)$ will tend to be "laterally inhibited" by all the other outputs. If the argument α of the function $f_t(\alpha)$ is positive, then the output $\mu_j(t + 1)$ will also be positive, but all outputs for which α is negative will be driven to zero.

The effect of this processing is to boost the value of the largest output relative to the value of the others. Even though this effect is quite easy to understand, it is nevertheless quite remarkable to observe. Given even a small difference, the network will work to differentiate the largest node from the others and, sometimes after a slow buildup, will proceed quickly to drive all inputs except one to negative values with corresponding zero outputs. The one surviving positive output will be at the node that had the greatest initial input. The subnet stops processing when such "convergence" is attained. The dramatic effect of this type of processing is illustrated by the results reported by Lippman and shown in Figure 7.2. These results show how, in the case of a Hamming net with 1000 binary inputs and 100 output nodes or classes, all outputs but one are suppressed

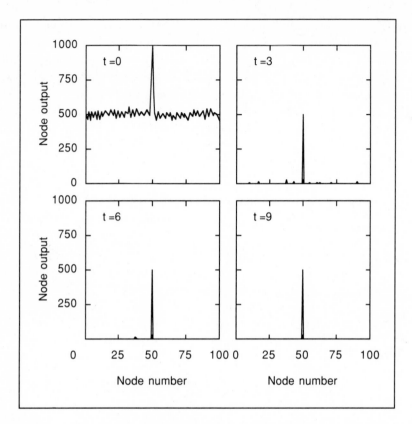

Figure 7.2 Illustration of the effectiveness of MAXNET in picking out node with maximum output (taken from Figure 7 of Lippman, Gold, and Malpass [1987]).

to zero. The input pattern was the exemplar pattern corresponding to output node 50. The output values of all 100 nodes are presented at time zero and after three, six, and nine iterations. We see that convergence was obtained after nine iterations, in the sense that there were no positive inputs except the one at node 50.

Incidentally, the activation function of MAXNET nodes, as described in expression (7.4), is nonlinear and is of the functional form shown in Figure 7.3. It is often referred to as the *threshold logic activation* function. In our discussion, we have taken the threshold to be zero and we assume that we operate below the saturation level.

MAXNET is a useful subnet. There is reason to believe that it is an emulation of an effect that is active in biological neural nets; it is known in that context as the "on center, off surround" effect.

In use of MAXNET, timing is of importance. The Hamming net exercises a straightforward feedforward operation and the matching scores can be calculated in one or two cycles of computing. In contrast, MAXNET may require processing times that are orders of magnitude longer. Therefore, mechanisms are required for disabling the Hamming-net outputs until MAXNET has converged and is ready for a new set of inputs.

Lippman, Gold, and Malpass [1987], in reporting the results of a comparative study of Hamming and Hopfield neural nets for pattern classification, point out that the Hamming net has a number of obvious advantages over the Hopfield net. The Hamming net implements the optimum minimum error classifier when bit errors are random and independent; thus, the performance of the Hopfield net is either worse than or equivalent to that of the Hamming net for such circumstances. Lippman, Gold, and Malpass demonstrate this effect for a number of pattern-recognition problems.

Lippman also points out that, more important, the Hamming net requires considerably fewer connections than does the Hopfield net. For example, with 100 inputs and 10 classes the Hamming net requires 1000

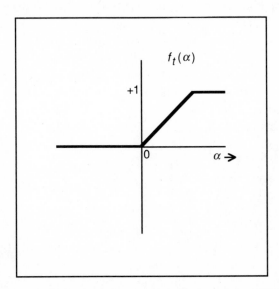

Figure 7.3   Threshold logic activation function used in MAXNET.

internode connections, whereas a Hopfield net requires 10,000 such connections. In the former case, the number of connections increases linearly with the number of nodes; whereas in the latter case, the dependence is quadratic.

These comparisons are valid only if the objective is confined to *classification*. The Hopfield net is an associative memory and its principal function is that of automatic recall of one of the stored exemplars in its entirety, even when the input (cue) is distorted. The Hamming net is not designed to function in that manner.

MAXNET is used in nets for discovering cluster structure in sets of patterns, as described in the next section.

7.3 Nets for Discovering Cluster Structure

Because we view patterns as points in N-dimensional feature space, then we might expect that patterns that are similar in some respect, on the basis either of class membership or of other attribute values, might also be close to each other in the N-dimensional pattern space. For example, all patterns belonging to class c_i might cluster closer to one another than to any pattern belonging to class c_j.

In supervised learning, the pattern-recognition device is presented with labeled patterns so that it can learn the mapping between N-dimensional feature space and the interpretation space, the classification space. However, there are circumstances where it might be appropriate to discover how the ensemble of patterns observed in a problem situation is distributed in pattern space. If the mechanism giving rise to the patterns also segregates them into clusters in a meaningful manner, then clearly any procedure that identifies the location and distribution of these clusters is also meaningful and valuable. Such unsupervised-learning procedures try to identify several prototypes or exemplars that can serve as cluster centers. A prototype may be one of the actual patterns or a synthesized prototype centrally located in the respective cluster.

The very act of clustering necessitates a choice of metric; that is, we must decide how distance is to be measured.

In Chapter 2, we saw that the choice of Euclidean distance would lead to the K-means algorithm or to the ISODATA algorithm. However, the Hamming distance or the Mahalanobis distance [Duda and Hart, 1973], or any other suitable measure of distance, also might be used as appropriate.

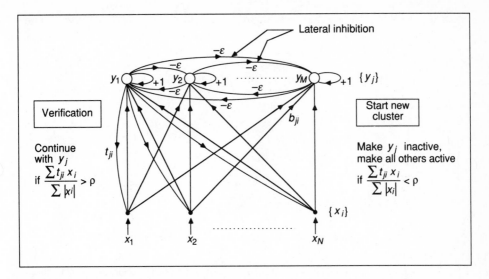

Figure 7.4 Schematic representation of net for unsupervised learning (top-down links t_{ji} shown for only one of the top nodes). (Adapted from ART1 architecture of Carpenter and Grossberg, [1987].)

In addition, we know that often it is helpful to know the probabilities of class memberships, rather than just the class memberships themselves. In other words, for a pattern $\underline{x}$, what is the probability that $\underline{x}$ is a member of cluster i? This question was discussed in Chapter 3 in the context of the use of fuzzy-logic techniques in pattern recognition.

Some neural-net algorithms have been suggested for cluster formation; in this section we describe a generic net that is adapted from the Adapative Resonance Theory (ART) structure Carpenter and Grossberg [1987], but can also accommodate the ideas of Kohonen. A special case of such nets is shown schematically in Figure 7.4. It is essentially an ART1 net [Carpenter and Grossberg, 1987].

The algorithm is as follows:

Step 1. Present a new pattern $\underline{x} \equiv \{x_i\}$ to input nodes ($x_i = \pm 1$ for all i).

Step 2. Use bottom-up processing to obtain a weighted sum

$$y_j = \sum b_{ji} x_i \qquad (7.6)$$

Step 3. Use the MAXNET procedure to find the upper-level node with the largest y_j value.

Step 4. Verify that $\underline{x}$ truly belongs to the jth cluster by performing top-down processing; that is, form the weighted sum

$$\sum_i t_{ji} x_i$$

Then, $\underline{x}$ belongs to jth cluster if

$$\frac{\sum_i t_{ji} x_i}{\|\underline{x}\|} > \rho \tag{7.7}$$

where ρ is a vigilance parameter. If so, proceed to step 5; otherwise, go to step 6.

In (7.7), $\|\underline{x}\|$ is the norm of the $\underline{x}$ vector. For ART1, $\|\underline{x}\| = \sum_i |x_i|$.

Step 5. Update b_{ji} and t_{ji} for that specific j and all i.

Step 6. Since $\underline{x}$ does not belong to the one node that was the most likely, deactivate that node and go back to step 2 to start another cluster center.

For ART1 the initiation and update procedures are

$$t_{ji}(o) = 1 \tag{7.8}$$

$$b_{ji}(o) = \frac{1}{1+N} \tag{7.9}$$

$$t_{ji}(n+1) = t_{ji}(n) x_i \tag{7.10}$$

$$b_{ji}(n+1) = \frac{t_{ji}(n) x_i}{0.5 + \sum_{i=1}^{N} t_{ij}(n) x_i} \tag{7.11}$$

This algorithm seems to be quite reasonable in the case of patterns with binary-valued features in ART1. The set of weights $\{b_{ji}\}$ for any specific node j constitutes the short-term memory of the prototype pattern for cluster j, and the set of weights $\{t_{ji}\}$ is essentially that also.

The quantities b_{ji} and t_{ji} serve different purposes. For example, after all clusters have been formed, the function of the b_{ji} is to determine the exemplar that is *most like* the input $\underline{x}$. Of itself, however, this step does not guarantee that the pattern $\underline{x}$ truly should be considered a member of that cluster. An explicit verification needs to be carried out; this verification is done using the top-down weights t_{ji}.

The quantity $\Sigma t_{ji} x_i$ is essentially a count of the number of coincidences of unit-valued features between the jth pattern and the input pattern. The quantity $\Sigma |x_i|$ is the number of unit-valued features in the input pattern. The quantity $\Sigma t_{ji} x_i / \Sigma |x_i|$ will always be less than or equal to unity, and it provides a measure of how well the input pattern meets expectation.

If the value of ρ is set high, then conformation requirements are high and a body of patterns is likely to be split up into a large number of separate clusters. On the other hand, if the value of ρ is lowered, then larger departures from expectations are tolerated and the same set of patterns might be organized into a much smaller set of clusters.

In the case of continuous-valued features, the criterion for comparing similarity would have to be different from that of ART1. That is, if $\{b_{ji}\}$ constitutes the short-term memory of the cluster prototype of cluster j, then the similarity between $\{b_{ji}\}$ and $\{x_i\}$ is not necessarily best measured by $\Sigma b_{ji} x_i$, as it is in the case of ART1. Similarly, the procedures for initializing and updating $\{t_{ji}\}$ and $\{b_{ji}\}$ also would be different. Carpenter and Grossberg have described ART2, which accommodates analog patterns, but we shall not discuss that algorithm except to note that we have greater freedom in our choice of metric for measuring similarities if we are not limited to biological nets. In particular, instead of counting the number of matching features, we calculate the Euclidean distances between the input pattern and the exemplars, $\{b_{ji}\}$, and determine that node for which the quantity (N − Euclidean distance) is the greatest, where N is the number of elements in the input pattern and the numeric values of the elements lie between 0 and 1. In that manner, MAXNET sorts all the input patterns into clusters belonging to the various nodes. We can maintain "vigilance" by setting radii for the cluster centers. A pattern lying outside of a hypersphere would not be accepted as belonging to that cluster even if MAXNET assigned it to that node. An algorithm for effecting clustering in this manner is given in Appendix B together with a sample program.

The behavior of ART2 is similar to that of ART1 as far as the magnitude of the vigilance parameter is concerned. The results exhibited in Figures 7.5 and 7.6 were obtained by Carpenter and Grossberg for 50 analog input patterns using algorithm ART2. Figure 7.5 shows that the 50 patterns were grouped into 34 different categories with a high value of the vigilance parameter. Coarser grouping was obtained when the vigilance was lowered. In Figure 7.6, the same 50 input patterns are shown, organized with 20 recognition categories.

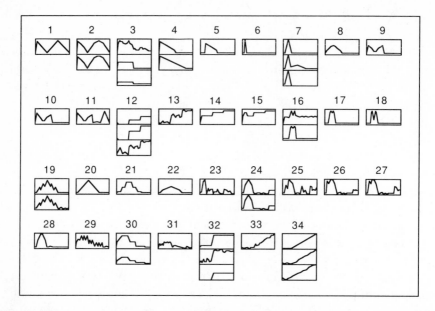

Figure 7.5   Category grouping of 50 analog input patterns into 34 recognition categories. (Carpenter, G. A. and S. Grossberg, ART2: Self-organization of stable category recognition codes for analog input patterns, *Applied Optics,* Vol. 26, p. 4920, 1987. Adapted from and reprinted with permission of The Optical Society of America.)

7.4 Kohonen's Studies of Ordered Mappings

We can consider the operation of self-organized clustering to be a mapping through which points in N-dimensional pattern space are mapped into a smaller number of points in an "output space." The mapping is achieved autonomously by the system without external supervision. In other words, the clustering is achieved in a self-organized manner.

Such mappings may have interesting and useful topological properties. Kohonen has reported the results of some one- and two-dimensional mappings that had the characteristic of being "topologically correct." It would seem that such mappings could be generalized to higher dimensions. However, even in the one-dimensional case, Kohonen showed, through simulation, that an array of units connected to an input array of resonators of moderate bandwidth could organize itself such that after a number of iterative steps, the array units started to become sensitized to different frequencies in an ascending or descending order. The model system bore a striking resemblance to the tonotopic maps formed in the auditory cortices of mammals.

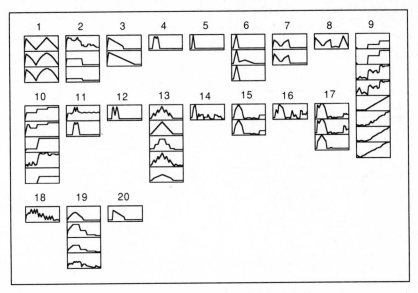

Figure 7.6 Demonstration that lower vigilance implies coarser groupings. The same ART2 system used for results shown in Figure 7.5 grouped the same 50 inputs into 20 recognition categories when the vigilance ratio was lowered. Note, for example, that categories 1 and 2 of Figure 7.5 are here joined in category 1; categories 14, 15, and 32 are here joined in category 28; and categories 19 through 22 are here joined in category 13. (Carpenter, G. A. and S. Grossberg, ART2: Self-organization of stable category recognition codes for analog input patterns, *Applied Optics*, Vol. 26, p. 4921, 1987. Adapted from and reprinted with permission of The Optical Society of America.)

The essential features of the systems that Kohonen used in his studies are illustrated in Figures 7.7 and 7.8 for one-dimensional and two-dimensional output arrays.

Ordered Mappings

Let a number of events in the external world be represented by patterns $\underline{a}_1, \underline{a}_2, \underline{a}_3, \ldots$. Each pattern has N features, and these values are applied to the inputs of the system shown in Figure 7.7. The inputs go through an intermediary relaying network and generate sets of *sensory signals* to an array of processing units, each of which has one output response. The processing units are arrayed in a one-dimensional array, but interact among themselves as specified.

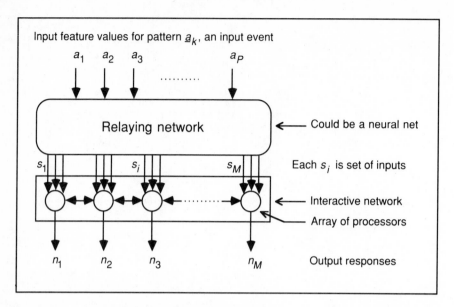

Figure 7.7   Schematic illustration of components of a one-dimensional system that implements an ordered mapping.

For any input event $\underline{a}_p$, the *sets* of sensory signals s_i distributed to each processing unit i may be nonidentical and the number of signals in each s_i may be different; however, these signals are assumed to be *coherent* in the sense that they are uniquely determined by the same $\underline{a}_p$.

Assume that the events $\underline{a}_p$ can be *ordered* in some metric or topological way such that $\underline{a}_1 R \underline{a}_2 R \underline{a}_3 \ldots$, where R stands for a general ordering relation that is transitive (that is, the ordering $a_i R a_2 R a_3$, implies that $\underline{a}_1 R \underline{a}_3$). In addition, assume that the processing units produce outputs in response to the events $\underline{a}_1, \underline{a}_2, \ldots$, such that, in response to events $\underline{a}_k$, the outputs of the linear array are $\eta_1(\underline{a}_k), \eta_2(\underline{a}_k), \ldots$.

Definition 7.1 *The system of Figure 7.7 is used to implement a one-dimensional ordered mapping if for* $\underline{a}_1 R \underline{a}_2 R \underline{a}_3 \ldots$, *and for* $i_1 > i_2 > i_3 \ldots$

$$\eta_{i_1}(\underline{a}_1) = \max_{j}\{\eta_j(\underline{a}_1) \mid j = 1, 2, \ldots, m\}$$

$$\eta_{i_2}(\underline{a}_2) = \max_{j}\{\eta_j(\underline{a}_2) \mid j = 1, 2, \ldots, m\} \qquad (7.12)$$

$$\eta_{i_3}(\underline{a}_3) = \max_{j}\{\eta_j(\underline{a}_3) \mid j = 1, 2, \ldots, m\}$$

and so on.

Definition 7.1 may be generalized to two- and higher-dimensional arrays of processing units. In those cases, some *topological* order must be defined for the set of events $\underline{a}_i$ in terms of ordering relationships with respect to different attributes. However, the topology of the array is simply defined by the definition of neighbors to each other.

If the unit with the maximum response to a particular event is regarded as the image of the latter, then the mapping is said to be ordered *if the topological relations of the images and the events are similar.* Such mappings are also referred to by Kohonen as being *topological correct*; our interest is in how such mappings are achieved through self-organization.

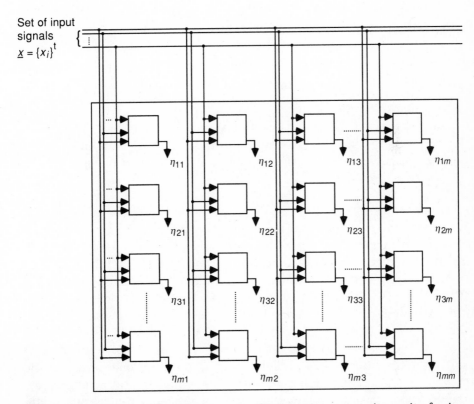

Figure 7.8 A two-dimensional array of interacting processing units for implementing an ordered mapping. In one study, the same set of input signals $\{x_i\}$ connected to all processors. If test vector $\underline{x}$ were chosen in an ordered two-dimensional array, then images of the test vectors (the outputs) were also ordered in a topologically similar array.

In summary, the essential constituents of the systems are as follows:

1. A relaying network that acts in response to the occurrence of an event in event space and generates *sets* of sensory signals as outputs. (These sets of signals may or may not be identical, but they are *coherent* in the sense that they are uniquely determined by the same input event.) The relaying network also distributes these sets of signals to an array of identical processors, one set to each processor.

2. An ordered array of identical processors each of which receives a set of signals (hereon viewed as a pattern) as its external input and generates an output that is a function of its external input, inputs from its interacting neighboring processors and the values of some local parameters (such as the components of the weight vector). This function is known as the discriminant function.

3. A mechanism that compares the discriminant-function values of all the processors and selects the unit with the greatest function value to designate the location of that output as the image of the initial event.

4. An adaptive process that adjusts the parameters of the processors such that the discriminant-function values are altered with the objective of increasing the value of the output of each of the units. (The lateral interactions determine which unit finally wins out over all the others.)

More explicitly, for the two-dimensional array shown in Figure 7.8 let $\underline{x}$ be an input pattern (an input set of signals) due to the occurrence of an event in event space. In this case, all processors receive the same input. In addition, we note that if the event was simply the specification of a point in two-dimensional space, then the spatial coordinates of that location would constitute the input to the array of processors. The task of the relaying network would indeed be simple under such circumstances.

Let $\underline{m}_i$ be a weight vector associated with processor (and output) unit i. In the interest of simplicity we will use only one index for the processors and corresponding outputs. The actual spatial arrangements and the topology of the interactions can be specified through appropriate indexing of the interprocessor interactions.

Unit i has input weights or parameters $\mu_{i1}, \mu_{i2}, \ldots, \mu_{in}$, which are expressible as a column vector $\underline{m}_i = [\mu_{i1}, \mu_{i2}, \ldots, \mu_{in}]^t \in R^N$. The local excitation, due to the input signal set $\underline{x}$, is simply

$$\phi_i = \sum_{j=1}^{n} \mu_{ij} x_j = \underline{m}_i^t \underline{x} \tag{7.13}$$

The net excitation to unit i with all the lateral interactions taken into account is

$$net_i = [\phi_i + \sum \gamma_k \eta_k] \tag{7.14}$$

where γ_k represents the strength of the laternal (interprocessor) interactions, and the nonlinear output of unit i is

$$\eta_i = f[\phi_i + \sum \gamma_k \eta_k - \delta] \tag{7.15}$$

The quality δ is a threshold taken by Kohonen to be

$$\delta = \max_i \{\eta_i\} - \varepsilon \tag{7.16}$$

with ε as a small positive constant.

The threshold δ is a floating bias function common for all units. Kohonen [1982] describes two other approaches to modelling the discrimination process (Expression 7.15), but states that the results of the self-organizing procedure do not seem to be sensitive to how the details of that thresholding procedure are specified.

An additional discrimination mechanism singles out that unit ℓ among all the i units that has the greatest (output) value

$$\eta_\ell = \max_i \{\eta_i\} \tag{7.17}$$

and $\underline{x}$ is then considered to have been "mapped" onto that unit ℓ.

If there is only one such $\underline{x}$, then it would be immaterial as to how it is mapped onto the array of processors—presumably any one of the processors will do. However, if there is an ordered set of such input events giving rise to ordered set $\{\underline{x}\}$ patterns, then, under some circumstances, it is important that topological structures present in the input space be conserved in the mapping process so that the self-organized output space will exhibit the same topological relationships. The issues are how what types of lateral interactions can lead to ordered self-organization and how

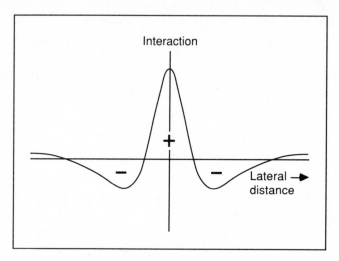

Figure 7.9   Schematic representation of lateral interaction around an arbitrary point of excitation as a function of distance.

the discriminant vectors $\underline{m}_i$ are to be learned so that the ordered relationships are preserved.

Kohonen found that self-organizing topologically correct mappings can be obtained, at least for one- and two-dimensional spaces, if the processor units are allowed to interact laterally in appropriate ways, or in ways analogous to those observed in biological systems, consisting of

1. A short-range lateral excitation, reaching laterally up to a radius of 50 to 100 μm (in primates)

2. A wider ring of inhibitory action surrounding the central excitatory area, reaching up to a radius of 200 to 500 μm

3. A weaker excitatory action surrounding the inhibitory penumbra, reaching up to a radius of several centimeters

This type of lateral interaction is illustrated in Figure 7.9. In Kohonen's quantitative work, this type of lateral interaction was approximated by a discrete set of coefficients, as shown in Figure 7.10.

In Kohonen's work, adaptation, for the purposes of self-organization, is introduced through the supposition that each local $\underline{m}$ vector tries to rotate in the direction of the input pattern vector $\underline{x}$, keeping its amplitude normalized, one of the adaptive laws investigated being

$$\mu_{ij}(t+1) = \frac{\mu_{ij}(t) + \alpha\eta_i(t)(x_j - x_b)}{\left\{\sum_{j=1}^{n}[\mu_{ij}(t) + \alpha\eta_i(t)(x_j - x_b)]^2\right\}^{1/2}} \qquad (7.18)$$

where

$\mu_{ij}(t+1) =$ the jth component of the weight vector $\underline{m}$ of unit i at discrete time $(t+1)$

$\eta_i(t) =$ the discrimination function value for processor unit i at discrete time t

$x_j =$ the jth component of the input pattern to unit i

$x_b =$ a background value, independent of processor index, which can be made zero

$\alpha =$ a gain parameter used in the adaptation process often decreased gradually as the process proceeds so as to force covergence

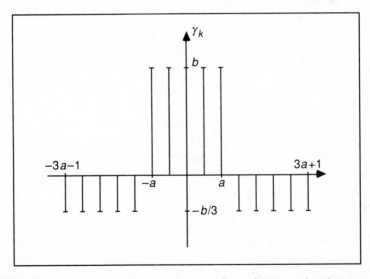

Figure 7.10   Coefficients used to represent lateral interaction in some quantitative simulations (Kohonen [1982]).

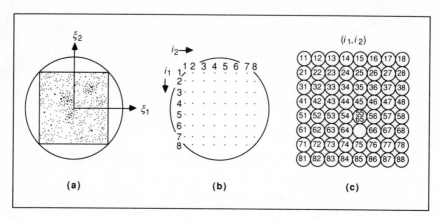

Figure 7.11 (a) Distribution of training vectors (front view of the surface of a unit sphere in R^3). The distribution had edges, each of which contained as many vectors as the inside. (b) Test vectors which are mapped into the outputs of the processing unit array. (c) Images of the test vectors at the outputs. (Kohonen, T., Self-organized formation of topologically correct feature maps, *Biological Cybernetics*, Vol. 43, p. 61, ©1982, Springer-Verlag. Adapted from and reprinted with permission.)

If there is only one event, namely only one signal pattern $\underline{x}$, then it might be imagined that it will be essentially a matter of chance as to what processor will represent it in image space. However, as the different members of an ordered set of events are cycled through the self-organization process, the question is whether equations (7.12) to (7.18) suffice to bring about an ordering of the processor units that reflect the order among the event.

Kohonen [1982] reports on the results of several interesting investigations. In one instance, he used a randomly chosen sequence of $\underline{x}$ vectors to order a two-dimensional array of processor outputs. The random sequence was selected from a continuous distribution of all radially arrayed vectors with tips within a rectangular area on the surface of a sphere of unit radius. Insofar as the tips of the $\underline{x}$ vectors were concerned, the array was two dimensional, as was the arrangement of the output processors. The two distributions are shown in Figures 7.11(a) and 7.11(b).

In the training phase, a random sequence of $\underline{x}$ vectors was selected from the continuous distribution shown in Figure 7.11(a), and $\underline{m}$ vectors were "learned" for each of η_{ij} processor outputs. In a subsequent test phase, a two-dimensional ordered array of $\underline{x}$ vectors was mapped into the processors, with the results shown in Figure 7.11(c). It is clear that somehow the system had organized itself so that the topological relationships in the input were conserved in the output.

In another instance, Kohonen plotted lines joining the tips of the m vectors. Initially, the m vectors were randomly oriented and the lines joining the tips accordingly formed random patterns. After a large number of training steps, the weight vectors formed regular arrays, as evidenced by the pattern formed by lines joining the tips of these vectors, shown in Figure 7.12.

In another experiment, Kohonen studied the responses of a simulated

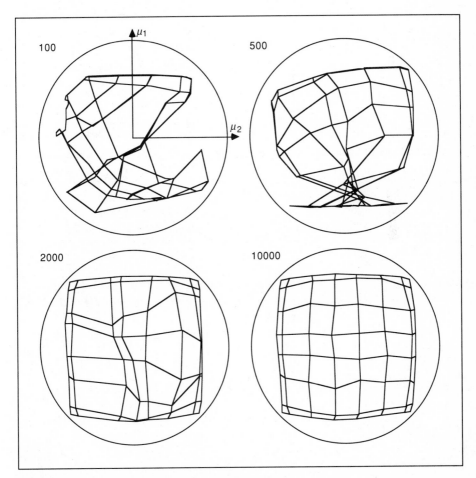

Figure 7.12 Distribution of the weight vectors $m_i(t)$ at different times as revealed by the positions of lines joining the tips of the vectors. The number of training steps is shown above the distribution. Interaction is between nearest neighbors only. (Kohonen, T., Self-organized formation of topologically correct feature maps, *Biological Cybernetics*, Vol. 43, p. 62, ©1982, Springer-Verlag. Adapted from and reprinted with permission.)

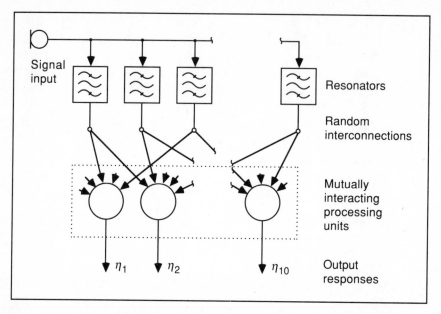

Figure 7.13   Illustration of the one-dimensional system used in the self-organized formation of a frequency map. (Kohonen, T., Self-organized formation of topologically correct feature maps, *Biological Cybernetics*, Vol. 43, p. 62, ©1982, Springer-Verlag. Adapted from and reprinted with permission.)

one-dimensional array of 10 mutually interacting processors (nearest neighbors only) connected to the outputs of a linear array of 20 tuned filters, as shown in Figure 7.13. The tuned filters (resonators) collectively play the role of the relaying network.

The resonators (20 in number) corresponded to second-order filters with quality factor $q = 2.5$ and resonant frequencies selected at random from the range [1,2]. The signal generator—the input—generated single-frequency signals in the range [0.5,1], meaning that any one of the single-frequency signals was attenuated to varying degrees by the different filters. Five inputs to each array unit were picked up at random from the resonator outputs, so that there was no initial correlation or order in any structure or parameter. In the training session, frequencies were selected at random from the range [0.5,1], and the array adapted its mapping, in this case the sensitivities. That is, each of the units learned a weight vector, so that, with nearest neighbor interactions taken into account, in accordance with system equations (7.13) to (7.17), the units exhibited characteristics of a tuned receiver. Each unit had its own value for the frequency at which it was most sensitive.

Table 7.1 Discrete Joint Probabilities

Unit i	1	2	3	4	5	6	7	8	9	10
Frequency map in experiment 1, 2000 steps	0.55	0.60	0.67	0.70	0.77	0.82	0.83	0.94	0.98	0.93
Frequency map in experiment 2, 3500 steps	0.99	0.98	0.98	0.97	0.90	0.81	0.73	0.69	0.62	0.59

The results were truly remarkable. After a number of iterated training steps, the array of processing units started to become sensitized to different frequencies in an ascending or descending order, as shown in Table 7.1.

In these investigations, Kohonen decreased α in a manner proportional to $1/t$ so as to ensure "convergence." However, it is clear that this matter of convergence, or equivalently the issues of local and global stabilities of self-organized orderings, merit further detailed study.

7.5 Comments and Bibliographical Remarks

To pattern-recognition researchers accustomed to working with the K-means and ISODATA algorithms, the follow-the-leader type of clustering or unsupervised learning procedures described in this chapter might not seem to be terribly innovative, at first glance. However, there are novel features. The top-down verification step proposed by Carpenter and Grossberg [1985; 1987] is indeed very important.

MAXNET merely indicates which cluster prototype is most similar to the input patterns; the actual resemblence may be very slight. Therefore, unless there were a verification step, the system would not know that an error had been made.

The customary attitude to the use of the ISODATA algorithm is that the human information processor is very much "in the loop," making judgments and decisions. In contrast, neural-net processing is envisioned for autonomous network processing of patterns, with no conscious intelligent agent involved.

The ART systems of Carpenter and Grossberg [1985; 1987] are particularly powerful in the context of *systems* of such nets. Complex and powerful pattern-information-processing functionalities can be built up, provided additional controls and associations are implemented.

We note that the ART architecture consists of a flat net, or a "slab," with no "hidden" layers, different from the architecture of the generalized delta rule net, and also from that of associative memories, such as the Hopfield nets. This diversity results not in richness, but rather in awkwardness. In contrast, as we show in Chapter 8, the functional-link net suited to the learning of associated pairs also has a flat or slab architecture that can be intermingled with the ART architecture.

We can get an inkling of what Grossberg perceives to be possible by listing, without further discussion, a number of the distinctive characteristics of the ART architectures and those of others (unnamed) architectures:

1. Real-time (on line) learning versus lab-time (off-line) learning

2. Nonstationary unexpected world versus stationary, controlled world

3. Self-organization versus teacher as a source of expected output

4. Self-stabilization versus capacity catastrophe

5. Maintain plasticity in an unexpected world versus externally shut-off plasticity

6. Self-scaling computational units

7. Learn internal expectations versus impose external costs

8. Active attentional focussing and priming versus passive weight change

9. Closing versus opening the fast–slow feedback loop

10. Expectant priming versus grinding all memory cycles

11. Learning in the approximate match phase versus in the mismatch phase: hypothesis testing avoids the noise catastrophe

12. Fast or slow learning: the oscillation catastrophe

13. Self-adjusting parallel memory search and global energy landscape upheaval versus search tree and local minima

14. Rapid direct access versus increase of recognition time with code complexity

15. Asynchronous versus synchronous learning

16. Discriminative tuning via attentional vigilance

17. Towards a general-purpose machine for cognitive hypothesis testing, data search, and classification [Grossberg 1988, pp. 40–45]

By listing and discussing these items, Grossberg suggests, in effect, that the ART architecture would go quite a way toward a general-purpose machine for hypothesis testing, data search, and classification. Grossberg's discussions are stimulating. However, we have much research to do if we wish to evaluate such behavioral characteristics with pattern-recognition networks, ART or otherwise.

7.6 References and Bibliography

1. Amari, S.I., 1977. Neural theory of association and concept-formations, *Biological Cybernetics*, Vol. 26, pp. 175–185.

2. Carpenter, G.A. and S. Grossberg, 1985. Category learning and adaptive pattern recognition, a neural network model, *Proc. Third Army Conference on Applied Mathematics and Computing*, ARO Report 86-1, pp. 37-56.

3. Carpenter, G.A. and S. Grossberg, 1986. Neural dynamics of category learning and recognition: Attention, memory consolidation, and amnesia. In J. Davis, R. Newburgh, and E. Wegman (Eds.), *Brain Structure, Learning, and Memory*, AAAS Symposium Series, Vol. 105, Westview Press, Boulder, Colorado.

4. Carpenter, G.A. and S. Grossberg, 1987. ART2: Self-organization of stable category recognition codes for analog input patterns, *Applied Optics*, Vol. 26, pp. 4919–4930.

5. Duda, R.O. and P.E. Hart, 1973. *Pattern Classification and Scene Analysis*, Wiley, New York.

6. Fukushima, K., 1980. Neocognition: A self-organizing neural network model for a mechanism of pattern recognition unaffected by shift in position, *Biological Cybernetics*, Vol. 36, pp. 193–202.

7. Hebb, D.O., 1949. *The Organization of Behaviour*, Wiley, New York.

8. Kohonen, T., 1987. Adaptive, associative, and self-organization functions in neural computing, *Applied Optics*, Vol. 26, pp. 4910–4918.

9. Kohonen, T., 1982. Self-organized formation of topologically correct feature maps, *Biological Cybernetics*, Vol. 43, pp. 59–69.

10. Lippman, R.P., 1987. An introduction to computing with neural nets, *IEEE ASSP Magazine*, Vol. 4, pp. 4–22.

11. Lippman, R.P., B. Gold, and M.L. Malpass, 1987. A comparison of Hamming and Hopfield neural nets for pattern classification. MIT Lincoln Laboratory Technical Report, TR-769, Massachusetts Institute of Technology, Cambridge, MA.

12. Nilsson, N.J., 1965. *Learning Machines: Foundations of Training Pattern Classifying Systems*, McGraw-Hill, New York.

CHAPTER 8

The Functional-Link Net: Basis for an Integrated Neural-Net Computing Environment

8.1 Introduction

The previous three chapters have been concerned with neural nets for supervised learning, for associative storage and recall, and for unsupervised learning. As indicated in our discussions, the network models for the first two tasks suffer from limitations. In particular, the learning rate for the generalized delta rule net is often unacceptably low, and the model does not scale well for patterns with large number of elements. The storage capacity of the basic Hopfield net is also low, and the net is subject to error if capacity is exceeded, or if some of the stored patterns are similar in some respects.

As mentioned in Chapters 5 and 6, we can alleviate some of these difficulties by making use of "higher-order" terms in these network models. In the case of the generalized delta rule net, the introduction of such terms may be thought of as sigma-pi units [Rumelhart, Hinton, and Williams, 1986] or as links influenced by the output of a correlation node, as in the meta–generalized delta rule model [Pomerleau, 1987]. Introduction of such terms generally results in dramatic increases in learning rates.

Similarly, Chen and colleagues [1986] and Lee and colleagues [1986] report that the storage capacity of the Hopfield net is considerably improved when higher-order synaptic links are included. Sejnowski [1986] reports that the efficiency of the Boltzmann machine, a probabilistic variant of the Hopfield net, is also improved by inclusion of higher-order interactions.

In this chapter, we describe another approach to improving the performance of the generalized delta rule net. In fact, after we have incorporated the "improvements," we often find that there is no longer any need for a generalized delta rule—a delta rule suffices.

There are different ways of thinking about the processing action of the generalized delta rule net. In one view, the nodes in the first hidden layer construct hyperplanes, the nodes in the second layer construct hypervolumes, and those in other layers specify the AND or OR decision rules [Lippman 1987]. From another, equally valid, viewpoint [Nilsson 1965] the successive layers carry out a sequence of mappings until we find a representation—that is, a mapping in a suitable space—where the desired separation is possible.

Our approach to improving the supervised learning net is based on the second viewpoint. Instead of groping around until we find a suitable sequence of transformations, we ask whether it might be possible to enhance the original representation right from the start, in a linearly independent manner, so that hyperplanes for separation might be learned more readily.

One way of enhancing the initial representation of a pattern is to describe it in a space of increased dimensions. Then, the questions are (1) how are additional dimensions to be chosen?, and (2) what are the values to be ascribed to a pattern along these new coordinate axes?

We describe our approach in terms of functional links. In contrast to the linear weighting produced by the linear links of the generalized delta rule net, the functional link acts on an element of a pattern or on the entire pattern itself by generating a set of linearly independent functions, then evaluating these functions with the pattern as the argument. In one sense, no new ad hoc information has been inserted into the process; nonetheless, the representation has definitely been enhanced, and separability becomes possible in the enhanced space.

We find that use of functional links not only increases learning rates [Klassen and Pao, 1988], but also has an unexpected effect of simplifying the learning algorithms and unifying the architecture for all three types of nets. That is, the new net is capable of accommodating the three tasks of supervised learning, associative storage and recall, and unsupervised learning.

On occasion, we use the term *higher-order* in our discussion of the functional-link net, but it is clear that we are not solely or specifically interested in joint or higher-order activations. In one instance of the functional-link net, the action of the functional link is to multiply each element of the input pattern by the entire pattern vector. The overall result is to generate a tensor, the outerproduct, from the original pattern vector, and the higher-order performance characteristics that Giles and Maxwell [1987] had reported previously are reproduced and rediscovered. Somewhat unexpectedly, we find that the higher-order correlation route to augmenting the net can be viewed as a special case of the functional-link net. In general, the functional-link net is not primarily concerned with incorporating higher-order effects of the correlation type.

8.2 Functional Transform Along a Nonlinear Link

The standard Rumelhart, Hinton, and Williams net has only linear links; it is, of course, very tempting to relax this limitation. As scientists, however, we may find it repugnant to go about that task in an ad hoc manner.

In place of an ad hoc approach, we can either appeal to neurobiology for guidance or try to find an approach that is mathematically simple and general. The functional-link approach is more biased to the latter than to the former, although, as we shall see, the results might be compatible with what is known of biological neural nets.

The overall concept is that of a *functional* link. Thus, in this mathematically based conceptual model of a net suitable for parallel distributed processing, different additional functionalities may be activated once a node is activated. As illustrated in Figure 8.1, activation of node k offers the possibility that processes $f_0(o_k), f_1(o_k), \ldots, f_n(o_k)$ may also be activated.

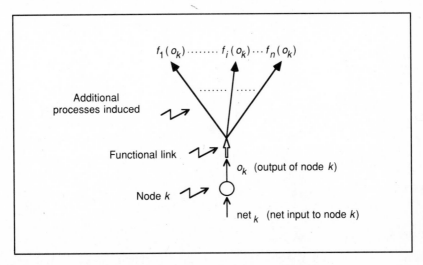

Figure 8.1   Schematic illustration of a functional link.

Different effects are obtained depending on the details postulated for the functional link. We consider two models, the functional expansion model and the tensor (or outerproduct) model, respectively. The latter is but a special case of the general method. We treat it because we have found that the results so obtained are of the same nature as those obtained by other methods that introduce correlation terms directly.

In the functional expansion model, the functional link acts on each node singly. It might induce the same additional functionalities for each node in the input pattern. This concept is illustrated schematically in Figure 8.2. In this model, each component of the input vector is acted on by the functional link to yield the quantities $f_1(o_k), f_2(o_k), \ldots, f_n(o_k)$.

Under some circumstances, $f_1(x)$ might simply be x and $f_2(x)$ might be x^2 and so on. Or the functions might be a subset of a complete set of orthonormal basis functions spanning a n-dimensional representation space, such as $\sin \pi x$, $\cos \pi x$, $\sin 2\pi x$, $\cos 2\pi x$, and so on. The net effect is to map the input pattern into a larger pattern space. We associate and represent each component x with the quantities $x, x^2, x^3, \ldots$ or with $x, \sin \pi x, \cos \pi x$, and so on, depending on the set of functions that we deem to be appropriate. No intrinsically new ad hoc information is introduced, but the representation is enhanced. We may think of going from $\sin \pi x$ to

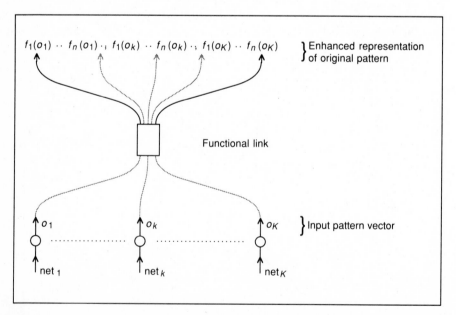

Figure 8.2   Schematic illustration of the functional-expansion model for a functional-link net.

$\sin 2\pi x$ and to $\sin 3\pi x$ and so on as making use of *higher-order terms*, but clearly the connotation in this case is quite different from that of previous usage in the literature.

In a sense, the tensor or outerproduct model is simply a special case of the functional-expansion model.

In the tensor or outerproduct model, each component of the input pattern multiplies the *entire* input pattern vector. The functional link in this case generates an entire vector from each of the individual components. The same process may be described in terms of the formation of an outerproduct between two vectors, one being the original pattern vector and the other being the same vector augmented by an additional component of value unity. Augmenting the vector allows the original pattern to be regenerated, along with the higher-order effects.

In both models, the process of representation enhancement may be used repeatedly (that is, recursively), as appropriate, or both modes may be used simultaneously and in combination, as appropriate.

In the tensor model, the effect of the nonlinear functional transform is to change the representation of the input pattern so that, instead of being described in terms of a set of components $\{x_i\}$, it is described as

$$\{x_i, x_i x_j\}_{j \geq i}$$

or as

$$\{x_i, x_i x_j, x_i x_j x_k\}_{j \geq i \quad k \geq j \geq i}$$

and so on. In a sense, no new information has been added, but joint activations have been made explicitly available to the net.

Such functional transforms greatly increase the number of components in terms of which of the input pattern is described. We can simplify the enhanced pattern by omitting terms with two or more equal indices, and also terms for which there is no correlation over an ensemble of input patterns. So, we consider the sequence of transformations

$$\{x_i\} \Rightarrow \{x_i, x_i x_j\}_{j \geq i} \Rightarrow \{x_i, x_i x_j, x_i x_j x_k\}_{j \geq i \quad k \geq j \geq i} \Rightarrow \dots \tag{8.1}$$

and omit terms for which

$$\sum_{p=1}^{P} (x_i x_j)_p \to 0 \tag{8.2}$$

Table 8.1   Increase of Number of Pattern Components with Enhancement

Number of Components in Initial Pattern $\{x_i\}$	Number of Components in $\{x_i, x_i x_j\}$ $j > i$	Number of Components in $\{x_i, x_i x_j\}, x_i x_j x_k\}$ $j > i \, k > j > i$
2	3	3
3	6	7
4	10	14
5	15	25
10	35	155

In (8.1) the values of x_i and x_j range from -1 to $+1$. Similar considerations apply to the higher-order terms.

In practice, the pruning action is important because, if only the diagonal terms are omitted, the increase of complexity may still be intolerable, as shown by Table 8.1. However, higher-order terms beyond the second order often are not required as the number of components are increased.

The effects of such an enhancement are dramatic; we shall describe them in examples later in this chapter. For supervised learning, not only is the learning rate usually increased greatly, but also often a flat net with no hidden layers suffices. Supervised learning thus can be carried out with the same net architecture as that used for unsupervised learning (as in the case of nets using the ART algorithm). In addition, associative storage and recall also can be achieved with such nets.

Example 8.1 is particularly illuminating in illustrating the benefits obtained through enhancement of the representation of the pattern. Whereas the parity-2 (XOR) problem could not be solved without a hidden layer, the same problem is easily solved if the patterns are represented in three dimensions in terms of an enhanced representation. The learning rate is significantly increased.

Example 8.2 is another demonstration of simplification of network architecture accompanied by enhanced learning rate. These results are similar to those of Giles and Maxwell [1987].

The outerproduct model truly introduces higher-order terms in the enhanced representation in the sense that some of these terms represent joint activations. In contrast, the functional-expansion model merely expands the dimension of the representation space without introducing joint activations. Experience indicates that, at low degrees of enhancement, the two approaches result in significantly different results. Direct enhancement of each component individually results at first primarily in increased resolution of the classification or estimation actions on the set of patterns involved. In contrast, the outerproduct-enhancement mode determines more quickly the qualitative nature of the outcome—namely, whether classification is indeed possible with a net with no hidden layer. Examples 8.3 and 8.4, however, are representative of instances where the outerproduct-enhancement mode would have been ineffective by itself.

The question, then, is whether there is any theoretical basis for the choice of method or for determining the degree of enhancement. Sobajic [1988] has carried a theoretical discussion of the functional-link methodology; he proves that the functional-expansion model is always capable of yielding a flat-net solution. Moreover, his analysis also provides guidance on how to proceed, if we wish to obtain simple solutions. A synopsis of his analysis is contained in Section 8.3.

Example 8.3 is concerned with a task that is more in the nature of estimation rather than of classification. The question is whether a net can learn a network representation of a continuous function given the values of the function $f(\underline{x})$ at only a finite number of points $\underline{x}$, possibly a rather small and irregularly spaced number of points. The actual task is that of estimating the value of the attribute, $f(\underline{x})$, given the pattern $\underline{x}$. It is a well-defined task and constitutes an important and useful capability of such networks.

The results of Example 8.3 are interesting in their own right, demonstrating that pattern enhancement through functional expansion can indeed be effective. However, there is ambiguity in the procedure because of the fact that there is only one component in the input pattern and because of the nature of the orthogonal functions chosen for the expansion.

In contrast, we gain further insight by considering the procedure in Example 8.4, where a net is asked to synthesize a net representation of a complex two-dimensional curved surface. The task is again that of estimation. Given a finite number of associated pairs $\{(x, y)/f(x, y)\}$, the net attempts to synthesize a network representation of a continuous function that is a generalization of the input data, the finite set of sampled data $\{(x, y)/f(x, y)\}$. It is also expected to be a good approximation of the original function $f(x, y)$, of which only a finite number of sampled values are available.

For the task of Example 8.4, we found that acceptable learning could not be achieved at a reasonably low order of functional expansion. However, when the outerproduct was used in combination with the functional expansion procedure, good results were obtained readily.

8.3 A Brief Consideration of the Mathematical Basis for the Functional-Link Net

We shall not indulge in a lengthy discussion of Sobajic's analysis, but shall merely cite enough of his results to indicate that, in principle, it is indeed always possible to solve supervised learning problems with a "flat net"—that is, one with no hidden layers—provided we use the functional-link approach. This finding constitutes a drastic departure from the credo that hidden layers are all-important.

Let us consider the possibility of learning with a flat net. Let there be P patterns, each with N elements. For a net with one output, let the net configuration be as shown in Figure 8.3. For pattern p, the pattern components are $x_i^{(p)}$ and the output is $y^{(p)}$. The weighting factors along the links are w_i, and the node threshold is θ, these being true for all the patterns, $p = 1, 2, 3, \ldots, P$.

Thus, in general,

$$y = \frac{1}{1 + e^{-\alpha \mathrm{net}}} \tag{8.3}$$

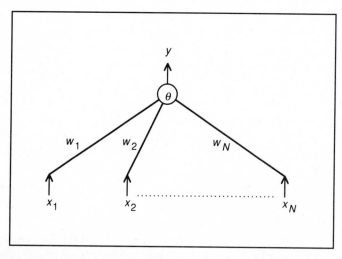

Figure 8.3   Delta-rule processing for the functional-link net.

or

$$net = \ell n \left(\frac{y}{1-y} \right)^{1/\alpha} = z \qquad (8.4)$$

That is,

$$w_1 x_1^{(p)} + \ldots + w_N x_N^{(p)} + \theta = z^{(p)} \qquad p = 1, 2, \ldots, P \qquad (8.5)$$

or, for all P patterns,

$$\begin{bmatrix} x_1^{(1)} & \cdots & x_N^{(1)} & 1 \\ \vdots & \ddots & \vdots & \vdots \\ x_1^{(P)} & \cdots & x_N^{(P)} & 1 \end{bmatrix} \begin{bmatrix} w_1 \\ w_2 \\ w_N \\ \theta \end{bmatrix} = \begin{bmatrix} z^{(1)} \\ \vdots \\ z^{(P)} \end{bmatrix} \qquad (8.6)$$

Thus, finding the weights for a flat net consists of solving a system of simultaneous linear equations for the weights w_i and the threshold θ. In the following discussion, we drop the distinction between w and θ and consider the sum of the number of weights and threshold to be N. This action simplifies the notation.

That is, we need to solve the linear matrix equation

$$\underline{X}\,\underline{w} = \underline{z} \qquad (8.7)$$

where the dimensions of $\underline{X}$ are $P \times N$.

We note that if $P = N$ and the determinant of X is not zero, that is Det $\underline{X} \neq o$, then

$$\underline{w} = \underline{X}^{-1}\underline{z} \qquad (8.8)$$

If $P < N$, then we can partition $\underline{X}$ to obtain a matrix $\underline{X}_F$ of dimension $P \times P$. We set $w_{P+1} = w_{P+2} = \ldots = w_N = o$ and, if Det $\underline{X}_F \neq o$, then

$$\underline{w} = \underline{X}_F^{-1}\underline{z} \qquad (8.9)$$

If we do not do this partitioning explicitly, we will find that we can obtain a large number of solutions, perhaps an infinite number of them, all of which satisfy the given constraints for the few patterns provided as examples.

The more interesting case is where $P > N$. Then, we have

$$\begin{matrix} [\underline{X}] & [\underline{w}] \\ (P \times N) & (N \times 1) \end{matrix} = \begin{matrix} [\underline{z}] \\ (P \times 1) \end{matrix} \qquad (8.10)$$

Because the functional link can generate an infinitely large number of orthonormal functions, we can "enhance" the columns of $\underline{X}$ so that N is increased to N_{FL}, and N_{FL} can always be made to be equal to or greater than P. We then have

$$
\begin{array}{ccc}
[\underline{X}_{FL}] & [\underline{w}_{FL}] & [\underline{z}] \\
(P \times N_{FL}) & (N_{FL} \times 1) & = & (P \times 1)
\end{array}
\tag{8.11}
$$

Thus, if $N_{FL} = P$ and Det $\underline{X}_{FL} \neq o$, then

$$
\underline{w}_{FL} = \underline{X}_{FL}^{-1} = \underline{z},
\tag{8.12}
$$

Expression (8.11) is an exact flat-net solution.

If $N_{FL} > P$, and rank $\underline{X}_{FL} = P$, we proceed as in equation (8.9). When $P > N$, we can proceed in the "conventional" manner, to obtain

$$
\underline{w} = (\underline{X}^t \underline{X})^{-1} \underline{X}^t \underline{z}
\tag{8.13}
$$

Pseudoinversion does indeed give a best fit solution. That solution is often unacceptable, however, as indicated by the high error value at the end of the learning process.

This analysis indicates that the functional-expansion model always yields a flat-net solution if a sufficiently large number of additional orthonormal functions are used in the enhancement and if data-compression preprocessing is used to remove redundant patterns.

8.4   Supervised Learning with the Functional-Link Net

In this section, we use four examples to illustrate the characteristics of the functional-link net when used for supervised learning. In the first two examples, the patterns are enhanced with use of the outerproduct approach, whereas in the third example, functional enhancement is the more effective mode. In the fourth example, the learning task is so challenging that both the outerproduct and functional enhancement modes of enhancement are used in combination. Some of the elegance and superior qualities of the functional-link net are demonstrated in these examples.

Example 8.1 The Parity-2 Problem.   In the parity-2, or XOR, problem the patterns and the associated outputs are as follows:

Pattern Number	x_1	x_2	Associated Output y
1	-1	-1	1
2	-1	1	-1
3	1	-1	-1
4	1	1	1

The patterns can be plotted in a two-dimensional space as shown in Figure 8.4(a). We note that the even-parity patterns have an associated output value of 1 and the odd-parity patterns have an output of -1. The associated input–output pairs were learned both with the functional-link approach and with the generalized delta rule approach. The network architectures for the functional-link net and for the semilinear generalized delta rule net are compared in Figures 8.4(b) and 8.4(c). The rate of decrease of system error with the number of presentations of the set of all four patterns is shown in Figure 8.5. The improvement in the rate of learning is dramatic. ■

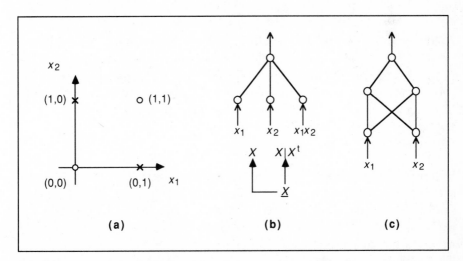

Figure 8.4   The parity-2 or XOR problem. (a) The four patterns to be classified XOR problem. (b) Functional-link net without hidden layer. (c) The generalized delta rule net.

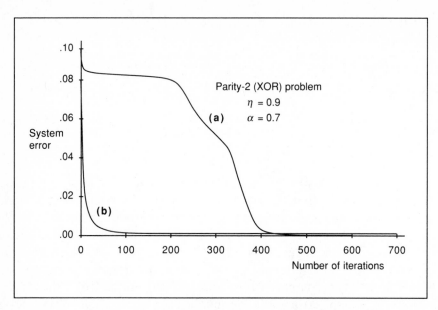

Figure 8.5 Comparison of rates of learning. (a) Generalized delta rule net with one hidden layer. (b) Functional-link net without internal layers.

Example 8.2 The Parity-3 Problem.

Results obtained in the parity-3 problem are similar to those in the parity-2 cases. These results are shown in Figures 8.6 and 8.7. Note that, in the case of the parity-3 problem, it was essential that two successive outerproduct operations be carried out. If we had stopped at the first step, the flat net and the delta rule would not have been able to solve the problem. This latter point is shown in Figure 8.8. ∎

Example 8.3 Learning a Function of One Variable.

The task of learning a function is a stringent one. In this task, we present the net with 20 sampled points of a curve and ask that the net learn the input–output pairs and then generate an estimate of the original function. In essence, we use a net to represent a function.

In this case, we use the functional-expansion model and map the one component of the input pattern onto a larger space spanned by $\sin(\pi x)$, $\cos(\pi x)$, $\sin(2\pi x)$, $\cos(2\pi x)$, $\sin(3\pi x)$, and so on, except that we retained only the terms shown in Figure 8.8(a). Other terms could have been retained also. The architectures of the flat functional-link net and the multilayered semilinear generalized delta rule net are compared in Figure 8.9.

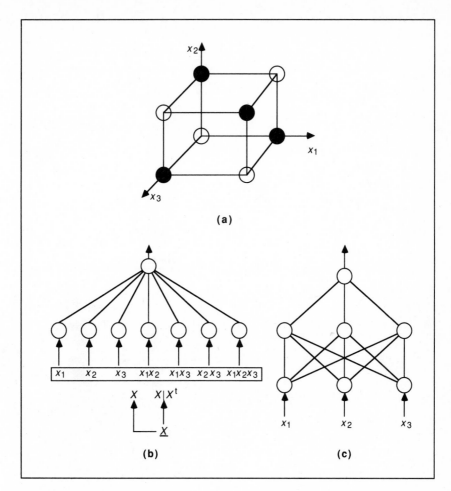

Figure 8.6   The parity-3 problem. (a) Patterns in the parity-3 problem. (b) Functional-link net with no hidden layers. (c) Generalized delta rule net.

The respective learning rates attained with these nets are shown in Figure 8.10. The representations learned are shown in Figure 8.11.   ■

Example 8.4 Learning a Function of Two Variables.   We obtained 100 sampled points of a surface synthesized from two two-dimensional Gaussians, shown in Figure 8.12, and tried to learn a network representation of that surface using the functional-link approach.

We found that a combined use of the functional expansion and outerproduct-pattern-enhancement procedures sufficed to enable us to use a flat-net architecture for learning a representation of the surface.

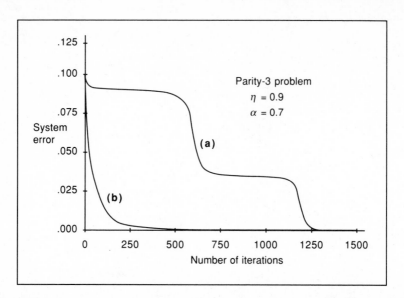

Figure 8.7   Comparison of rates of learning. (a) Generalized delta rule net with one hidden layer. (b) Functional-link net without a hidden layer.

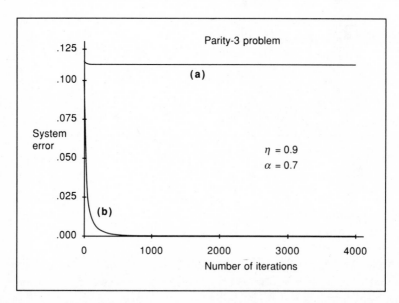

Figure 8.8   Comparison of learning rates in the net with successive outer-product-enhancement transformations. (a) With only one stage of outer product transformation. (b) With two successive stages of outer product transformation.

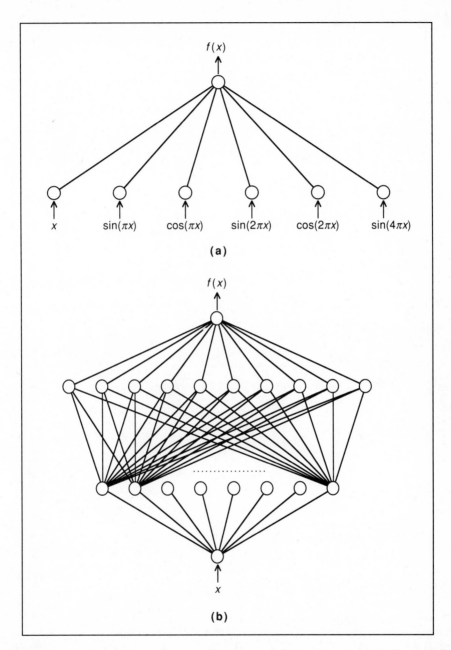

Figure 8.9   Comparison of net architectures. (a) The functional-link net. (b) The generalized delta rule.

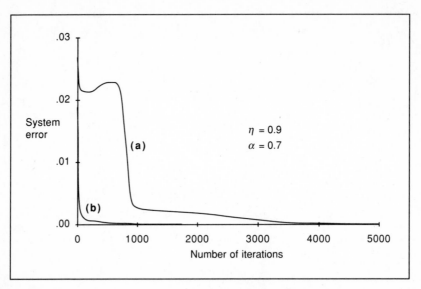

Figure 8.10   Comparison of rates of learning. (a) Generalized delta rule net.
(b) Functional-link net without hidden layers.

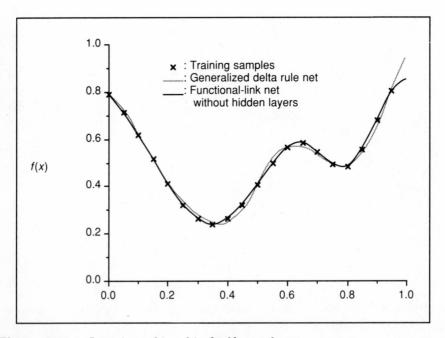

Figure 8.11   Learning achieved in feedforward nets.

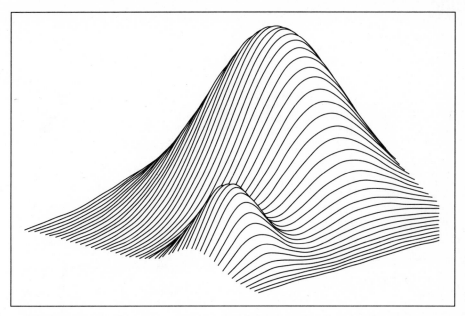

Figure 8.12   Schematic representation of a three-dimensional surface for which a network representation was to be learned.

The original two-component input pattern (x, y) was enhanced to a 19-component pattern with components: x, $\sin(\pi x)$, $\cos(\pi x)$, $\sin(2\pi x)$, $\cos(2\pi x)$, $\sin(3\pi x)$, $\cos(3\pi x)$, y, $\sin(\pi y)$, $\cos(\pi y)$, $\sin(2\pi y)$, $\cos(2\pi y)$, $\sin(3\pi y)$, $\cos(3\pi y)$, xy, $x\sin(\pi y)$, $x\cos(\pi y)$, $y\sin(\pi x)$, and $y\cos(\pi x)$.

As shown in Table 8.2, a comparison of the values of the surface function estimated with the functional-link net with those of the actual function indicates that a simple but accurate network representation of the function had been learned. A single set of weights suffices to provide accurate estimates of the surface not only at the training set points, but also at other points. A representation was also learnt using the generalized delta rule for the non-enhanced pattern. Two hidden layers were used, with eight nodes in the first hidden layer and 10 nodes in the second hidden layer.

A comparison of the learning rates for the two types of nets is shown in Figure 8.13. Again, there is a significant increase in the rate of learning in the case of the functional-link net.

Table 8.2 Comparison of network-estimated values and actual values of function $f(x_1, x_2)$.

Input	Estimated $f(x_1, x_2)$		Target
(x_1, x_2)	Functional-link net	Generalized delta rule net	Actual $f(x_1, x_2)$
(0.0,0.3)	0.2668	0.2437	0.2435
(0.0,0.6)	0.1441	0.1888	0.1673
(0.1,0.4)	0.4514	0.4678	0.4549
(0.1,0.6)	0.4308	0.4932	0.4549
(0.2,0.4)	0.4818	0.5002	0.4549
(0.2,0.7)	0.6743	0.6879	0.6619
(0.2,0.9)	0.2444	0.2775	0.2435
(0.3,0.8)	0.7408	0.6841	0.7501
(0.4,0.1)	0.1041	0.0984	0.1150
(0.4,0.7)	0.6799	0.6377	0.6619
(0.5,0.0)	0.4426	0.4020	0.4550
(0.5,0.1)	0.2476	0.2012	0.2436
(0.5,0.5)	0.0563	0.0891	0.0697
(0.6,0.2)	0.1655	0.1909	0.1718
(0.7,0.2)	0.2180	0.3543	0.2002
(0.7,0.4)	0.0729	0.0941	0.0701
(0.8,0.1)	0.1212	0.1765	0.1177
(0.8,0.5)	0.1680	0.1141	0.1627
(0.9,0.1)	0.0328	0.0456	0.0330
(0.9,0.4)	0.2894	0.2021	0.2652
(0.9,0.9)	0.0012	0.0120	0.0012
(1.0,0.4)	0.0459	0.0538	0.0411
(1.0,0.8)	0.0342	0.0629	0.0332
(1.0,1.0)	0.0002	0.0093	0.0002

8.5 Combined Supervised and Unsupervised Learning

The functional-link approach aims at producing a sufficiently enhanced representation for the input patterns so that the associated (enhanced input–output) pairs can be learned with a flat net; that is, with a net that has no hidden layers.

One advantage of using a flat net for supervised learning is that both supervised and unsupervised learning can be carried out with the same net architecture, with no reconfiguring and no shuffling of data from one

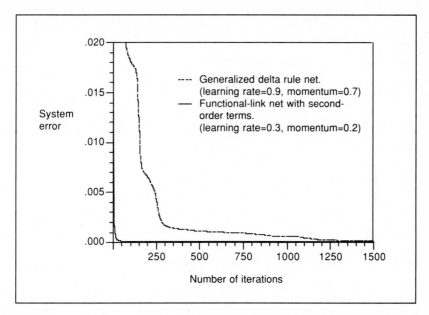

Figure 8.13 Comparison of system errors for the generalized delta rule net and the functional-link net for learning the function $\underline{f}(\underline{x}_1, \underline{x}_2)$.

net to another. This ability is important in any real pattern-recognition task. Such a pattern-recognition task might require the ability to deal with a very large number of patterns and to infer classification procedures for several different classes or categories.

A flat-net algorithm similar to that of ART2 [Carpenter and Grossberg 1987] can be used to sort the patterns into clusters that are similar to one another.

Taking each cluster, one at a time, we can examine the class labels of the patterns to see whether they are indeed "similar" to the extent of class membership also being the same. If they are, then we might conclude that the patterns are being described in a meaningful manner, and we could also synthesize a set of weights that will yield the desired output whenever one of those patterns is presented as input. The output model is (or models are) "associated" with the node used for unsupervised learning. During the supervised learning, only a few of the possibly many patterns need to be considered, since they are all nearly alike. All others can, in fact, be discarded, and only a few representative patterns need to be used in the

<u>Unsupervised Learning Phase</u>

1. Activate all output nodes j, $j = 1, 2, ..., J$

2. Initialize weights $b_{ji} = \varepsilon_{ji}$, where ε_{ij} are random numbers ($-1 < \varepsilon_{ij} < 1$)

3. Input pattern $\{y_i\}$, $i = 1, ..., N$

4. Calculate square of Euclidean distance: $ED_{ji}^2 = \sum_i (b_{ji} - y_i)^2$

5. Determine that j for which $ED_{ji}^2 < ED_{ki}^2$ for all $k = 1, 2, ..., J,$ $k \neq j$

6. Assign pattern $\{y_i\}$ as belonging to node j if ED_{ji}^2 also is equal to or less than ED_{ji}^2 (limit), where ED_{ji}^2 (limit) is a more or less arbitrarily chosen limiting radius beyond which patterns are not considered to be of that cluster

7. Update $b_{ji}(n+1) = \dfrac{n}{n+1} b_{ji}(n) + \dfrac{1}{n+1} y_i$ ($n = 0$ at initialization)

   Therefore, after input of first pattern $b_{ji}(1) = y_i$

8. Input next pattern, determine to which unsupervised learning node it belongs, and update corresponding $\{b_{ji}\}$.

<u>Supervised Learning</u>

1. *Classification*: All patterns belonging to the same cluster node j should produce same associated outputs $\{t_k\}$. This is carried out with a flat net, with a special set of output nodes "associated" with cluster node j.

2. *Estimation of attribute values*: All patterns belonging to the same cluster node j in fact have slightly different attribute values $\{t_k\}$. This is also carried out with a flat net, with a special set of output nodes "associated" with cluster node j.

Figure 8.14   Algorithm for combined supervised and unsupervised learning using the functional-link.

supervised training. The supervised learning then consists of learning how to estimate values of attributes in the neighborhood of that cluster. This circumstance of combined supervised and unsupervised learning is described in greater detail in Figure 8.14.

Another circumstance arises when patterns that are not alike in fact have the same class label. This circumstance should not be surprising, because all that is being signaled is that the disjoint volumes in pattern space that are labeled with the same class label are in fact "similar" on the basis of class label rather than in explicit pattern description.

This easy coexistence between supervised learning and unsupervised learning relieves a net of the burden of trying to associate many dissimilar patterns with the same output. In addition, often, if two groups that are not alike happen to end up in the same cluster, the message is that either the pattern description is not adequate or the vigilance factor is not adequately stringent. Or we need to acknowledge the stochastic nature of the phenomenon.

8.6 Associative Storage and Recall

In this section, we describe the use of a functional-link net for associative storage and recall. The functionality is similar to that of the Hopfield net, but the situations are significantly different.

Memorization consists of supervised learning. A pattern is stored if the associated output is specified; that is, we specify $t_k = 1$, for example. Many different patterns can be stored in this manner. Also, we need not specify that the desired output be 1; we might specify it as 0.8 equally well.

Now, if a distorted cue is fed to such a net, the output will not be 0.8. It might be 0.9 or 0.65, in which case the values of the error $(t_k - o_k)$ would be -0.10 and $+0.15$, correspondingly. Irrespective of whether the error is positive or negative, the input bits of the unenhanced pattern are changed asynchronously until the error is reduced to zero or to near zero and no further changes result in lower errors. One of the original stored patterns is then recovered.

Note that altering the value of one of the components of the original pattern changes the values of several of the components of the enhanced pattern. In assessing whether or not that change should be made, we need only to determine whether the partial sums of all those weighted components combine to decrease the error. If the answer is yes, then that change is made and retained. This procedure is demonstrated by the illustrations shown in Figures 8.15, 8.16, and 8.17.

The context is that of storing the letters T and C in a 3×3 memory. As shown in Figure 8.15, the net learns an enhanced pattern consisting of the nine pixel values and joint activations between each pixel and the four nearest neighbors. Learning is achieved readily. In Figure 8.16, we present the supervised learning flat net with a distorted T and also with a distorted C. In each case, the distortion consists of one bit being in error.

The errors (rather than the changes in error) are shown for various trial corrections attained as the bits were flipped asynchronously. Clearly, in this idealized case, minimum error was obtained when one of the correct patterns was recovered. In the case of T, the residual error was minimum for a correction made in the value of bit 5. A similar result was obtained in the case of C, except that in this case the value of the error was zero.

Similar results are shown in Figure 8.17 for distorted cues containing two error bits. Again for zero error, the original patterns were recovered.

These are but isolated results, and we do not know enough about this approach to assess its significance. We introduce it at this juncture merely to suggest that there may be virtue in keeping system architecture simple, even if more nodes are used or if some of the nodes are complex.

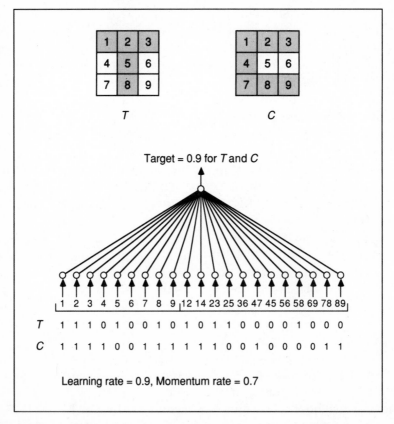

Figure 8.15   Illustration of associative recall of correct pattern on presentation of distorted pattern (1 error bit).

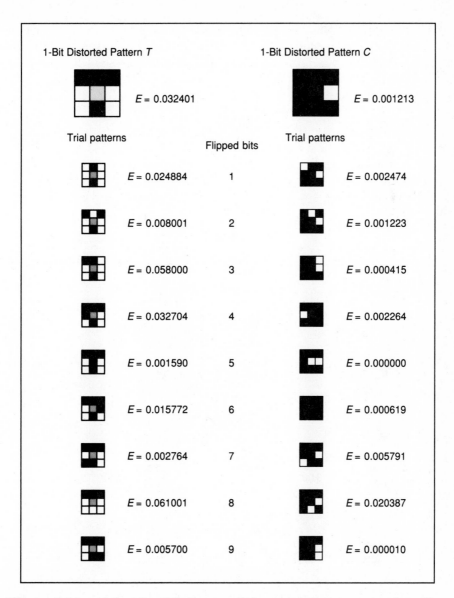

Figure 8.16   A functional-link net used for associative storage and recall.

8.7   Comments and Bibliographical Remarks

The functional link transforms the initial pattern representation to another one, usually to one of larger dimensions. Classes that cannot be separated in the original space are often separable in higher-dimension space. The transformations involved in the functional-link net are definitely nonlinear and the mathematical issue is therefore that of *nonlinear*

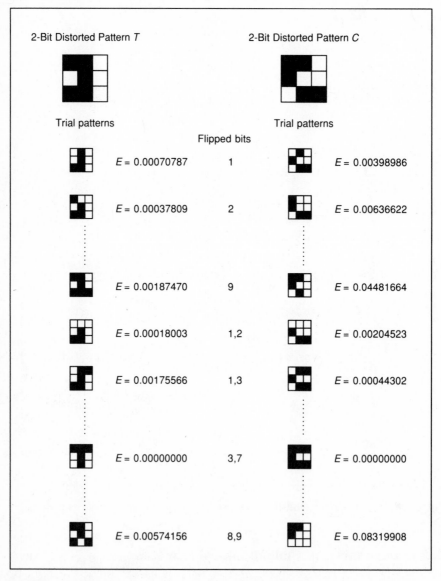

Figure 8.17   Illustration of associative recall of correct pattern on presentation of distorted pattern (with 1 and 2 error bits).

separability. Duda and Hart [1973] mention this possibility, and Sklansky and Wassel [1981] also provide important insight into these matters.

It is enlightening to focus on the special case (not a very restrictive one) where sufficient functional enhancement has been carried out so that a flat, or slab, net architecture can be used; that is, the delta rule can be used in place of the generalized delta rule. For this special case, the combined techniques of unsupervised and supervised learning can be used effectively to ensure that the number of linearly independent patterns presented to the functional-link net is neither overly large ($P >> N + 1$) nor overly small ($P << N + 1$). In the former case, establishment of linear independence and minimization of least-mean-square error may take a great deal of time; in the latter case, there is no unique solution for the weights for the link in the delta rule net. This latter situation is acceptable, but may lead to incorrect generalization.

Adaptive pattern-recognition *systems*, as implemented with artificial neural nets, are indeed likely to be an important aspect of modern computing. Because those systems will be composed of collections of subsystems carrying out diverse tasks, it is important—for hardware as well as software reasons—that the heterogeneous subsystems have certain aspects of commonality. This requirement is one of the reasons why the functional-link net approach and the resulting simplications in network architecture may be worthy of further serious investigation.

8.8 References and Bibliography

1. Carpenter, G.A. and S. Grossberg, 1987. Art 2: Self-organization of stable category recognition codes for analog input patterns, *Applied Optics*, Vol. 26, pp. 1–23.

2. Chen, H.H., Y.C. Lee, G.Z. Sun, H.Y. Lee, T. Maxwell, and C.L. Giles, 1986. High order correlation model for associative memory, *American Institute of Physics Conference Proceedings, No. 151: Neural Networks for Computing,* Snowbird, Utah, pp. 398–403.

3. Duda, R.O. and P.E. Hart, 1973. *Pattern Classification and Scene Analysis*, Wiley, New York.

4. Giles, C.L. and T. Maxwell, 1987. Learning, invariance, and generalization in higher-order neural networks, *Applied Optics*, Vol. 26, pp. 4972–4978.

5. Klassen, M.S. and Y.H. Pao, 1988. Characteristics of the functional-link net: A higher order delta rule net, *IEEE Proceedings of 2nd Annual International Conference on Neural Networks*, June, San Diago, CA.

6. Lee, Y.C., G. Doolen, H.H. Chen, G.Z. Sun, T. Maxwell, H.Y. Lee, and C.L. Giles, 1986. Machine learning using a higher order correlation network, *Physica 22D*, pp. 276–306, North-Holland, Amsterdam.

7. Lippmann, R.P., 1987. An introduction to computing with neural nets, *IEEE ASSP Magazine*, Vol. 4, pp. 4–22.

8. Nilsson, N. J., 1965. *Learning Machines: Foundations of Trainable Pattern Classifying Systems*, McGraw-Hill, New York.

9. Pomerleau, D.A., 1987. The meta-generalized delta rule: A new algorithm for learning in connectionist networks. Computer Science Dept. Report, CMU-CS-87-185, Carnegie-Mellon University, Pittsburgh, PA.

10. Rumelhart, D.E., G.E. Hinton, and R.J. Williams, 1986. Learning internal representations by error propagation. In D.E. Rumelhart and J.L. McClelland (Eds.), *Parallel Distributed Processing: Explorations in the Microstructures of Cognition,* Vol. 1: *Foundations.* MIT Press, Cambridge, MA.

11. Sejnowski, T.J., 1986. Higher-order Boltzmann machines. *American Institute of Physics Conference Proceedings, No. 151: Neural Networks for Computing,* Snowbird, Utah. pp. 398–403.

12. Sklansky J. and G.N. Wassel, 1981. *Pattern Classifiers and Trainable Machines*, Springer-Verlag, New York.

13. Sobajic, D., 1988. *Neural Nets for Control of Power Systems*, Ph.D. Thesis, Computer Science Dept., Case Western Reserve University, Cleveland, OH.

CHAPTER 9

Linking of Symbolic and Subsymbolic Processing: The Roles of Fuzzy Logic, Pattern Recognition, and Neural Nets

9.1 Introduction

Fuzzy logic provides a means for linking symbolic processing and numeric computations, two quite different matters. Symbolic processing is usually done in terms of linguistic symbols and is concerned with concepts and qualitative relationships, whereas numeric computations are concerned with precise, detailed algorithmic manipulations of quantitative information. Both aspects of information processing are essential to computer information-processing systems dealing with real-world tasks.

The membership function is an important aspect of this linkage. It is defined in the domain of the numeric variables and gives a measure of how compatible the numeric description is with a qualitative entity. Or, it gives a measure of the possibility that the concept in question might correspond to the set of numeric data in question.

The membership function plays a critical role in establishing that linkage, but it is also a source of weakness. "Nonbelievers" generally are uneasy about how membership functions are to be synthesized or specified and maintained self-consistent within the scope of a task. There are also questions of whether any one general extension principle is in fact general enough for all circumstances. It would seem that the answer would depend on how the membership functions were obtained in the first place.

In this chapter, we point out that neural nets can perform an important role in such matters by providing quantitative representations of the qualitative concepts and by maintaining these representations correctly throughout the processing undergone by the qualitative, linguistic symbols.

9.2   Network Representations of Membership Functions

We saw in Chapter 8 that a neural net can synthesize a network representation of a continuous function given a reasonable number of isolated instances of that function. The network takes the associated input–output pairs consisting of {dependent variable, function value} and synthesizes a network representation of the continuous function. This means that a neural network can utilize a finite number of instances to build a membership function that might represent the concept in question in a valid manner over a wide range of possibilities. We discuss this matter in some detail in this chapter.

Membership functions implemented in these manners are no longer arbitrary, subject to change at a whim. Set operations, syllogisms, and extension principles, for example, all need to be represented in terms of the neural nets and of the patterns that are the inputs and outputs of these neural nets. There is a strengthening of the entire formal structure of the linkage, but with that strengthening also come constraints. We use an example to bring together in one discussion various related matters. The example is that of hiring a floor supervisor.

The personnel manager of a moderate-sized business is informed by the owner that the plant needs a warehouse floor supervisor and that she should hire a suitable person for that position as soon as possible. She is also told by the owner that the floor supervisor needs to be "tall" and "not clumsy." It is a fact that such vague directions are often sufficient in real-world situations. As the company is not large, the personnel manager knows the owner well and believes that she and the owner have a common idea of what constitutes "tall" and "not clumsy." These qualitative (vague) concepts would be fuzzy sets defined in the domain of height and defined by the membership functions shown in Figure 9.1.

The personnel manager certainly does not have factual data to back up her idea of what the membership functions should be. But she does have a few data points provided by previous incidents, and she fills in the rest.

Several details deserve attention at this point. First, we assume that we indeed do synthesize some sort of membership function for our own

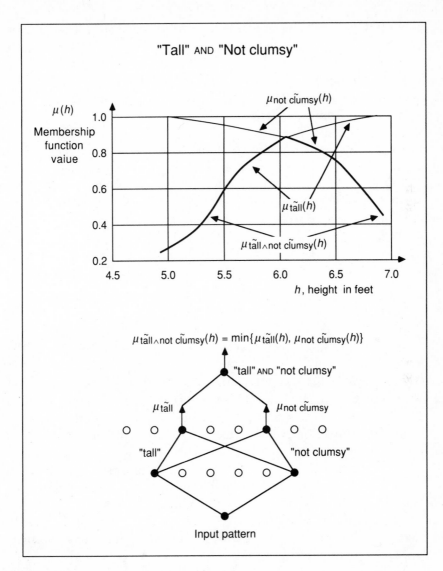

Figure 9.1 Membership function for the intersection of two fuzzy sets.

use when we reason or make decisions. In computer implementations of such decision making processes, however, we need to make these representatives explicit. As we demonstrated in Chapter 8, this specification can be done with a neural net. *The neural net is then a network representation of that membership function.*

Second, the membership function so determined is not arbitrarily represented by an ad hoc functional form and a few haphazardly chosen parameters. It is tightly constrained by the known instances supplied as examples of the possibility distribution. It can and must be updated as new examples become available. For example, the personnel manager can and must learn from experience if she finds that her idea of "tall" is significantly different from that of her employer.

Third, given that she can judge on the basis of "tall" and on the basis of "not clumsy," how is the personnel manager to rate candidates on the basis of "tall" AND "not clumsy"? From a variety of views, fuzzy logic arrives at the same result; namely, that the membership function of the intersection of the two fuzzy sets should be given by

$$\mu_{\tilde{A} \wedge \tilde{B}}(x) = \min\{\mu_{\tilde{A}}(x), \mu_{\tilde{B}}(x)\} \qquad (9.1)$$

Thus,

$$\mu_{\widetilde{\text{tall}} \wedge \text{not } \widetilde{\text{clumsy}}}(h) = \min\{\mu_{\widetilde{\text{tall}}}(h), \mu_{\text{not } \widetilde{\text{clumsy}}}(h)\} \qquad (9.2)$$

This membership function represented by the heavy line shown in Figure 9.1.

We know that this result is suitable mathematically in that it has all the requisite characteristics of being distributive, associative and so on. This result also makes sense. The possibility-distribution meaning of the membership function requires that we accord significance to only the lower of the two membership-function values.

For example, at height 5 feet, we have to recognize that the possibility of the candidate being suitable needs be judged on only the basis of the requirement that he be "tall." We are confident that he is not clumsy. This is an inexorable fact and there is absolutely no reason to consider using some other combination of the two membership functions to provide some other evaluation of the situation.

In terms of neural-net computing, the entire task of evaluating the candidate could be represented in terms of three neural-net computations, as shown schematically in Figure 9.2. MINNET is similar to MAXNET. However, it not only identifies the minimum value of all the inputs, but also it passes on that value.

Similarly, let us suppose that the owner had specified instead that the floor supervisor should be "reasonably tall" OR "agile," having in mind that agile persons can compensate quite well for lack of height.

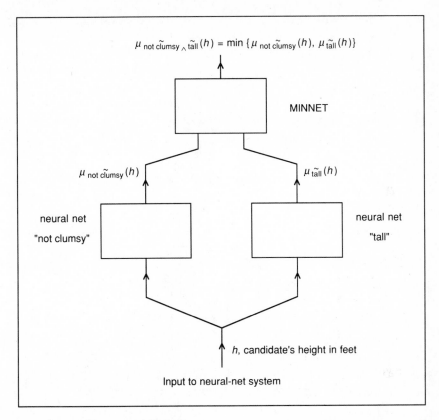

Figure 9.2   Fuzzy sets and fuzzy logic intersection operation represented in terms of neural nets.

Again, the personnel manager might have an idea that she knows what the owner has in mind when he says "reasonably tall" AND "agile." However, neural net representations of these fuzzy sets, learned from actual examples, might be those shown in Figure 9.3.

Again, there is a question of how a candidate is to be evaluated on the basis of "reasonably tall" OR "agile." Fuzzy logic prescribes that a membership function of the union of two fuzzy sets be

$$\mu_{\tilde{A} \cup \tilde{B}}(x) = \max\{\mu_{\tilde{A}}(x), \mu_{\tilde{B}}(x)\} \tag{9.3}$$

This expression is represented by the darker curve in Figure 9.3.

We point out that this solution makes eminent sense because it agrees with what we would want the result to be on the basis of semantics. After all, since either quality is sufficient, we need to focus on only what will qualify the candidate, and we need not penalize him for other shortcomings. Therefore,

$$\mu_{\widetilde{\text{reasonably tall}} \cup \widetilde{\text{agile}}}(h) = \max\{\mu_{\widetilde{\text{reasonably tall}}}(h), \mu_{\widetilde{\text{agile}}}(h)\} \qquad (9.4)$$

The entire process can be represented in terms of a network of neural

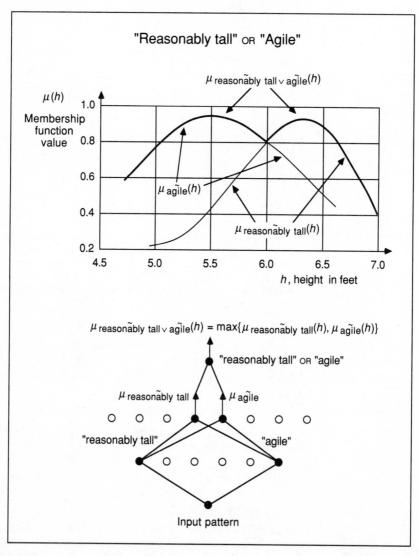

Figure 9.3   Membership function for the union of two fuzzy sets.

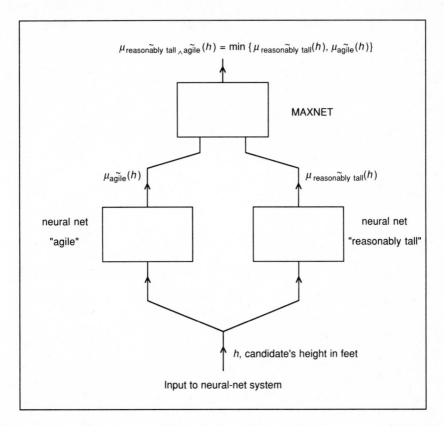

Figure 9.4 Fuzzy sets and fuzzy logic union operations represented in terms of neural nets.

nets, as shown in Figure 9.4. Note that we have now represented fuzzy logic as well as fuzzy sets in terms of neural nets.

9.3 Modeling the Extension Principle

There is need for an extension principle that is of general validity. It so happens that one or more such principles have been proposed, but one or more would have to be invented if there had been none. The reason for this statement is as follows. Consider an explicit function that constitutes a mapping from the space of the input variables into the space of the output variables. It is a crisp relationship in the sense that, for any one instance, the input variables have precise values and the output also has precise values(s). Under some circumstances, however, it may be more meaningful to acknowledge explicitly that there is uncertainty in the values of the input variables. Thus, the temperature might be approximately 300° C meaning that there is possibility that it is 290° C or any other value within a range of values. In other words, temperature might be defined more accurately as a fuzzy set, a vague quantity named "approximately 300° C." Similarly, pressure, another input variable, might also be a fuzzy set, and so on. The crisp functional form of the original relationship is still of interest. The principal question is, what are the possibilities or membership-function values of the outcome?

The general extension principle as proposed by Zadeh [1975] and as stated in Chapter 3 follows.

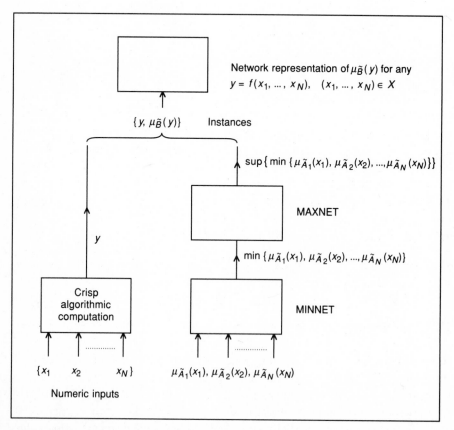

Figure 9.5 Illustration of procedure for synthesis of network representation of a fuzzied functional relationship.

Definition 9.1 *A general extension principle for finding fuzzy set analogs of crisp procedures may be defined as follows: Let X be a Cartesian product of universes $X = X_1, \ldots, X_r$, and let $\tilde{A}_1, \ldots, \tilde{A}_r$ be r fuzzy sets in $X_1, \ldots, X_r$, respectively. The function f is a mapping from X to a universe Y, $y = f(x_1, \ldots, x_r)$. Then, a fuzzy set $\tilde{B}$ in Y is defined by*

$$\tilde{B} = \{(y, \mu_{\tilde{B}}(y)) | y = f(x_1, \ldots, x_r), (x_1, \ldots, x_r) \in X\}$$

where

$$\mu_{\tilde{B}}(y) = \begin{cases} \sup \; \min\{\mu_{\tilde{A}_1}(x_1), \ldots, \mu_{\tilde{A}_r}(x_r)\} & \text{if } f^{-1}(y) \neq 0 \\ & \{(x_1, \ldots, x_r) \in f^{-1}(y)\} \\ 0 & \text{otherwise} \end{cases}$$

where f^{-1} is the inverse of f and sup *denotes the least upper bound.*

The physical meaning of $f^{-1}(y)$ is that it is that value of x (or possibly that set of values of x) for which $f(x)$ would be y.

Despite its somewhat formal nature, this principle is an easily understandable logical consequence of the two fuzzy-set operations encountered previously—those of intersection and union. The extension principle states that an output has no greater possibility than the smallest of all the possibilities of the individual components that constitute the input to the computations in question. This reasoning is compatible with the reasoning underlying the fuzzy intersection operation, even though in this case we are dealing with a product space. However, there may be many ways of arriving at any one numeric output, and the possibility for the outcome should be the largest value of all the various possibilities—hence the provision for taking the least upper bound. This second step is in accord with the fuzzy union operation.

A neural-net representation of the procedure for synthesis of a network representation of a fuzzied relationship is illustrated schematically in Figure 9.5. The most difficult part is determining the least upper bound of min $\{\mu_{\tilde{A}_1}(x_1), \mu_{\tilde{A}_2}(x_2), \ldots, \mu_{\tilde{A}_N}(x_N)\}$. That is, the procedure needs to be certain that it has considered all combinations of $\{x_1, x_2, \ldots, x_N\}$ for which $f(x_1, x_2, \ldots, x_N) \to y$. This is generally a tiresome task and realistically can be carried out thoroughly in only a few isolated instances. The information for these instances, in the form of associated input–output pairs, is then passed to another neural net, which finally learns the relationship between y and $\mu_{\tilde{B}}(y)$.

9.4 Fuzzy Syllogisms

The study of how crisp syllogisms might be fuzzied is also interesting and rewarding, especially in illuminating the different roles that a neural network can play in representing such relationships. We shall see that, in fuzzifying the relationship A implies B, we can implement not only the transitions

$$A \to \tilde{A} \quad \text{and} \quad B \to \tilde{B}$$

but also the transition of implies $\to$ $\widetilde{\text{implies}}$. We shall describe these matters next.

To facilitate our understanding of the different roles that neural nets can play in the instance, we display in Figure 9.6 a graphical representation of the crisp syllogism

if A implies B

and B implies C

then A implies C

We use the language of fuzzy sets to describe the completely crisp situation. This language should cause no confusion, and the slight degree of artificiality is more than compensated for by the ease of the subsequent transition to truly fuzzy sets.

For example, in Figure 9.6, we say that the concept of A is represented by the neural net A. It is a crisp concept because the output is $\mu_A(\underline{x}) = 1$ for a certain $\underline{x}$. (For the present purposes, we put aside questions of degeneracy in representation.) For all other possible $\underline{x}$, $\mu_A(\underline{x}) = 0$. Similarly, a specific $\underline{y}$ is acknowledged to be a crisp representation of B. The relationship that A implies B is represented by the fact that, when $\underline{x}$ is presented to the neural net A, do we not only obtain $\mu_A(x) = 1$, but also an output $\underline{y}$, and that $\underline{y}$ is acknowledged by neural net B by a value of $\mu_B(\underline{y}) = 1$. Therefore, $A \to B$. Similar remarks apply to the relationship $B \to C$. The only question left in this graphical depiction of a crisp syllogism is whether in a neural net implementation we should eventually also have A generate $\underline{z}$ as well as $\underline{y}$. In latter case C would recognize the $\underline{z}$ from A, as well as a $\underline{z}$ from B and the syllogism would have been implemented.

It is a straightforward matter to go from this depiction of a crisp syllogism to a fuzzy one. In the case of a fuzzy set $\tilde{A}$, input patterns $\underline{x}$ do not yield $\mu_{\tilde{A}}(\underline{x})$ values of 1 or 0. Rather, the values of $\mu_{\tilde{A}}(\underline{x})$ fall in the range of 0 to 1 and $\mu_{\tilde{A}}(\underline{x})$ is the membership function that defines the

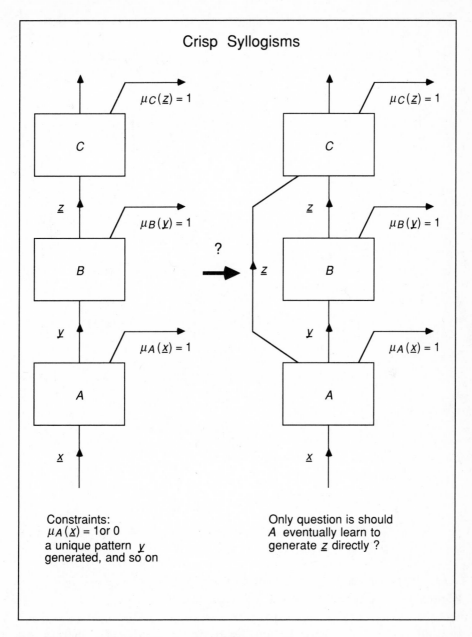

Figure 9.6 Network illustration of a crisp syllogism.

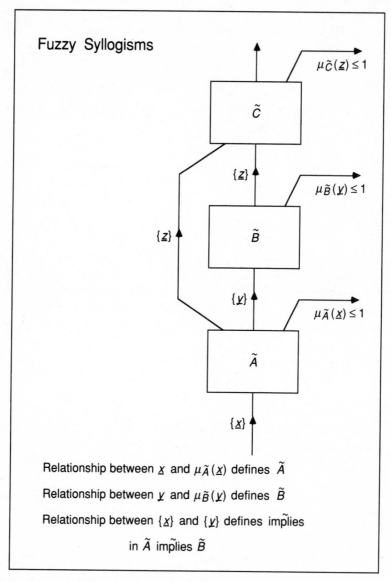

Fuzzy Syllogisms

$\mu_{\tilde{C}}(\underline{z}) \leq 1$

$\mu_{\tilde{B}}(\underline{y}) \leq 1$

$\mu_{\tilde{A}}(\underline{x}) \leq 1$

Relationship between $\underline{x}$ and $\mu_{\tilde{A}}(\underline{x})$ defines $\tilde{A}$

Relationship between $\underline{y}$ and $\mu_{\tilde{B}}(\underline{y})$ defines $\tilde{B}$

Relationship between $\{\underline{x}\}$ and $\{\underline{y}\}$ defines $\widetilde{\text{implies}}$

in $\tilde{A}$ $\widetilde{\text{implies}}$ $\tilde{B}$

Figure 9.7   Network illustration of fuzzy syllogisms.

concept $\tilde{A}$. Similarly, the relationship between $\underline{y}$ and $\mu_{\tilde{B}}(\underline{y})$ defines the fuzzy set $\tilde{B}$, and corresponding remarks apply to $\tilde{C}$.

It is the relationship between the set $\{\underline{x}\}$ and the set $\{\underline{y}\}$ that defines the fuzzy relationship $\widetilde{\text{implies}}$. It is quite independent of the definitions of

$\tilde{A}$ and $\tilde{B}$, and may be taught to the network $\tilde{A}$ through associated pairs of $\{\underline{x}/\underline{y}\}$.

A graphical depiction of the fuzzy syllogism

$$\text{if } \tilde{A} \ \widetilde{\text{implies}}_1 \ \tilde{B}$$

$$\text{and } \tilde{B} \ \widetilde{\text{implies}}_2 \ \tilde{C}$$

$$\text{then } \tilde{A} \ \widetilde{\text{implies}}_3 \ \tilde{C}$$

is given in Figure 9.7. Again, there is a question of whether to modify $\tilde{A}$ to generate a $\underline{z}$ as well as a $\underline{y}$, appropriately.

The situation can become quite complicated if we bestow a higher degree of fuzziness to $\widetilde{\text{implies}}$. A single $\underline{x}$ could, for example, generate a distribution function for $\underline{y}$—a "cloud" of $\underline{y}$, so to speak. The recognition of this cloud as $\tilde{B}$ would involve the convolution of two membership functions, one characterizing the uncertainty represented by the cloud generation and the other in the recognition of any $\underline{y}$ as possibly being $\tilde{B}$. Both matters can be implemented with neural nets.

The central thrust of the discussion in this chapter is that neural-net representations of the use of fuzzy logic in pattern information processing are useful both in clarifying concepts and in providing means for implementing such processing.

9.5 Comments and Bibliographical Remarks

The material contained in this chapter is original. It touches on an extremely important aspect of pattern recognition that is only dimly realized and is rarely articulated well: When we try to recognize a pattern, it helps if we know what we are looking for. The really difficult problems of perception will not be solved by any simple pattern-recognition algorithm acting alone; the algorithm must instead act in combination with other stored knowledge. Pattern recognition needs to be adaptive not only in terms of any one algorithm, but also in terms of interactions between "knowledge" and perception. The former will include knowledge in the form of sensory data [McClelland and Rumelhart 1981], as well as of other forms of knowledge, expressed in the equivalent of linguistic symbolic statements and related to quantitative phenomena through fuzzy sets.

This challenging area of adaptive pattern recognition deserves our attention.

9.6 References and Bibliography

1. McClelland, J. L. and D. E. Rumelhart, 1981. An interactive activation model of context effects in letter perception: Part 1. An account of basic findings, *Psychological Review*, Vol. 88, pp. 375–407.

2. Zadeh, L., 1975. The concept of a linguistic variable and its application to approximate reasoning, Parts 1, 2, and 3, *Information Sciences*, Vol. 8, pp. 199–249, pp. 301–357, Vol. 9, pp. 43–80.

CHAPTER 10

Issues in the Use of Adaptive Pattern Recognition

10.1 Introduction

In this chapter we reexamine the nature and scope of adaptive pattern recognition and examine the issues that arise when we use adaptive pattern recognition in various tasks.

The word *adaptive* in the terminology of adaptive pattern recognition is used to emphasize the importance of being able to deal with patterns that are distorted by noise, of being able to modify classification procedures adaptively in accordance with changing circumstances, and of being able to self-organize internal structures of memories and pattern classifiers adaptively in accordance with the structure of pattern data. There is, therefore, no hard and fast intrinsic connection between adaptive pattern recognition and parallel processing, or between the former and neural-net computing or distributed processing. For example, all the algorithms—such as the Hopfield associative memory, the generalized delta rule, ART, and the functional-link net—can be executed with conventional serial digital processing, as indeed they have been.

Nevertheless, neural-net concepts are relevant because patterns may be large and detailed, and parallel processing with interconnected multiprocessors might eventually become an essential part of any practicable scheme of adaptive pattern recognition. Given this highly probable eventuality, it becomes important that algorithms and pattern information-processing structures be cast in the form of network processes.

In this chapter, we examine several categories of tasks that have been attempted with the adaptive pattern-recognition approach, and we address the basic issues and intrinsic difficulties. We place equal emphasis on the issues and on the tasks because, in our view, this approach gives us a better intuitive understanding of the technical challenges and opportunities.

Basic issues of prime importance and interest are

1. Structures within patterns

2. Patterns of linguistic symbols

3. Structures in patterns of linguistic symbols

4. Associations with varying degrees of belief

5. Estimation versus classification—need for accuracy

6. Temporal correlation between inputs and outputs—conditioning, learning and control

7. Possibility of using adaptive pattern recognition to solve truly difficult problems

These issues will be discussed in the following sections in the context of related generic tasks. In some instances, we demonstrate techniques for dealing with specific problems. In general, we do not intend to imply that such techniques are the preferred ones. The demonstrations are principally to illuminate the nature of the issues.

10.2 Dealing with Structure Within Patterns

In the realm of *geometric* pattern recognition, patterns are represented as vectors. That is, situations are coded into the form of a sequence of real numbers. The sequences are of a fixed length, although some flexibility can be accommodated through *masking*, and the names or meanings of the individual components of the patterns are left implicit. The situation is very different in the cases of signal processing, image processing, language processing and other tasks of similar nature. In such situations, the relevant parts of a pattern generally are not specified and, in many cases, it is the structural relationships between parts of a pattern that are of interest.

For example, in image processing, we might want to recognize the presence of a rectangle in the field of view independent of the position or orientation of the rectangle or of the size of the rectangle. Similarly, in the recognition of handwritten letters, our interest is the structure within the letter rather than the size or location or orientation of that letter.

In the past, concern with this type of task gave rise to a type of pattern recognition called *syntactic pattern recognition*. That approach is based on mathematical linguistics and formal language theory, the idea being that we should be able to think of pattern in terms of sentences or strings of symbols. Strings may be of any length, and the classification task is that of deciding whether or not that sentence belongs to the language in question; that is, whether the sentence obeys the constraints of the grammar of that language. The pattern-recognition procedure is transformed into the task of parsing the sentence to see whether the latter could have been generated with the grammar of that language—that is, with the terminal symbols and production rules of the grammar. The syntactic pattern-recognition approach has had limited success in dealing with the general problem of recognizing structures in patterns. Only regular or context-free grammars can be inferred in a general systematic manner, and only "before" or "after" structural relationships can be accommodated in the format of the theory.

The neural-net approach to pattern recognition has inspired the formulation of other approaches to the recognition of structure in patterns, some of which are invariant to scale, position (translation), and orientation.

We discuss one such approach that is influenced by concepts contained in Minsky's and Papert's book on computational geometry [1969], in a series of papers by Lee and colleagues, [1986], Giles and Maxwell [1987], and Maxwell and colleagues, [1986] on the use of higher-order effects in learning, and on concepts incorporated in our functional-link net approach.

Translational Invariance

Consider a one-dimensional binary-valued pattern of 16 pixels, shown as a two-dimensional 4×4 display in Figure 10.1(a). The task is to recognize the presence of two contiguous dark pixels (with the value of 1), independent of the position of the array. The background pixels have a value of 0. In terms of the two-dimensional display, the task is that of recognizing the presence of a horizontal 2-pixel array, independent of the position of that array.

Boundary conditions are important, we will examine that matter in detail at a later stage of this discussion. For convenience, at the present

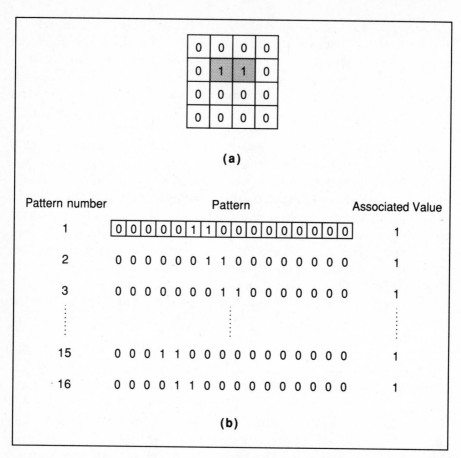

Figure 10.1   Sixteen patterns that form the equivalence class of a translational group.

we assume periodic boundary conditions. This means that we can focus our attention on a unit cell of 16-pixels, which is also our *observation space*. It is but one of an infinite array of such unit cells. All of these unit cells are identical, and focusing our attention on one such cell suffices for all purposes, both theoretical and pragmatic. In this model, what is lost from the display or observation space at the right-hand boundary appears on the left. In terms of the two-dimensional display, what disappears at the bottom right-hand corner of the display reenters the display at the top left-hand corner.

The sixteen one-dimensional patterns displayed in Figure 10.1(b) represent all the circumstances in which two dark contiguous pixels appear in observation space. For the present, we include pixels at the two boundaries as also being contiguous.

The task of recognizing that particular feature—the 2-pixel horizontal array—in a translationally invariant manner, can be regarded to be the same, in part, as that of synthesizing a net that will recognize all the sixteen patterns shown in Figure 10.1(b) to be equivalent, giving an output of 1, for example.

We think of the functional-link net in terms of a flat-net without a hidden layer. In order that a single set of weights may be able to recognize any and all of the translated patterns correctly, the equalities shown in Figure 10.2 must be true. The sum of those relationships is also true.

In learning the weights for the net, we could indeed follow the usual procedure of presenting the patterns sequentially and letting the weights converge to a stable set of values. However, in this simple case we can also view the process from another perspective.

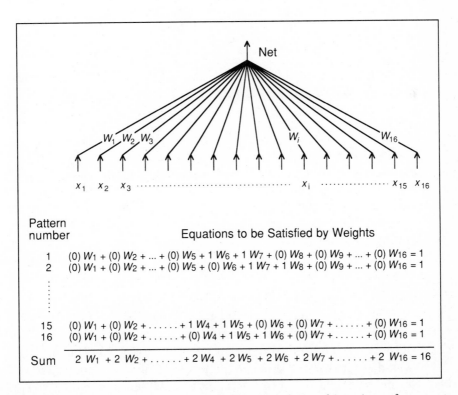

Pattern number	Equations to be Satisfied by Weights
1	$(0) W_1 + (0) W_2 + ... + (0) W_5 + 1 W_6 + 1 W_7 + (0) W_8 + (0) W_9 + ... + (0) W_{16} = 1$
2	$(0) W_1 + (0) W_2 + ... + (0) W_5 + (0) W_6 + 1 W_7 + 1 W_8 + (0) W_9 + ... + (0) W_{16} = 1$
⋮	
15	$(0) W_1 + (0) W_2 + ... + 1 W_4 + 1 W_5 + (0) W_6 + (0) W_7 + ... + (0) W_{16} = 1$
16	$(0) W_1 + (0) W_2 + ... + (0) W_4 + 1 W_5 + 1 W_6 + (0) W_7 + ... + (0) W_{16} = 1$
Sum	$2 W_1 + 2 W_2 + ... + 2 W_4 + 2 W_5 + 2 W_6 + 2 W_7 + ... + 2 W_{16} = 16$

Figure 10.2 Procedure for accomplishing translational invariance for an output unit.

After summing the sixteen equations, we have only one equation for the sixteen weights, namely

$$\left[\sum_g (x_1)_g\right] W_1 + \left[\sum_g (x_2)_g\right] W_2 + \ldots + \left[\sum_g (x_{16})_g\right] W_{16} = 16 \qquad (10.1)$$

That is, *any* initial one-dimensional 16-pixel pattern is subjected to all possible nonequivalent horizontal translations so that all possible different positions of the contiguous 2-pixel array are generated. The value of a pixel is observed for each of these configurations and the sum of the values over all possible configurations is obtained. That sum then constitutes the input to one node of a sixteen-node functional-link net.

Expression (10.1) is the condition for determining the sixteen weights for the sixteen input-node net. We note that the inputs are all equal in value. The sixteen weights are so underconstrained that we might as well set $W_i = W$ for all i, to obtain

$$W \sum_i \left[\sum_g (x_i)_g\right] = 16 \qquad (10.2)$$

We see that in reality we only have a single-node net with a single weight.

For the problem illustrated in Figure 10.1, this weight is evaluated to be

$$W = 0.5 \qquad (10.3)$$

The order of the two summations in Equation (10.2) may be interchanged. Thus, in training the net, we evaluate each pixel over all configurations and subsequently sum over all pixels. However, in processing any particular display in observation space, all we need to do is to sum over all pixels, and the criterion for acceptance is

$$W \sum_i (x_i) = 1 \qquad (10.4)$$

as stipulated initially and illustrated in Figure 10.2. The crucial point is that the sum-over-all-pixels operation is translationally invariant and there is, therefore, no need to repeat it over all translated configurations.

It would seem that recognizing the presence of a contiguous array of two dark points might be an easy task indeed. All one has to do is to sum all the pixel values in observation space! However, we hasten to add that this procedure yields a necessary result, but is not of itself sufficient to

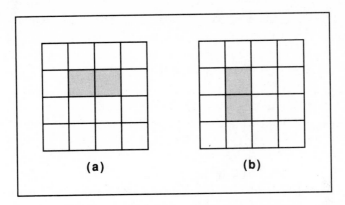

Figure 10.3 Patterns of horizontal (a) and vertical (b) bars.

ensure that there is indeed a *contiguous* array in the pattern. After all, the presence of any 2 dark pixels would have yielded the same result. Additional processing is required to ensure detection of contiguity.

The conditions represented in Figures 10.1 and 10.2 are minimal in the sense that they are necessary but are not sufficient for recognizing further structural details.

Consider the situation where it is necessary to differentiate between the horizontal array of Figure 10.3(a) and the vertical array of Figure 10.3(b). In this case, we try to incorporate into the pattern description terms that capture the spatial structure of the array. For example, the terms x_i, $i = 1, 2, \ldots 16$ do not capture any information regarding the contiguity of the two pixels, the relationship being horizontal in one case and vertical in the other.

To capture that information, we take the correlation terms $x_i x_{i+j}$, $i = 1, 2, \ldots, 16$, $j = 1, 2, 3, 4$, and so on. We note that the motivation for introducing these additional terms in this case is to capture structural information and not to provide enhancement in the sense of functional-link enhancement. In addition, a term of the nature of $x_i x_{i+j}$ for a specific value of i must be averaged over all possible transformations if we wish to have the value of that local evaluation invariant with respect to all allowed horizontal translations. Assuming that wraparound is accepted at the boundaries, we find that we can replace the sixteen sum-over-all configurations operation with a single sum-over-all-pixels operation. An additional item is now obtained for each value of j. The set of such items constitute a new type of pattern capable of differentiating between the two structures.

A new net can then be synthesized to differentiate between the two new patterns. Additional functional-link enhancement could be used for this new net if necessary. These matters are illustrated in Figure 10.4, where we see that the five components of the new preprocessed patterns are $\Sigma_i x_i$, $\Sigma_i x_i x_{i+1}$, $\Sigma_i x_i x_{i+2}$, $\Sigma_i x_i x_{i+3}$, and $\Sigma_i x_i x_{i+4}$. In this simple instance, no additional enhancement was required.

To repeat, to capture a description of spatial structure, we take the original pattern and, for each initial pixel, we average that value over all transformations with respect to which the pattern is invariant insofar as structure is concerned. Then, in addition, for each pixel we consider in turn, to as high an order as needed, the second-order, third-order, and higher-order correlation terms. *Each* of these is averaged over all transformations of the group. Depending on the nature of the transformations, considerable simplification can result and, for the two structures in Figure 10.3, we end up with the task each having to sum the result of simple local operations over all pixels. There is, therefore, only the need to

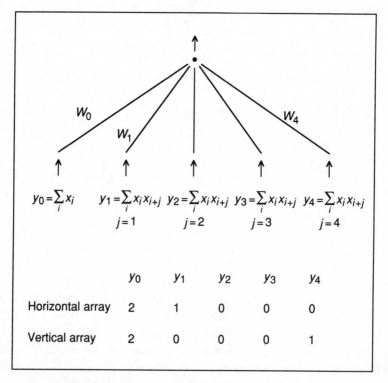

Figure 10.4   Patterns that represent structure and translational invariance.

consider global operators, the results of which are translationally invariant. As illustrated in Figure 10.4, the new patterns are both comprised of five components and the task is to determine if these patterns can differentiate between the two structures. This economy in representation is in contrast to having two patterns, each of $16 \times 5 = 80$ components, but is gained at a cost of considerable additional processing.

Information regarding temporal sequential structures can be captured and recognized in the same manner.

This discussion indicates that recognition of structure in patterns, including images, will be handled in ways significantly different from previous conventional approaches.

Boundary Conditions

In translational invariant processing, adoption of periodic boundary conditions leads to a considerable simplification of our approach. The properties of the translational group for a periodic lattice are well known. The fact that the lattice is an infinite array of replicas of a standard unit cell means that the otherwise infinite translational group is reduced to a finite group of distinct operators and, in addition, we only need to confine our observation to one unit cell. What happens in that cell happens identically in all the other cells.

We now describe the matter of transformation invariance more formally and more generally for circumstances of periodic boundary conditions and observation within a unit cell. This is in preparation for what we must do if the boundary conditions are not periodic, so that we might be able to distinguish between valid and invalid procedures.

Let $G \equiv \{g\}$ be a finite group of transformations, such that

1. For all g in G and for all patterns $\underline{x}$ in the problem domain, $g\underline{x} = \underline{v}$ is also a pattern in the problem domain.

2. G is closed under composition; namely

$$g_1, g_2 \in G \Rightarrow g_1 g_2 \in G \qquad (10.5)$$

3. There exists an inverse transformation g^{-1} such that if

$$g \in G \qquad (10.6)$$

then

$$g^{-1} \in G \qquad (10.7)$$

and

$$gg^{-1}\underline{x} = \underline{x} \tag{10.8}$$

or equivalently

$$I\underline{x} = \underline{x} \tag{10.9}$$

where I is the identity operator and is also a member of the group.

A set of patterns $\{\underline{x}^s\}$ forms an equivalence class of G iff

$$\{\underline{x}^s\} = \{g\underline{x}^s | g \in G\} \tag{10.10}$$

An observation Y is G-invariant if it gives the same output for all members of an equivalence class of pattern $\underline{x}^s$. That is, $Y(\underline{x})$ is G-invariant $\Leftrightarrow$ $Y(\underline{x}^s) = Y(g\underline{x}^s)$ for all $g \in G$.

Let us define an invariance operator

$$I_G = \sum_G g \tag{10.11}$$

Clearly

$$gI_G \equiv I_G \tag{10.12}$$

Now for any observation operator O and any pattern $\underline{x}$, we can always write

$$O(I_g\underline{x}) = O(gI_G\underline{x}) \tag{10.13}$$

And so we see that the effect of *any* observation operator becomes transformationally invariant if it is made to operate on the pattern $I_g\underline{x}$ rather than on $\underline{x}$ itself.

In neural-net processing, we achieve transformational invariance in pattern recognition by averaging the input of each node over an appropriate transformation group so that the ability to detect features incompatible with the required invariance is eliminated. In circumstances where periodic boundary conditions are not realistic, processing procedures need to be modified, but insight gained from the study of periodic-boundary problems is still helpful.

For more realistic and more stringent conditions, the objective is to recognize the presence of some local structure in the pattern (that is, in observation space) regardless of where that local structure might be located within the observation space. One approach is to design a number of local structure detection operations, which results in inputs to a neural net. For seemingly opaque, stochastic circumstances, unsupervised learning might be used to sort out the different modes in which the local structure might manifest itself. In more orderly circumstances, supervised learning would provide a recognition method of higher precision.

Regardless of the manner in which the design procedure is approached, all translationally invariant operators have certain characteristics in common. The operation is usually some local operation centered on a pixel in the display space and repeated over all pixels (or nearly all pixels) in the display space. The local results are summed, or averaged, to yield a single input to a neural net. The operator as a whole might be viewed as an operator acting on the entire pattern's and the design's objective is that the operation's results yield the same result irrespective of the structure's location within the display.

As indicated by the procedures followed in the example of Figure 10.1, insight can be gained in the design procedure by enumerating the various configurations in which the local structure might occur, carrying out a pixel-centered evaluation for each configuration and averaging the results of such evaluations, for each and every pixel, over all configurations. The final step of the feature extraction operation would vary depending on the nature of these averaged results. The objective is to replace the sum over all configurations with a sum over all pixels, or nearly all pixels. Boundary conditions will indicate what sets of pixels should be included for any specific global operator.

In these suggestions for the design of transformation invariance structure detectors, we emphasize that there is no dependence on periodic boundary conditions, and we deal with sets of possible positions rather than groups of transformations.

10.3 Dealing with Linguistic Symbols

Traditionally, AI research has relied principally on symbolic processing. One of the strengths of the basic AI languages such as LISP or PROLOG is that the symbols used are natural-language words. With that approach, the user of the programming language is able to work in an environment not alien to the language environment of ordinary, everyday activities. The intended meaning and purpose of statements, rules, and data structures are thus often easy to understand intuitively. The neumonic aspects of the representation serve to remind the programmer of what the symbols are likely to be representing. The price we pay for this benefit is that such linguistic symbols need to be recognized readily in a content-addressable manner.

In LISP, for example, it is possible to recognize all "atom" symbols on the oblist (object list) in a content-addressable manner. This recognition is usually achieved through hashing, but could be achieved in a number of other ways, like pattern recognition in a parallel-processing manner. Also, the location of an atom on the oblist does help us to locate all the other instances in which it might appear—in frames and on property lists.

Similarly, in symbolic processing, in exercising an IF–THEN rule, the IF part needs to be verified through pattern matching before the THEN part can be identified. In PROLOG, in unification, we must do a great deal of matching of strings of linguistic symbols so that variables can be bound appropriately.

Clearly, a genuine high-speed hardware associative memory based on pattern matching could function effectively in all such instances.

As parallel processing becomes a reality, researchers have shown increased interest in the question of how linguistic symbols might be or should be represented in data structures.

There is some concern that the "localistic" representation might not be appropriate for parallel processing, and some researchers believe that a more distributed representation would be more robust against the destruction of any small random subset of the units or connections used in representing a pattern of linguistic variables, and also would be more suitable for parallel processing.

One such distributed representation scheme is the "coarse-coding" approach studied by Hinton and collaborators [Hinton 1981; Hinton et al. 1986; Touretzky and Hinton 1986]. We shall describe this approach briefly.

The intent of the technique is to smear the representation of a linguistic symbol over a large number of memory units, rather than representing it locally in a few units. Typically, a working memory might consist of 2000 binary-state units. Each unit has a receptive-field table, such as the one shown in Figure 10.5. A unit's receptive field is defined to be the cross-product of the six symbols in each of the three columns, giving 6^3 or 216 triples per field. The unit described in Figure 10.5 has the triples (C K R) and (F A B) in its receptive field, along with 214 others.

We can store a triple in working memory by turning on all the receptors representing that triple. With 2000 working-memory units, any specific triple will, on an average, be in $(6/25)^3 \times 2000$, or roughly 28, receptors. Of course, this value is only the average, and the actual number will vary slightly from one triple to the next if the field tables are generated randomly initially. Also, the field tables are used only to determine the connections between these memory units and other units in the system. Once these connections have been established, the tables are no longer needed or used.

An external observer can test whether a particular triple is present in working memory by checking the percentage of active receptors for it. If this value is close to 100 percent, the triple may be assumed to be present.

For example, if the triple (F A B) were stored in working memory, the unit in Figure 10.5 would be active, along with about 27 other units. But, although (C K R), for example, is also in the field, the number of receptor units the two unrelated triples have in common would be small. Therefore, when (F A B) is stored in the memory of all 28 receptors containing (C K R), only one receptor is activated—namely, the one that contains both (F A B) and (C K R).

In principle, if we have a list of the total number of receptors for each triple, we need only to evaluate the percent of receptors that are actually active and to determine whether or not the triple is present. For example if the triples (F A B) and (F C D) were stored in working-memory, and if the working memory units were in a 40×50 array, then 55 of the units might be active, as shown in Figure 10.6. The actual positions of the units are

C	A	B
F	E	D
M	H	J
Q	K	M
S	T	P
W	Y	R

Figure 10.5   An example of a randomly generated receptive-field table for a working-memory unit. The receptive field of the unit is defined as the cross-product of the symbols in the three columns. (Touretzky, D.S. and Hinton, G.E. (1988) A distributed connectionist production system. *Cognitive Science* 12(3), p. 427. Reprinted with permission of Ablex Publishing Corp.)

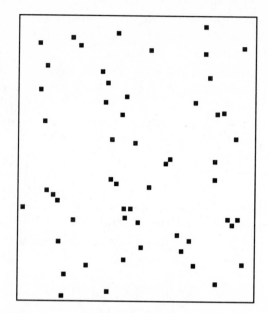

Figure 10.6   The state of working memory after the triples (F A B) and (F C D) have been stored. Active working-memory units are indicated by black squares; 55 of the 2000 units are active. (Touretzky, D.S. and Hinton, G.E. (1988) A distributed connectionist production system. *Cognitive Science* 12(3), p. 428. Adapted from and reprinted with permission of Ablex Publishing Corp.)

not important, because the units' receptive fields were generated randomly initially.

The working memory shown in Figure 10.6 can also be interpreted in terms of the likelihood that various triples might be stored. For example, the first dozen triples with the strongest representations might have the percent activities listed in Table 10.1.

In a sense, it is immaterial how the working memory is deciphered. We could achieve that step by using a Hopfield or Boltzmann machine algorithm or by linking all units to respective triples. The important point is that a linguistic symbol is represented by a number of units "smeared" over a working memory. A holographic scheme is attained. If a unit or two is damaged, the presence of that symbol might still be detected. A vast number of different triples could be stored, but only a relatively small number can be stored at any one time. Also, deletion of one symbol can decrease the representation of other symbols by so much that, after a while, a symbol has to be reinserted if it is to be in the memory.

Table 10.1   The First Dozen Triples with the Strongest Representations when Working Memory is the State Shown in Figure 10.6. (Touretzky, D.S. and Hinton, G.E. (1988) A distributed connectionist production system. *Cognitive Science* 12(3), p. 429. Reprinted with permission of Ablex Publishing Corp.)

Triple	Percent active	Active receptors	Total receptors
(F A B)	100	28	28
(F C D)	100	28	28
(F A D)	40	11	27
(F B D)	38	10	26
(F A X)	37	11	29
(S A B)	37	10	27
(F Q D)	37	10	27
(F C N)	37	10	27
(F C B)	37	10	27
(F C M)	35	10	28
(F T D)	35	10	28
(N C D)	34	10	29

10.4 Dealing with Structures in Patterns of Linguistic Symbols

We distinguish between structure in patterns of symbols and structure in patterns of *linguistic* symbols. The difference is profound. In both cases, the relative positions of symbols within the patterns represent critical information. That is, the structure within the pattern is more important than are the absolute locations of symbols. In the latter case, however, semantics and syntax are intermingled. That is, the individual "meaning" of a work or symbol can change in accordance with how that symbol is arrayed with respect to other such symbols. Furthermore, as the meanings of the individual symbols change, the meaning of the entire array changes. In terms of pattern recognition, the "classification" of a pattern becomes dependent not only on the identity of the symbols, and not only on the relative structure between the symbols, but also on the "meaning" of the symbols that change as the structures change.

Initially, syntactic pattern recognition relied strongly on what could be achieved with the formal methods of mathematical linguistics and on "parsing" as the principal pattern-classification paradigm. This reliance in turn led to the need for inferring what the production rules might be, with many attendant difficulties. Subsequent computational-linguistics research has explored the relative merits of use of augmented transition networks, case grammars, and language-processing approaches based on formal templates and expectations.

In this section, we content ourselves with presenting an alternative to detailed parsing. We show that it is possible to differentiate between sentences generated by two different grammars, each of which is capable of generating a fragment of all conceivable English-language sentences. This work is taken from an illustration contained in the doctoral thesis of Klassen [1988].

The two grammars of interest G_1 and G_2 are from Nilsson [1980] and Winston [1984], respectively, and both are context-free.

For **grammar** G_1, we have

$$\text{Starting symbol: } S$$
$$\text{Nonterminal symbols: } \{S, DNP, VP, V, PP, P, DET, NP, A, N\}$$
$$\text{Representative terminal symbols: } \{new, president, company, sale, of, approves, the\}$$

The **production rules** are as follows:

$$
\begin{aligned}
\{S &\longrightarrow DNP \quad VP \\
VP &\longrightarrow V \quad DNP \\
PP &\longrightarrow \underline{P} \quad DNP \\
DNP &\longrightarrow DET \quad NP \\
DNP &\longrightarrow DNP \quad PP \\
NP &\longrightarrow A \quad NP \\
NP &\longrightarrow N \\
A &\longrightarrow new \\
N &\longrightarrow president | company | sale \\
DET &\longrightarrow the \\
P &\longrightarrow of \\
V &\longrightarrow approves\}
\end{aligned}
$$

A typical sentence is

The president of the company approves the sales.

Similarly, for **grammar** G_2, we have,

Starting symbol: S

Nonterminal symbols: $\{S, DNP, VP, V, PP, P, DET, NP, A, N\}$

Representative terminal symbols: $\{moved, a, the, this, that, silly, red, big, robot, pyramid, top, table, to, of\}$

The **production rules** are as follows:

$$
\begin{aligned}
\{S &\longrightarrow DNP\ \ VP \\
VP &\longrightarrow VP\ \ PP \\
VP &\longrightarrow V\ \ DNP \\
PP &\longrightarrow P\ \ DNP \\
DNP &\longrightarrow DET\ \ NP \\
NP &\longrightarrow A\ \ NP \\
NP &\longrightarrow N \\
DET &\longrightarrow a|the|this|that \\
A &\longrightarrow silly|red|big \\
N &\longrightarrow robot|pyramid|top|table \\
V &\longrightarrow moved \\
P &\longrightarrow to|of\}
\end{aligned}
$$

A representative sentence is

The silly robot moved the red pyramid to the big table.

The point we want to make in this discussion is that it is possible to replace or augment the parsing approach in the processing of such patterns with a truly parallel pattern-processing approach utilizing "surface" structures.

For example, a general sequence that can be generated by grammar G_1 is

$$
\begin{array}{llllllllllll}
Symbol: & \# & DET & (A)^q & N & (P & DET & (A)^m & N)^y & V & DET & (A)^n & N \\
Coded\ as: & 1 & 2 & 3 & 4 & 5 & 2 & 3 & 4 & 6 & 2 & 3 & 4 \\
& : & (P & DET & (A)^{m'} & N)^x & & \$ \\
& : & 5 & & 2 & 3 & 4 & \phi & q, m, y, n, m', x \geq 0
\end{array}
$$

Table 10.2   Sample Sequences Used for Training of Neural Net that Discriminates Between Sentences of Grammars G_1 AND G_2

Training Samples Inputs in Coded Form					Sequence of Length 5 Outputs (G_1)	(G_2)
1	2	3	4	5	1	ϕ
2	3	4	5	2	1	1
3	4	5	2	3	1	1
4	5	2	3	4	1	1
5	2	3	4	6	1	ϕ
2	3	4	6	2	1	1
3	4	6	2	3	1	1
4	6	2	3	4	1	1
6	2	3	4	5	1	1
5	2	3	4	ϕ	1	1
1	2	3	4	6	ϕ	1

A general sequence that can be generated by grammar G_2 is

$$\textit{Symbol: } \#\ DET\ (A)^n\ N\ V\ DET\ (A)^n\ N(P\ \ DET\ (A)^m\ N)^q\ \ \$$$
$$\textit{Coded as: }\ 1\quad 2\quad\ \ 3\quad 4\ 6\quad 2\quad\ \ 3\quad 4\quad 5\quad\ \ 2\ 3\quad\ \ 4\quad\ \ \phi$$

$$q, n, m, x \geq 0$$

A functional-link net was trained with the examples listed in Table 10.2. The two outputs values of 0 or 1 indicated whether the sequence of symbols in question could have been generated with that grammar.

This is just one illustration of the use of structure-sensitive pattern-recognition techniques for handling tasks that are conventionally relegated to syntactical analysis. Other results from Klassen [1988] indicate that context-sensitive grammars also can be handled in this manner.

There are many additional adaptive measures that we need to understand before we can use this approach to language processing. For example, it might be critically important that the adaptive technique be able to discover for itself what lengths of sequences are important or under what circumstances contextual structures are likely to occur. In the absence of such autonomous unsupervised-learning capabilities, it might still be possible to distinguish between languages, as Klassen has begun to show. The power of the approach would certainly be much enhanced if the methodology could be taught at a higher level and then could adapt to build up detailed techniques.

10.5 Associations with Varying Degrees of Belief

Measures of belief can be incorporated in parallel-processing adaptive pattern recognition in two ways.

In one case, the values of the individual pattern inputs are actually belief values, or membership values, as illustrated in Figure 10.7. This type of pattern recognition would be particularly suitable for fuzzy control or for sensor data fusion.

In another situation, a degree of belief can be attributed to a particular pattern itself. In training a net to classify patterns or to estimate values of an attribute, we can evaluate the system error in a manner somewhat different from the conventional approach.

Conventionally, for example, in supervised learning, the system error is the average of the individual pattern errors. That is, the desired value of the kth output is t_k and, if the actual output is o_{pk} for the pattern p, then the system "error" to be minimized is

$$\langle E^2 \rangle = \frac{1}{2}\frac{1}{p}\sum_k \sum_p (t_k - o_{pk})^2 \tag{10.14}$$

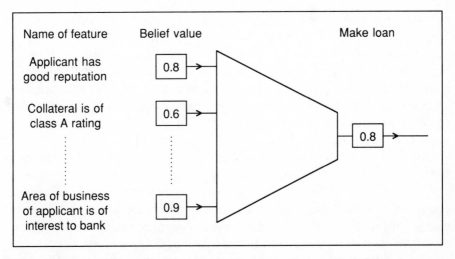

Figure 10.7 Evaluating a bank loan application; use of belief values.

However, if expression (10.14) is modified to incorporate a measure of our belief in the validity or relevance of each of these patterns, then the average of the effective squared error values can be written as

$$\langle E^2 \rangle = \frac{1}{2} \frac{1}{p} \sum_k \sum_p B_p (t_k - o_{pk})^2 \tag{10.15}$$

where B_p is the belief attributed to pattern $\underline{x}_p$.

B_p values provides a convenient and powerful means for modifying pattern-recognition discriminants. For example, setting $B_p = o$ constitutes a convenient way to remove the influence of $\underline{x}_p$ without having to do detailed deletion operations in the pattern database.

There are, of course, many other methods for incorporating uncertainties in neural-net computations and for using neural nets to represent uncertainties. Chapter 9 discussed, for example, how membership functions might be synthesized with the use of neural nets. Hopfield [1987] has also considered the task of incorporating objective probabilities in specifying the learning task, and he has discussed how that step modifies the supervised-learning algorithm.

10.6   Estimation Versus Classification—Need for Accuracy

The power of any pattern-recognition algorithm lies in its ability to deal with noise or distortion. That is, after being trained on representative patterns of a class, the algorithm is able to recognize all other patterns of that same equalivance class.

In the Hopfield associative-memory approach, a set of patterns are stored and any input pattern that is reasonably similar to one of the stored patterns is changed into that stored pattern. If the input pattern is viewed as a distorted version of that associated stored pattern, then the function of the memory is to provide an estimate of what the noisy pattern actually should be.

In supervised learning, the output is an estimated value of the class index. Thus, if we had trained the net to yield an output of 1 for all class A patterns, and of 0 for all non–class A patterns, an actual test-set pattern might cause an output of 0.86 and would be considered to be of class A. Again the basic act is that of estimation, although the final result might be clothed in the guise of classification.

This distinction is important because, more often than not, the act of direct interest is that of estimation rather than of classification. In Chapter 5, we saw that, in the parity-2 problem, if the even- and odd-parity patterns were assigned values of 1 and 0, respectively, and if the network was generalized to be valid for all points in the 1×1 two-dimensional square of unit area, then each point in that square would have an output value associated with it.

The different estimation outcomes exhibited in Figure 5.13 of Chapter 5 indicate clearly that there may be uncertainties in the generalization procedure. Additional reference points are needed to serve as the basis for estimations of generalized values.

Although more reference points are useful, it is interesting that the choice of the algorithm used for learning also influences the result. For the same parity-2 problem of Chapter 5, we get the generalized results shown in Figure 10.8, instead of those of either Figure 5.13(a) or 5.13(b), if we use the functional-link net for supervised learning, instead of the generalized delta rule.

In many respects, the values shown in Figure 10.8 would seem to be more reasonable than the previously estimated values shown in Figure 5.13.

When a net is used to learn a network representation of a function, the basic task is also that of estimation. We discussed instances of those tasks in Chapter 8.

It is interesting that adaptive pattern recognition and neural-net processing can therefore be used for implementing a large number of signal

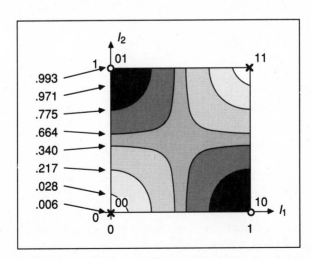

Figure 10.8   The generalized understanding of the input space with pruned functional link net.

interpolation and extrapolation tasks that are quite difficult when approached with other conventional means.

10.7 Temporal Correlation Between Inputs and Outputs

Time enters into the consideration of neural-net implementations of pattern recognition in several different ways. If a set of operations is carried out asynchronously, then there is neither a notion of time nor indeed one of sequential order, insofar as that set is concerned. If a specific sequence of operations, or of set of operations, needs to be carried out the manner of a linear string of events, there is again no real notion of time; we need only the concept of sequential ordering. However, if there are two or more sequence operations in progress at the same time, and if there are sychronization points at different stages of the processing to establish correct procedure or to transfer information, then relative time is of importance. Finally, in such circumstances, if there is a "natural" time constant associated with one or more of the types of operations involved, then the entire operation is of "real" time.

For example, we can make an autoassociative Hopfield network heteroassociative by arranging for the network to evolve from a normal set of $\{t_{ij}\}$ values automatically to another set $\{T_{ij}\}$ after input of a pattern $\underline{x}'_p$. The input pattern $\underline{x}'_p$ is corrected and becomes $\underline{x}_p$ through autoassociation, after which the weights $\{t_{ij}\}$ begin to evolve with "time" to become $\{T_{ij}\}$, and $\underline{x}_p$, becomes transformed into $\underline{y}_p$, a heteroassociative process. However, this type of time is definitely not "real" time, unless the rate of evolution is constrained by other temporal considerations.

In yet another consideration of time, there is a natural time constant and the output of the net is determined by the state of the input at several time intervals prior to the time of the output. Such a network can serve as a predictor, and such behaviour can represent "conditioned" response [Klopf 1987].

10.8 The Possibility of Using Adaptive Pattern Recognition to Solve Truly Difficult Problems

An algorithm is a recipe or a process for solving problems. Generally speaking, problems and related algorithms can be divided into two classes, the tractable and the intractable, as illustrated in Figure 10.9.

We determine the division between a reasonable and an unreasonable algorithm by the manner in which the algorithm depends functionally on N—typically the number of units involved in the problem. We must distinguish between *polynomial* and *superpolynomial* functions. A polynomial function of N is bounded from above by N^k for some fixed k. All other functions are superpolynomial. Since many of superpolynomials are exponential functions, the term *exponential* is often used synonymously with the term *superpolynomial*.

Algorithms that vary in exponential manner with N are truly bad. Such problems may indeed be intractable, because the number of steps required for their solution, even for a relatively small number of inputs (N), quickly become unimaginably large. The growth rates of six polynomial and exponential functions are plotted in Figure 10.10. These plots show clearly that such algorithms are utterly unimpracticable; making a computer run a thousand times faster would help hardly at all!

There is a class of problems called *NP-complete* [Harel 1987]. The naive solution is exponential, but such problems are not provably intractable and, in fact, the lower bound, if known, might be linear with N. The traveling-salesman problem is of this nature and so are a great num-

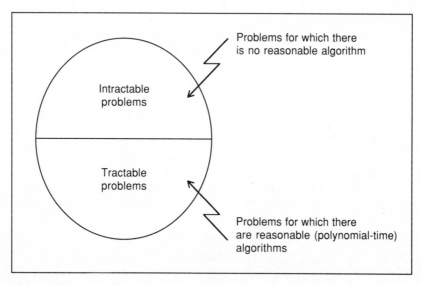

Figure 10.9   Division of algorithmic problems into tractable and intractable problems (after Figure 7.6 of Harel [1987]).

ber of the other problems of practical interest and importance. Many scheduling problems belong to this category.

Another interesting aspect to this situation, is that if one NP-complete problem could be shown to be tractable, then all NP-complete problems would be proven to be tractable!

The question is whether parallel-processing adaptive pattern recognition can provide a new approach to the solution of some classes of truly

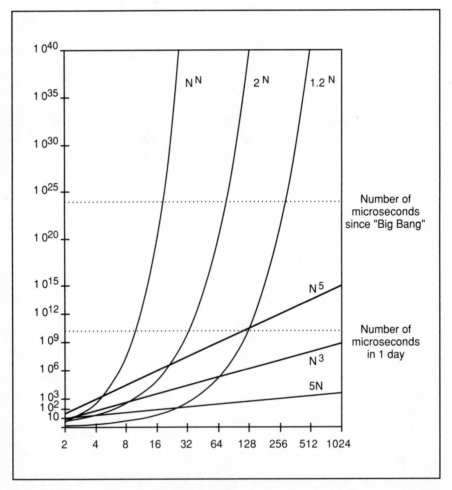

Figure 10.10　　Growth rates of polynomial and exponential functions. (Reprinted with permission from Fig. 7.4 of *Algorithmics: The Spirit of Computing* by David Harel, © 1987 Addison-Wesley Publishing Co., Wokingham, U.K.)

	Day $\longrightarrow$				
City	1	2	3	4	5
A	0	1	0	0	0
B	0	0	1	0	0
C	0	0	0	0	1
D	1	0	0	0	0
E	0	0	0	1	0

Figure 10.11 Illustration of solution of the traveling-salesman problem in the form of a pattern for which a Liapunov function is minimized.

difficult problems, one of them being the NP-complete problems. Hopfield and Tank [1985] formulated one such project. They cast the traveling-saleman problem in the form of determining the values at the nodes of an interconnected network. The nodes can be viewed in terms of an $N \times N$ pattern.

For example, as shown in Figure 10.11, the row index denotes the identity of the city in which the traveling salesman is located, and the column index denotes the day on which he is in that city.

The desired result was a pattern where certain nodes had value 1 and all others had value 0. That pattern indicated the location of the salesman on the successive days. Given the physical constraints, it was clear that there should be only N nodes with value 1, that no row should have more than one node with value 1, and that no column should have more than one node with value 1. These constraints ensured that N cities visited altogether, that no city would be visited more than once, and that the salesman would not be at two places at the same time.

In their approach to the problem, Hopfield and Tank synthesized a Liapunov function that had four parts. Minimization of the first three parts ensured satisfaction of the physical constraints. The fourth part represented the value of the sum of the intercity paths taken by the salesman in making the tour represented by the pattern of nodes.

An algorithm was devised that changed the values of the nodes so that the value of the Liapunov function was always decreased by a change. This approach is appealing because, if changes always cause a decrease in the Liapunov function, then all changes will continue to drive that function to lower and lower values until the problem is indeed solved. In other words, that state should correspond to the correct solution, with all cities visited just once in sequence and with the shortest distance traveled.

The flaw in this argument is that there may be, and there usually are, many local minima, so it is not possible to be sure that we have attained the global minimum. If the system had only one minimum, then this new approach would be interesting indeed.

In addition, Wilson and Pawley [1988] have investigated the "stability" of the traveling-salesman algorithm of Hopfield and Tank, and have returned a rather pessimistic verdict with regard to the possibility of scaling the procedure to large N. Wilson and Pawley found that there were a great many ways of being trapped in aimless cyclic wandering in solution space, or of being trapped at what amounts to local minima. However, Takefuji and his colleagues [1988] find that many of the procedural difficulties experienced by Wilson and Pawley can be alleviated by suitable reformulation of the Liapunov function. Accordingly, they are considerably more optimistic than Wilson and Pawley.

Just as Hopfield and Tank [1985] generalized Hopfield's content-addressable memory to computation, Baum [1986] similarly generalized the backpropagation procedure of Rumelhart, Hinton, and Williams [1986]. Baum's aim was to find a way to discover computational algorithms by using a constrained gradient descent in *algorithm* space. The idea is that even local minima in that space may still correspond to a fast parallel effective heuristic of considerable interest and importance. Although valuable insights were obtained, Baum was not successful in his overall goal. In particular, he could not obtain a procedure for handling the traveling-salesman problem. Despite this discouraging result, this issue is of great importance and is worthy of continued effort.

10.9 Comments and Bibliographical Remarks

This chapter is concerned with issues rather than with specific applications. We believe that this emphasis is much more enlightening, even if we are specifically interested in applications. The point is that adaptive pattern recognition, as implemented with neural nets, will indeed contribute critically to the solution of important problems, but facile or superficial approaches will not suffice. We need to understand the underlying issues first.

Three application areas are becoming defined. One generic application area is that of *image* processing. The task is to detect and recognize structured objects of a specific class in a large, cluttered field of other objects. Recognizing speech and reading handwritten text are examples. The task is not simple; it involves levels of complexity, starting from the rather low-level tasks of being able to detect a subpattern and extract it from the background despite changes in scale, position, orientation, distortions, and partial obscuration. Giles and Maxwell [1987] and Maxwell and associates [1986], for example, report on the use of "higher-order" terms to achieve invariance; Fukushima [1980; 1987] discusses dealing with observations and omissions.

At higher levels of processing, we need to account for the fact that existing sensory-data knowledge is used in detection and recognition. For example, when we are trying to read scribbled handwriting, we may have to distinguish whether a letter is an "e" or a "c." If, however, the letter is in the sequence "l-ad" and we have no knowledge of any word "lcad," but we do have knowledge of the word "lead," then the appropriate gains will be fedback to result in recognition of "e."

There are yet higher levels of processing that involve cognitive processes. For example, if the competition had been between "e" and "o" and a simple lookup confirmed that both "lead" and "load" were admissible, more involved inferences would be necessary. Cohen and Grossberg [1986; 1987] give indications of the complexities of such matters. The pioneering work by Sejnowski and Rosenberg [1986] on NETtalk certainly constitutes an example of this type of work.

Another important application is that of controls and the learning of control strategies. One approach has been to generate many control paths, and to reward the successful ones and to penalize the failures. Some contributions of Barto and coworkers illustrate this approach [Barto and Sutton 1981; Barto, Sutton, and Anderson 1983; Barto and Sutton 1985]. To increase efficiency, we can employ heuristics to discourage paths known to be unrewarding, to prevent the occurrence of cyclic paths, and so on. The work by Anderson [1987] on learning the pole-balancing task is an instance of that approach.

Using a somewhat different approach, Pao and his colleagues have advocated using examples of successful and unsuccessful procedures to learn strategy and to generate control actions for all other circumstances. Thus, in dynamic control, a finite number of examples of correct control actions can be learned with use of a supervised learning, which can then be used to provide estimates of appropriate action for all other circumstances. Pao and his colleagues have reported this approach in the domains of robotics [Sobajic, Lu, and Pao 1987], electric-power systems [Sobajic and Pao 1988], and process control in general [Pao 1988]. Unsupervised learning can be used for discovery of control strategies. Patterns describing systems states are clustered and are examined to see whether the cluster structure corresponds to different types of control actions. If necessary, each such cluster of patterns may also be subjected to supervised-learning control, and dynamic control can be approached in this manner [Pao and Sobajic 1988].

Controls is, indeed, a rapidly developing application area for neural nets. A special issue of the *IEEE Control Systems* magazine, Vol. 8, Num-

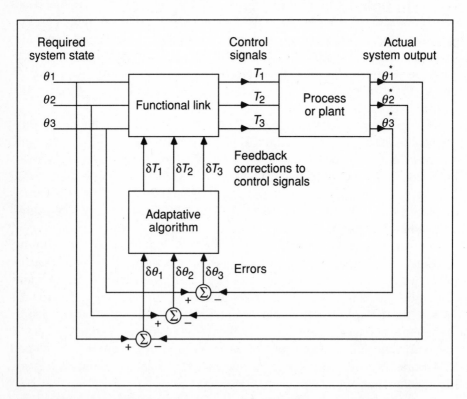

Figure 10.12   Architecture of a control system based on a neural net.

ber 2, April 1988, contains several introductory articles on neural nets in the context of control.

Chen [1988] has given an insightful discussion of neural-net approaches to implementing controls. As illustrated in Figure 10.12, there is no question that we wish to have a neural net that will recognize the system state and the control objective, and will generate the correct control actions. The only question is how this net is to be trained. As stated previously, it might be trained by reward or punishment, in the manner of Barto's work, or by prescription, or by the iterative corrections of Kawato and colleagues [1968], Psaltis and colleagues [1988], and Chen [1988]. Chen advocates the use of adaptive measures to make sure that the training of the functional-link net is always up to date. This practice also is used by Pao and Sobajic [1988]. Chen [1988] has shown that inverse kinematics and inverse dynamics can be incorporated in such controls for the control of robotic manipulators.

A third application area is perhaps more a research and development area, than it is an applications area. The need for it is so great, however, that we suspect research results will be applied even while immature. This research area is the matter of combining expert systems and neural nets, or, equivalently, of combining (linguistically expressed) symbolic processing with numeric feature-valued pattern information processing.

Discussions by Touretsky and Hinton [1986], Touretsky and Geva [1987], Fahlman and Hinton [1987], Derthick [1987], and Gallant [1988] all give indications of the work being done to that end.

10.10 References and Bibliography

1. Anderson, C.W., 1987. Strategy learning with multilayer connectionist representations. *Proceedings of the Fourth International Workshop on Machine Learning*, University of California at Irvine, pp. 103–114.

2. Barto, A.G. and R.S. Sutton, 1981. Landmark learning: An illustration of associative search, *Biological Cybernetics*, Vol. 42, pp. 1–8.

3. Barto, A.G., R.S. Sutton, and C.W. Anderson, 1983. Neuronlike adaptive elements that can solve difficult learning control problems, *IEEE Transaction on Systems, Man, and Cybernetics*, Vol. 13, pp. 834–846.

4. Barto, A.G. and P. Anandan, 1985. Pattern recognizing stochastic learning automata, *IEEE Transaction on Systems, Man, and Cybernetics*, Vol. SMC-15, pp. 360–375.

5. Baum, E.B., 1986. Generalizing back propagation to computation, *American Institute of Physics Conference Proceedings, No. 151: Neural Networks for Computing*, Snowbird, Utah, pp. 47–52.

6. Chen, V., 1988. Neural net implemented adaptive controls, Ph.D. thesis, Electrical Engineering and Applied Physics Dept., Case Western Reserve University, Cleveland, OH.

7. Cohen, M.A. and S. Grossberg, 1986. Neural dynamics of speech and language coding: Development programs, perceptual grouping, and competition for short-term memory, *Human Neurobiology*, Vol. 5, pp. 1–22.

8. Cohen, M.A. and S. Grossberg, 1987. Masking fields: A massively parallel neural architecture for learning, recognizing and predicting multiple groupings of patterned data, *Applied Optics*, Vol. 26, pp. 1866–1890.

9. Derthick, M., 1987. A connectionist architecture for representing and reasoning about structured knowledge, *Proceedings of the Ninth Annual Conference of the Cognitive Science Society*, Seattle, WA.

10. Fahlman, S.E. and G.E. Hinton, 1986. Connectionist architectures for Artificial Intelligence, *Computer*, Vol. 19, pp. 100–108.

11. Fakushima, K., 1987. Neural network model for selective attention in visual pattern recognition and associative recall, *Applied Optics*, Vol. 26, pp. 4985–4992.

12. Fukushima, K. and S. Miyaki, 1980. Neogocition: A self-organzing neural network model for a mechanism of pattern recognition unaffected by a shift in position, *Biological Cybernetics*, Vol. 36, pp. 193–202.

13. Gallant, S.I., 1988. Connectionist expert systems, *Communications of the ACM*, Vol. 31, pp. 182–169.

14. Giles, C.L. and T. Maxwell, 1987. Learning, invariance and generalization in high order neural networks, *Applied Optics*, Vol. 26, pp. 4972–4978.

15. Harel, D., 1987. *Algorithmics: The Spirit of Computing.* Addison-Wesley Publishing Co., Wokingham, U.K.

16. Hinton, G.E., 1981. A parallel computation that assigns canonical object-based frames of reference, *Proceedings of the Seventh Interna-

tional Joint Conference on Artificial Intelligence, Vol. 2, pp. 1088–1096, Vancouver BC, Canada.

17. Hinton, G.E., J.M. McClelland, and D.E. Rumelhart, 1986. Distributed representations. In D.E. Rumelhart and J.L. McClellands (Eds.), *Parallel Distributed Processing: Explorations in the Microstructure of Cognition*, Vol. 1: *Foundations*. MIT Press, Cambridge, MA.

18. Hopfield, J.J., 1987. Learning algorithms and probability distributions in feed-forward and feed-back networks, *Proceeding of the National Academy of Science*, USA., Vol. 74, pp. 8429–8433.

19. Hopfield, J.J. and D.W. Tank, 1985. Neural computation of decisions in optimization problems, *Biological Cybernetics*, Vol. 52, pp. 144–152.

20. Kawato, M., Y. Uno, M. Isobe, and R. Suzuki, 1988. Hierarchical neural network model for voluntary movement with application to robotics, *IEEE Control System Magazine*, Vol. 8, pp. 8–16.

21. Klassen, M.S., 1988. *Characteristics of Functional Link Net and Its Use in Character Recognition*. Ph.D. Thesis, Computer Science, Case Western Reserve University, Cleveland, OH.

22. Klopf, H.A., 1987. A neuronal model of classified conditioning. U.S. Air Force Wright Aeronautical Laboratories technical report, AFWAL-TR-87-1139, Dayton, OH.

23. Lee, Y.C., H.H. Chen, G. Doolen, C.L. Giles, H.Y. Lee, T. Maxwell, and G.Z. Sun, 1986. Machine learning using a higher order correlation network, *Physica*, 22D, pp. 276–306.

24. Maxwell, T., C.L. Giles, Y.C. Lee and H.H. Chen, 1986. Transformation invariance using high order correlations in neural net architecture, *IEEE Transaction on Systems, Man, and Cybernetics*, Vol. 86, pp. 627–632.

25. Minsky, M. and S. Papert, 1969. *Perceptrons: An Introduction to Computation Geometry*. MIT Press, Cambridge, MA.

26. Nilsson, N.J., 1980. *Principles of Artificial Intelligence*. Tioga, Palo Alto, CA.

27. Pao, Y.H., 1988. Autonomous machine learning of effective control strategies with connectionist-nets, *Journal of Intelligent and Robotic Systems*, Vol. 1, pp. 35–53.

28. Pao, Y.H. and D.J. Sobajic, 1988. Autonomous feature discovery for

critical clearing time assessment. *Proceedings of the Symposium on Expert System Applications to Power Systems*, Stockholm, Sweden.

29. Psaltis, D., A. Sideris, and A.A. Yamamura, 1988. A multilayered neural network controller, *IEEE Control System Magazine*, Vol. 8, pp. 17–21.

30. Rumelhart, D.E., G.E. Hinton and R.J. Williams, 1986. Learning internal representations by error propagation. In D.E. Rumelhart and J.L. McClelland (Eds.) *Parallel Distributed Processing: Explorations in the Microstructures of Cognition*. Vol. 1: *Foundations*. MIT Press, Cambridge, MA.

31. Sejnowski, T.J. and C.R. Rosenberg, 1986. *NETtalk: A Parallel Network that Learns to Read Aloud*. Electrical Engineering and Computer Science Technical Report, JHU/EECS-86/01, John Hopkins University, Baltimore, MD.

32. Sobajic, D.J. and Y.H. Pao, 1988. Artificial neural-net based security assessment for electric power systems. *IEEE Power Engineering Society*, Winter Meeting, New York, February; also published in *IEEE Transactions on Power Systems*, Vol. 3, pp. 647–653.

33. Sobajic, D.J., J.J. Lu, and Y.H. Pao, 1988. Intelligent control of the Intelledex 605T robot manipulators. *Proceeding of IEEE Second Annual International Conference on Neural Networks*, June, San Diego, CA.

34. Takefuji, Y., K.C. Lee, and C.W. Lin, 1988. Neural networks solving four-coulor problems, Case Western Reserve University, CAISR Technical Report TR 88-139.

35. Touretzky, D.S. and S. Geva, 1987. A distributed connectionist represention for concept structures. *Proceedings of the Ninth Annual Conference of the Cognitive Science Society*, Seattle, WA.

36. Touretzky, D.S. and G.E. Hinton, 1986. A distributed connectionist production system. Carnegie-Mellon University report, CMU-CS-86-172, Pittsburgh, PA.

37. Wilson, G.V. and G.S. Pawley, 1988. On the stability of the travelling salesman problem algorithm of Hopfield and Tank, *Biological Cybernetics*, Vol. 58, pp. 63–70.

38. Winston, P.H., 1984. *Artificial Intelligence*, 2nd Ed., Addison-Wesley, Reading, MA.

A Generalized Delta Rule Net Program for Supervised Learning

A.1 Introduction

This appendix contains a C language program for readers to use as a point of departure for exploring the Generalized Delta Rule procedure for supervised learning. The algorithm and notation used are generally those of Chapter 5. The program provides code in support of the following tasks:

1. Specify net architecture.

2. Learn weights and thresholds with use of training set patterns.

3. Use net to obtain output values for new patterns, either for classification purposes or for estimation of values of associated attributes.

The program runs under VAX/VMS or PC-DOS/MS-DOS. Under PC-DOS or MS-DOS, the program was compiled with Microsoft C.

A.2 Program

```
/**
    PROGRAM DESCRIPTION:

    THIS PROGRAM ALLOWS A USER TO BUILD A GENERALIZED
```

[*] Appendix A is contributed by M.S. Klassen and Yoh-Han Pao.

```
       DELTA RULE NET FOR  SUPERVISED LEARNING. USER CAN
       SPECIFY THE NUMBER OF INPUT & OUTPUT UNITS, NUMBER
       OF HIDDEN LAYERS AND NUMBER OF UNITS IN EACH
       HIDDEN LAYER.

       AFTER THE NET IS BUILT, LEARNING TAKES PLACE IN THE
       NET WITH A GIVEN SET OF TRAINING SAMPLES. USER
       SPECIFIES VALUES OF THE LEARNING RATE ETA, THE
       MOMENTUM RATE ALPHA, MAXIMUM TOLERANCE ERRORS AND
       MAXIMUM NUMBER OF ITERATIONS.

       AFTER LEARNING, ALL THE INFORMATION RELEVANT TO THE
       STRUCTURE OF THE NET, INCLUDING WEIGHTS AND
       THRESHOLDS ARE STORED IN FILES.

       OUTPUTS CAN BE GENERATED FOR NEW PATTERNS BY READING
       FROM FILE AND BY RECONSTRUCTING  THE NET.

       TRAINING SET SAMPLES AND ADDITIONAL SAMPLES FOR
       PROCESSING ARE STORED IN FILES.
**/

#include <stdio.h>
#include <math.h>
#include <ctype.h>
#ifndef VAX
/* for declaration of calloc() on PC or compatible */
#include <malloc.h>
#endif


/* define constants used throughout  functions          */

#define    NMXUNIT     50 /* max no. of units in a layer*/
#define    NMXHLR      5  /* max no. of hidden layers   */
#define    NMXOATTR    50 /* max no. of output features */
#define    NMXINP      200 /* max no. of input samples  */
#define    NMXIATTR    50 /* max no. of input features  */
#define    SEXIT       3  /* exit successfully          */
#define    RESTRT      2  /* restart                    */
#define    FEXIT       1  /* exit in failure            */
```

```
#define   CONTNE      0  /* continue calculation        */

/* Data base : declarations of variables */

float eta;         /** learning rate                **/
float alpha;       /** momentum rate                **/
float err_curr;    /** normalized system error      **/
float maxe;        /** max allowed system error     **/
float maxep;       /** max allowed pattern error    **/
float *wtptr[NMXHLR+1];
float *outptr[NMXHLR+2];
float *errptr[NMXHLR+2];
float *delw[NMXHLR+1];
float target[NMXINP][NMXOATTR];
float input[NMXINP][NMXIATTR], ep[NMXINP];
float outpt[NMXINP][NMXOATTR];
int   nunit[NMXHLR+2], nhlayer, ninput, ninattr, noutattr;
int   result, cnt, cnt_num;
int   nsnew, nsold;
char  task_name[20];
FILE  *fp1, *fp2, *fp3, *fopen();
int   fplot10;


                /* random number generator
                   (computer independent) */

long randseed = 568731L;
int random()
{
   randseed = 15625L * randseed + 22221L;
   return((randseed >> 16) & 0x7FFF);
}


                /* allocate dynamic storage for the net */
init()
{
   int len1, len2, i, k;
   float *p1, *p2, *p3, *p4;
```

```
len1 = len2 = 0;
nunit[nhlayer+2] = 0;

for (i=0; i<(nhlayer + 2); i++) {
   len1 += (nunit[i] + 1) * nunit[i+1];
   len2 += nunit[i] + 1;
}
                                   /* weights */
p1=(float *) calloc(len1+1,sizeof(float));
                                   /* output  */
p2=(float *) calloc(len2+1,sizeof(float));
                                   /* errors  */
p3=(float *) calloc(len2+1,sizeof(float));
                                   /* delw    */
p4=(float *) calloc(len1+1,sizeof(float));

                  /* set up initial pointers    */
wtptr[0]  = p1;
outptr[0] = p2;
errptr[0] = p3;
delw[0]   = p4;

                  /* set up the rest of pointers */
for (i=1 ; i <(nhlayer +1) ; i++) {
   wtptr[i] = wtptr[i-1] + nunit[i] * (nunit[i-1] +1);
   delw[i]  = delw[i-1] + nunit[i] * (nunit[i-1] +1);
}
for (i = 1; i < ( nhlayer+2); i++)  {
   outptr[i] = outptr[i-1] + nunit[i-1] + 1;
   errptr[i] = errptr[i-1] + nunit[i-1] + 1;
}

                  /* set up threshold outputs */
for (i = 0; i < nhlayer + 1; i++) {
   *(outptr[i] + nunit[i]) = 1.0;
}
}
```

```
                    /* initialize weights with random
                        numbers between -0.5 and +0.5 */
initwt()
{
   int i,j;

   for (j = 0; j<nhlayer+1; j++)
      for (i=0; i<(nunit[j]+1) * nunit[j+1] ; i++) {
         *(wtptr[j]+i) = random()/pow(2.0,15.0) - 0.5;
         *(delw[j] + i) = 0.0;
      }
}


                    /* specify architecture of  net and
                        values of learning parameters */
set_up()
{
   int i;

   eta=0.9;
   printf("\nMomentum rate eta (default =0.9)?: ");
   scanf("%f",&eta);

   alpha=0.7;
   printf("\nLearning rate alpha (default =0.7)?: ");
   scanf("%f",&alpha);

   maxe=0.01; maxep=0.001;
   printf("\nMax total error (default=0.01)?: ");
   scanf("%f",&maxe);
   printf("\nMax individual error (default=0.001)?: ");
   scanf("%f",&maxep);

   cnt_num=1000;
   printf("\nMax number of iteration(default=1000)?: ");
   scanf ("%d", &cnt_num);

   printf("\nNumber of hidden layers?: ");
   scanf("%d", &nhlayer);
```

```c
    for (i=0; i<nhlayer; i++)  {
       printf("\n\tNumber of units for hidden layer %d?: ",
       i+1 );
       scanf("%d",&nunit[i+1]);
    }

    printf("\nCreate error file? If so type 1,or type 0 : ");
    scanf("%d",&fplot10);

    printf("\nExecution starts");

    nunit[nhlayer+1] = noutattr;
    nunit[0]=ninattr;
}

                /* read file for net architecture and
                   learning parameters. File name has
                   suffix _v.dat */
dread (taskname)
char *taskname;
{
    int    i,j,c;
    char   var_file_name[20];

    strcpy(var_file_name, taskname);
    strcat(var_file_name,"_v.dat");
    if (( fp1 = fopen(var_file_name,"r")) == NULL)
    {
       perror("\n Cannot open data file ");
       exit(0);
    }

    fscanf(fp1,"%d%d%d%f%f%d%d",&ninput,&noutattr,
       &ninattr,&eta,&alpha,&nhlayer,&cnt_num);

    for  ( i=0; i < nhlayer+2; i++)
       fscanf (fp1,"%d", &nunit[i]);

    if ((c=fclose(fp1)) !=0)
       printf("\nFile cannot be closed  %d ", c);
```

```
}


                /* read file containing weights
                   and thresholds. File name has
                   suffix _w.dat*/
wtread(taskname)
char *taskname;
{
   int   i, j, c;
   char  wt_file_name[20];

   strcpy(wt_file_name,taskname);
   strcat(wt_file_name,"_w.dat");

   if (( fp2 = fopen(wt_file_name,"r")) == NULL)
   {
      perror("\n Cannot open data file ");
      exit(0);
   }

   for (i =0; i <nhlayer +1; i++) {
      for (j =0; j < (nunit[i]+1) * nunit[i+1]; j++) {
         fscanf (fp2,"%f", (wtptr[i]+j));
      }
   }

   if ((c=fclose(fp2)) !=0)
      printf("\nFile cannot be closed  %d ", c);
}



                /* create file for net architecture
                   and learning parameters. File name
                   has suffix _v.dat */

dwrite(taskname)
char *taskname;        {
   int   i, j, c;
```

```c
        char  var_file_name[20];

        strcpy(var_file_name,taskname);
        strcat(var_file_name, "_v.dat");

        if (( fp1 = fopen(var_file_name,"w+")) == NULL)
        {
           perror("Cannot open data file ");
           exit(0);
        }
        fprintf (fp1,"%u %u %u %f %f %u %u\n",ninput,noutattr,
                                             ninattr,eta,alpha,
                                             nhlayer,cnt_num);

        for (i=0; i <nhlayer+2;i++) {
           fprintf(fp1,"%d ",nunit[i]);
        }

        fprintf(fp1,"\n%d %f", cnt,err_curr);
        fprintf(fp1,"\n");

        for(i=0;i<ninput;i++)
        {
           for(j=0;j<noutattr;j++)
              fprintf(fp1,"%f        ",outpt[i][j]);
           fprintf(fp1,"\n");
        }

        if ((c=fclose(fp1)) !=0)
           printf("\nFile cannot be closed  %d ", c);
}




                    /* create file for saving weights and
                       thresholds learned from training.
                       File name has suffix _w.dat */
wtwrite(taskname)
char *taskname;
{
```

```
int   i, j, c, k;
char  wt_file_name[20];

strcpy(wt_file_name,taskname);
strcat(wt_file_name, "_w.dat");

if (( fp2 = fopen(wt_file_name,"w+")) == NULL)
{
    perror("Cannot open data file ");
    exit(0);
}

k=0;
for (i=0; i <nhlayer+1; i++)
    for ( j=0; j <(nunit[i] +1) * nunit[i+1]; j++) {
        if(k==8) {
            k=0;
            fprintf(fp2,"\n");
        }
        fprintf(fp2,"%f ", *(wtptr[i] +j));
        k++;
    }
if ((c=fclose(fp2)) !=0)
    printf("\nFile cannot be closed  %d ", c);
}


                /* bottom_up calculation
                    of net for input pattern i */
void forward(i)
{
    int   m, n, p, offset;
    float net;

                    /* input level output calculation*/
    for (m=0; m<ninattr;m++)
        *(outptr[0]+m) = input[i][m];

            /* hidden & output layer output calculation*/
    for (m=1; m<nhlayer+2;m++) {
```

```
    for (n=0;n<nunit[m];n++)  {
       net=0.0;
       for (p=0; p<nunit[m-1]+1;p++) {
           offset = (nunit[m-1]+1) * n + p;
           net += *(wtptr[m-1]+offset)
               *(*(outptr[m-1]+p));
       }
       *(outptr[m]+n) = 1/(1+exp(-net));
    }
}
for (n=0; n<nunit[nhlayer+1];n++)
    outpt[i][n] = *(outptr[nhlayer+1]+n);
}


                /* several conditions are checked to
                   see whether learning should terminate */
int introspective (nfrom,nto)
int nfrom;
int nto;
{
   int i,flag;

                        /* reached  max. iteration ?*/
   if (cnt>=cnt_num) return(FEXIT);

                        /* error for each pattern
                           small enough? */
   nsnew = 0;
   flag = 1;
   for (i = nfrom; (i < nto) && (flag == 1); i++) {
      if (ep[i] <= maxep) nsnew++;
      else flag = 0;
   }
   if (flag == 1) return(SEXIT);

                        /* system total error small
                           enough? */
   if ( err_curr <= maxe) return(SEXIT);
   return(CONTNE);
```

```
}




                     /* threshold is treated as weight of
                         link from a virtual node whose
                         output value is unity */
int rumelhart(from_snum,to_snum)
int from_snum;
int to_snum;
{
    int    i,j,k,m,n,p,offset, index;
    float out;
    char  *err_file = "criter.dat";

    nsold = 0;
    cnt = 0;
    result = CONTNE;

    if (fplot10==1)
       if ((fp3=fopen(err_file,"w")) == NULL)
       {
          perror("Cannot open error file");
          exit(0);
       }
       do {
       err_curr = 0.0;
                        /* for each pattern    */
       for (i=from_snum; i<to_snum;i++) {

                        /* bottom_up calculation */
          forward(i);

                        /* top_down error propagation */
                        /* output_level error   */
          for (m=0; m<nunit[nhlayer+1]; m++)   {
             out= *(outptr[nhlayer+1] +m);
             *(errptr[nhlayer+1]+m) = (target[i][m]-out)
                                   * (1-out) * out;
          }
```

```
                  /* hidden & input layer errors  */
      for (m= nhlayer+1; m>=1; m--)  {
         for ( n=0; n< nunit[m-1]+1; n++)  {
            *(errptr[m-1]+n)= 0.0;
            for (p=0; p<nunit[m]; p++)  {

               offset = (nunit[m-1]+1) * p + n;

               *(delw[m-1]+offset)=eta * (*(errptr[m]+p))
                  * (*(outptr[m-1]+n))
                  +alpha * (*(delw[m-1]+offset));

               *(errptr[m-1]+n) += *(errptr[m]+p)
                     * (*(wtptr[m-1]+ offset));
            }
            *(errptr[m-1]+n) = *(errptr[m-1]+n) *
               (1- *(outptr[m-1]+n)) * (*(outptr[m-1]
               +n));
         }
      }


                  /* weight changes  */
      for (m=1 ; m<nhlayer+2; m++)  {
         for ( n=0; n<nunit[m]; n++)  {
            for (p=0; p<nunit[m-1]+1; p++)  {
               offset= (nunit[m-1]+1) * n + p;
               *(wtptr[m-1]+offset) += *(delw[m-1]
               +offset);
            }
         }
      }

      ep[i] = 0.0;
      for (m=0; m<nunit[nhlayer+1]; m++) {
         ep[i] += fabs((target[i][m] -
               *(outptr[nhlayer+1]+m)));
      }
      err_curr  += ep[i] * ep[i];
   }                /* normalized system error */
```

```
    err_curr = 0.5 * err_curr/ninput;

        /** save errors in  file to draw the system
            error with  plot10 **/
    if (fplot10==1)
    fprintf(fp3,"%1d, %2.9f\n",cnt,err_curr);
    cnt++;

                    /* check condition for terminating
                        learning */
    result = introspective(from_snum,to_snum);
} while (result == CONTNE);

/* update output with changed weights */
for (i=from_snum; i<to_snum;i++) forward(i);

for (i=0; i <nhlayer+1; i++) {
   index = 0;
   for ( j=0; j <nunit[i+1]; j++)
   {
      printf("\n\nWeights between unit %d of layer %d",
         j,i+1);
      printf(" and units of layer %d\n", i);
      for( k=0;k<nunit[i];k++)
         printf(" %f", *(wtptr[i] + index++));
      printf("\n  Threshold of unit %d of layer %d
      is %f",
                j,i+1, *(wtptr[i] + index++));
   }
}

for (i=0; i<ninput;i++)
   for (j=0;j<noutattr;j++)
      printf("\n\n sample %d output %d = %f target
      %d = %f",
         i,j, outpt[i][j],j,target[i][j]);

printf("\n\nTotal number of iteration is %d", cnt);
printf("\nNormalized system error is %f\n\n\n",
err_curr);
```

```c
      return(result);
}


                  /* read in the input data file
                     specified by user during the
                     interactive session*/
user_session()
{
   int    i, j, showdata;
   char   fnam[20], dtype[20];
   FILE   *fp;

   printf("\n Start of learning session");

                     /* for task with name task_name,
                        input data file of the task is
                        automatically set to be
                        task_name.dat by the program */
   printf("\n\t Enter the task name : ");
   scanf("%s", task_name);

   printf ("\n How many features in input pattern?: ");
   scanf ("%d",&ninattr);

   printf("\n How many output units?: ");
   scanf("%d",&noutattr);

   printf ("\n Total number of input samples?: ");
   scanf ("%d",&ninput);

   strcpy(fnam,task_name);
   strcat(fnam,".dat");

   printf("\n Input file name is %s ", fnam);
   if(( fp = fopen(fnam,"r"))==NULL)
   {
      printf("\nFile %s does not exist",fnam);
      exit(0);
   }
```

```c
        printf("\n Do you want to look at data just read?");
        printf("\n    Answer yes or no : ");
        scanf("%s",dtype);
        showdata = ((dtype[0] == 'y') || (dtype[0] == 'Y'));
        for ( i=0; i<ninput;i++)  {
           for (j=0; j<ninattr;j++)  {
              fscanf(fp,"%f",&input[i][j]);
              if (showdata) printf("%f  ",input[i][j]);
           }
           for (j=0; j<noutattr;j++) {
              fscanf(fp,"%f",&target[i][j]);
              if (showdata) printf("%f\n",target[i][j]);
           }
        }
        if((i=fclose(fp)) != 0)
        {
           printf("\nFile cannot be closed %d",i);
           exit(0);
        }
}


                /* main body of learning */
learning( )
{
    int result;

    user_session();
    set_up();
    init();
    do  {
       initwt();
       result = rumelhart(0,ninput);
    } while (result == RESTRT);
    if (result == FEXIT)
    {
       printf("\n Max number of iterations reached,");
       printf("\n    but failed to decrease system");
       printf("\n error sufficiently");
```

```
    }

    dwrite(task_name);
    wtwrite(task_name);
}


                /* main body of output generation */
output_generation( )
{
    int    i,m,nsample;
    char   ans[10];
    char   dfile[20];

            /* If task is already in the memory, data
                files for task do not need to be read in.
                But, if it is a new task, data files
                should be read in to reconstruct the net */
    printf("\nGeneration of outputs for a new pattern");
    printf("\n\t Present task name is %s", task_name);
    printf("\n\t Work on a different task?    ");
    printf("\n\t   Answer yes or no : ");
    scanf ("%s", ans);
    if ((ans[0]=='y') || (ans[0]=='Y'))
    {
        printf("\n\t Type the task name : ");
        scanf("%s", task_name);
        dread(task_name);
        init();
        wtread(task_name);
    }

                    /* input data for output
                        generation are created */
    printf("\nEnter file name for patterns to");
    printf(" be processed: ");
    scanf("%s",dfile);
    if ((fp1=fopen(dfile,"r")) == NULL)
    {
        perror("Cannot open dfile");
```

```
        exit(0);
    }


    printf("\nEnter number of patterns for processing: ");
    scanf("%d", &nsample);


    for(i=0;i<nsample;i++)
        for (m=0;m<ninattr;m++)
            fscanf(fp1,"%f",&input[i][m]);

                /*output generation calculation starts */
    for(i=0;i<nsample;i++)
    {
        forward(i);

        for (m=0;m<noutattr;m++)
            printf("\n sample %d output %d = %f",
                i,m,*(outptr[nhlayer+1]+m));

        printf("\n");

    }
    printf("\nOutputs have been generated ");

    if((i=fclose(fp1)) != 0)
        printf("\nFile cannot be closed %d",i);
}


/*************** MAIN *********************/
main()
{
    char select[20], cont[10];

    strcpy(task_name, "********");

    do {
        printf("\n** Select L(earning) or O(utput generation)
```

```
    **\n");
    do  {
       scanf ( "%s", select);
       switch(select[0]) {
           case 'o':
           case 'O':
              output_generation ();
              break;
           case 'l':
           case 'L':
              learning();
              break;
           default:
              printf("\nanswer learning or output
              generation ");
              break;
       }
    } while ((select[0]!='o') && (select[0]!='O')
          && (select[0]!='l') && (select[0]!='L'));
    printf("\nDo you want to continue?   ");
    scanf ("%s",cont);
  } while ((cont[0] =='y') || (cont[0] =='Y'));

  printf("\nIt is all finished. ");
  printf("\n Good bye  ");
}
```

A.3 Example

Input Data File for Parity-3 Learning : par3.dat

```
0 0 0    0.9
0 0 1    0.1
0 1 0    0.1
0 1 1    0.9
1 0 0    0.1
1 0 1    0.9
1 1 0    0.9
1 1 1    0.1
```

Data File for Output Generation: data.dat

```
0    0    0
1    1    1
0.0 0.0 0.2
0.0 0.0 0.8
0.0 0.2 0.0
0.0 0.8 0.0
0.0 0.2 0.2
0.0 0.8 0.8
```

Output from Program Run

```
** Select L(earning) or O(utput generation) **
L

 Start of learning session
 Enter the task name : par3

How many features in input pattern?: 3

How many output units?: 1

Total number of input samples?: 8

 Input file name is par3.dat
 Do you want to look at data just read?
    Answer yes or no : y
0.000000   0.000000   0.000000   0.900000
0.000000   0.000000   1.000000   0.100000
0.000000   1.000000   0.000000   0.100000
0.000000   1.000000   1.000000   0.900000
1.000000   0.000000   0.000000   0.100000
1.000000   0.000000   1.000000   0.900000
1.000000   1.000000   0.000000   0.900000
1.000000   1.000000   1.000000   0.100000

Momentum rate eta (default =0.9)?: 0.9

Learning rate alpha (default =0.7)?: 0.7

Max total error (default=0.01)?: 0.000001
```

Max individual error (default=0.001)?: 0.0000001

Max number of iteration(default=1000)?: 2000

Number of hidden layers?: 1

Number of units for hidden layer 1?: 3

Create error file? If so type 1,or type 0 : 1

Execution starts

Weights between unit 0 of layer 1 and units of layer 0
 -2.755273 -2.755553 -2.756222
  Threshold of unit 0 of layer 1 is 6.599238

Weights between unit 1 of layer 1 and units of layer 0
 -5.482076 -5.487528 -5.497730
  Threshold of unit 1 of layer 1 is 7.316314

Weights between unit 2 of layer 1 and units of layer 0
 -4.870187 -4.894925 -4.942179
  Threshold of unit 2 of layer 1 is 1.474228

Weights between unit 0 of layer 2 and units of layer 1
 7.695147 -7.613980 6.758780
  Threshold of unit 0 of layer 2 is -3.380892

 sample 0 output 0 = 0.899753 target 0 = 0.900000

 sample 1 output 0 = 0.100304 target 0 = 0.100000

 sample 2 output 0 = 0.100339 target 0 = 0.100000

 sample 3 output 0 = 0.899036 target 0 = 0.900000

 sample 4 output 0 = 0.100365 target 0 = 0.100000

 sample 5 output 0 = 0.898985 target 0 = 0.900000

sample 6 output 0 = 0.898907 target 0 = 0.900000

sample 7 output 0 = 0.103369 target 0 = 0.100000

Total number of iteration is 1384
Normalized system error is 0.000001

Do you want to continue?   y

** Select L(earning) or O(utput generation) **
O

Generation of outputs for a new pattern
 Present task name is par3 .
 Work on a different task?
   Answer yes or no : n

Enter file name for output generation: data.dat

Enter number of patterns for processing: 8

 sample 0 output 0 = 0.899753

 sample 1 output 0 = 0.103369

 sample 2 output 0 = 0.707187

 sample 3 output 0 = 0.077218

 sample 4 output 0 = 0.710287

 sample 5 output 0 = 0.078334

 sample 6 output 0 = 0.326657

 sample 7 output 0 = 0.893754

```
Outputs have been generated
Do you want to continue?    n

It is all finished.
 Good bye
```

Unsupervised Learning Based on Discovery of Cluster Structure

B.1 Introduction

This appendix contains a C language program for readers to use as a point of departure for unsupervised learning by discovering the cluster structure.

In this program, clustering uses the Euclidean distance metric for determining distances between patterns and cluster centers. The algorithm and notation used are generally that of Chapter 7. An example is provided for verification of the code.

The program runs under VAX/VMS or PC-DOS/MS-DOS. Under PC-DOS or MS-DOS, the program was compiled with Microsoft C.

B.2 Program

```
/* PROGRAM DESCRIPTION:
        THIS PROGRAM CARRIES OUT UNSUPERVISED LEARNING AND
        SORTS SAMPLES INTO CLUSTERS USING THE EUCLIDEAN
        DISTANCE METRIC.

        THE MAXIMUM NUMBER OF CLUSTERS WHICH CAN BE CREATED
        IS AS MANY AS THE NUMBER OF INPUT PATTERNS.
```

* Appendix B is contributed by M.S. Klassen and Yoh-Han Pao.

```
        INPUT PATTERNS AND LEARNED WEIGHTS ARE STORED
        IN FILES.

*/


#include <stdio.h>
#include <ctype.h>
#include <math.h>


#define NMXPATTERN    100  /* max number of input samples */
#define NMXATTR       100  /* max number of input
                              attributes */

int   ninput;             /* number of input patterns */
int   ninattr;            /* number of input attributes */
float threshold;          /* threshold  */
int   testing;            /* 0=training, 1=testing*/
float pattern[NMXPATTERN][NMXATTR];
float b[NMXPATTERN][NMXATTR];     /* bottom_up weights */
int   cluster_tbl[NMXPATTERN][NMXATTR];
float x[NMXATTR];         /* input pattern */
float ed[NMXPATTERN];     /* Euclidean distances to
                              cluster centers*/
int   active_nodes;       /* number of current clusters */
FILE  *in,*out;
int   debug_flag;
int   total_time;         /* number of iterations */


                /** get information from a user   **/
user_session()
{
   int i, j;
   char file_name[20];

   printf("\nDisplay Euclidean distances for each
```

```
   iteration?");
   printf("\n  Yes = 1,No = 0 : ");
   scanf("%d", &debug_flag);


   printf("\n\nPlease enter threshold: ");
   scanf("%f", &threshold);

   printf("\nEnter the name of the input data file: ");
   scanf("%s", file_name);
   if ((in = fopen(file_name,"r")) == NULL)
   {
      printf("\nCannot open input data file\n");
      exit(0);
   }
   printf("\nHow many input training patterns?: ");
   scanf("%d", &ninput);

   printf("\nHow many input attributes?: ");
   scanf("%d", &ninattr);

   testing = 0;
   total_time = 0;
}


                      /* read pattern data from input file */
read_all_patterns()
{
   int i, j;

   for (i = 0; i < ninput; i++)
      for (j = 0; j < ninattr; j++)
         fscanf (in, "%e", &pattern[i][j]);

   fclose(in);
}


                         /* create the first cluster
```

```
                                      with the first pattern */
first_node()
{
   int i;
                        /* bottom_up weights=first pattern */
   for (i = 0; i < ninattr; i++)
      b[0][i] = pattern[0][i];

   active_nodes = 1;                /* number of clusters */
   cluster_tbl[0][0] = 1;/*number of members in cluster0*/
}



                        /* create a new cluster node */
form_new_node(input_no)
int input_no;                    /* input pattern number */
{
   int i;

   for (i = 0; i < ninattr; i++)
      b[active_nodes][i] = pattern[input_no][i];

   cluster_tbl[active_nodes][0] = 1;/*number of member=1 */
   cluster_tbl[active_nodes][1] = input_no;
   active_nodes++;          /* increment number of clusters */
}



                  /* calculate Euclidean distances
                     from a pattern to cluster centers   */
compute_euc_dist()
{
   int i, j;

   if (debug_flag == 1)
      printf("\nEuclidean distances to cluster centers\n");
   for (j = 0; j < active_nodes; j++)
   {
      ed[j] = 0.0;
      for (i = 0; i < ninattr; i++)
```

```
                    ed[j] = ed[j]+((b[j][i]-x[i]) * (b[j][i]-x[i]));

            if (debug_flag == 1) printf("%.6f ", ed[j]);
        }
        if (debug_flag == 1) printf ("\n");
}
```

```
                              /* choose the cluster nearest to
                                 the pattern and return cluster
                                 number if pattern is within
                                 threshold radius. If none
                                 available, then return -99 */

int compare_min_ed(input_no)
{
    int i, cluster_no ;
    float min;

    min = 10000;

    for (i = 0; i < active_nodes; i++)
        if (ed[i] < min)
        {
            min = ed[i];
            cluster_no = i;
        }

    if (debug_flag == 1)
        printf("Ed= %.3f  Node= %d  Pat= %d \n",
            sqrt(ed[cluster_no]), cluster_no, input_no);

    if (sqrt(ed[cluster_no]) <= threshold)
        return(cluster_no);
    else return(-99);
}
```

```
                              /* include a new member in the
```

```
                                    cluster by updating weights*/
update_wts(cluster_no,input_no)
int cluster_no;
int input_no;
{
    int i,no_member;
    float n,m;

    n = cluster_tbl[cluster_no][0];
    m = n + 1;
    if (testing == 0)
    {
        for (i = 0; i < ninattr; i++)
            b[cluster_no][i]=((n/m) * b[cluster_no][i])
                            +((1/m) * x[i]);
    }
    no_member =  ++(cluster_tbl[cluster_no][0]);
    cluster_tbl[cluster_no][no_member] =input_no ;
}


report()
{
    int i, j, k, nbcol;

    printf("\n\n");
    printf("+------+-----+----------------------------+\n");
    printf("| Node |Count|        Pattern   numbers   |\n");
    printf("+------+-----+----------------------------+\n");

    k=0;
    nbcol = 6;
    for (i = 0; i < ninput; i++)
    {
        if (cluster_tbl[i][0] == 0)  break;
        printf("| %-4d | %-3d |", i, cluster_tbl[i][0]);
        for (j = 1; j <ninput+1; j++)
        {
            if ((cluster_tbl[i][j] != 0)
                || ((i == 0) && (j == 1)))
```

```
            {
                if (k > nbcol)
                {
                    printf("|\n|        |       |");
                    k = 0;
                }
                printf(" %-3d", cluster_tbl[i][j]);
                k++;
            }

        }
        for (j = k; j <= nbcol; j++) printf("     ");
        printf("|\n");
        printf("+------+-----+--------------------------+\n");
        k = 0;
    }
}


print_bot_up_wts()
{
    int i, j;
    char *file_name="weights.dat";

    if ((out = fopen(file_name,"w")) == NULL)
    {
        printf("\n Cannot open input data file\n");
        exit(0);
    }

    printf("\n\nBottom_up weights");
    for (i = 0; i <active_nodes; i++)
    {
        printf("\n  Cluster %d\n  ",i);
        for (j =0; j < ninattr; j++)
        {
            printf("%.3f ", b[i][j]);
            fprintf(out,"%.3f ", b[i][j]);
        }
        printf("\n");
```

```
    }

    fclose(out);
}


main()
{
    int cluster_no,q;
    int i;

    user_session();
    read_all_patterns();
    first_node();

    for (q = 1; q < ninput; q++)
    {
        for (i = 0; i < ninattr; i++)
            x[i] = pattern[q][i];
        compute_euc_dist();
        if ((cluster_no = compare_min_ed(q)) >= 0)
            update_wts(cluster_no,q);
        else
            form_new_node(q);
    }

    report();                 /* report clustering result */
    print_bot_up_wts();
}
```

B.3 Example

Input data file for clustering: 8x7.dat

```
0.0 1.0 2.0 3.0 4.0 5.0 6.0
0.0 1.0 2.0 3.0 4.0 5.0 5.0
0.0 1.0 2.0 3.0 4.0 4.0 4.0
6.0 5.0 4.0 3.0 2.0 1.0 0.0
6.0 5.0 4.0 3.0 2.0 1.0 1.0
6.0 5.0 4.0 3.0 2.0 2.0 2.0
1.0 1.0 1.0 1.0 1.0 1.0 1.0
0.0 0.0 0.0 0.0 0.0 0.0 0.0
```

Output from Program Run

Display Euclidean distances for each iteration?
  Yes = 1,No = 0 : 0

Please enter threshold: 3
Enter the name of the input data file: 8x7.dat
How many input training patterns?: 8
How many input attributes?: 7

```
+-------+-----+------------------------------+
| Node |Count|         Pattern   numbers    |
+-------+-----+------------------------------+
| 0    | 3   | 0   1   2                    |
+-------+-----+------------------------------+
| 1    | 3   | 3   4   5                    |
+-------+-----+------------------------------+
| 2    | 2   | 6   7                        |
+-------+-----+------------------------------+
```

Bottom_up weights
  Cluster 0
  0.000 1.000 2.000 3.000 4.000 4.667 5.000

  Cluster 1
  6.000 5.000 4.000 3.000 2.000 1.333 1.000

  Cluster 2
  0.500 0.500 0.500 0.500 0.500 0.500 0.500

Index

A and non-A, learning semantic
net descriptions of, 101–104
A posteriori conditional probability, 27
A posteriori odds, 50
A priori odds, 49
A priori probability, 27
Acoustic measurements, for
speech identification, 71
Activation functions, 122, 176
Active receptors, in coarse coding,
148–149
Adaptive bidirectional associative
memory (BAM), 166
Adaptive pattern recognition

focus of task, 9–11
major issues in, 19
motivation for study of, 3–6
objectives of task, 11–14
Adaptive Resonance Theory
(ART), characteristics of, 194
"Agile" predicate, 227–228
Algebraic product, 69
Algebraic sum, 68
α-level sets, 62, 63
α-Perceptron, 114
AQVAL, 84
ARCH, 101
ART1
algorithm, 179–181